The Quest for Ulysses

THE QUEST FOR ULYSSES

W. B. Stanford and J. V. Luce

PHAIDON

Frontispiece. Fragment of a marble statue from the Cave of Tiberius at Sperlonga, *c*. 175–150 BC (see p. 159). As there is a representation of Skylla in the magnificent group to which it belongs, the expression of horror is probably caused by the spectacle of Skylla snatching and devouring six of the Companions, described by Ulysses in *Odyssey* 12:245–59 as the most pitiful sight he had ever seen. Stylistically, the Sperlonga sculptures show marked resemblances to the famous Laocoön group by Rhodian sculptors, *c*. 160–130 BC.

Phaidon Press Limited
5 Cromwell Place, London SW7 2JL

First published 1974
© 1974 by Phaidon Press Limited
ISBN 0 7148 1616 7

Printed in the U.S.A.
Filmset in Great Britain by
Robert MacLehose & Co. Ltd
Glasgow, Scotland

Contents

Acknowledgements

We would like to record our gratitude to the following for help in preparing this book: T. V. Buttrey, F. A. G. Loesel, Michael and Danaë O'Regan, H. W. Parke, Dorothy and Philip Stanford, C. C. and E. T. Vermeule, J. L. White. Our special thanks are due to Rosemary Saunders, who suggested many improvements and collected the illustrations, and to Corinne Harrison for expeditiously typing our final versions. The following have kindly given permission to quote from the cited works: The Bodley Head Ltd., London: James Joyce, *Ulysses*; Robert Graves: Homer, *The Iliad*, translated by Robert Graves, Cassell & Co. Ltd., London; Harper & Row, Publishers, Inc., New York: Homer, *The Odyssey*, translated by Richmond Lattimore; Nikos Kazantzakis: *The Odyssey: a modern sequel*, translated by Kimon Friar, Martin Secker & Warburg Ltd., London, and Simon & Schuster Inc., New York: Copyright © 1958 by Simon & Schuster; Macmillan Ltd., London: A. Tennyson, *Ulysses*; Oxford University Press, New York: Homer, *The Odyssey*, translated by T. E. Shaw; Penguin Books Ltd., Harmondsworth: Homer, *The Odyssey,* translated by E. V. Rieu (Penguin Classics 1946): Copyright © E. V. Rieu 1946; University of Chicago Press, Chicago and London: Homer, *The Iliad*, translated by Richmond Lattimore: Copyright 1951: Copyright © 1962 by the University of Chicago. The translations in the text are by the authors unless otherwise acknowledged.

October 1973

W. B. S.
J. V. L.

Introduction

W. B. Stanford

FEW figures in European civilization have inspired so many master-pieces of secular literature and art as Ulysses. Continuously from the time of Homer, poets and artists have portrayed him with inexhaustible variety. Sometimes he appears as an admirable hero, sometimes as a repulsive villain. But whether we like him or not, there he is in every period of creative art, arousing our interest and challenging conventional ideas about what constitutes heroism and villainy. He even has a place in astronomy among the minor planets: one of the Trojan Group bears his Greek name, Odysseus.

Our purpose in the present book is to determine the truth about this fascinating personality. Our quest will operate in two different fields of inquiry, one belonging to the world of fact, the other to the world of imagination. Four chapters will explore what is now known about Greece and her neighbours in the early ages when the Trojan War was fought and won with the help of Ulysses, and when bards began to record his exploits in their songs and poems. The rest of the book will consider the large store of mythology, literature and art in which Ulysses plays a major role, beginning with the *Iliad* and the *Odyssey* and ending with the two outstanding writers on the Ulysses theme in the twentieth century, James Joyce of Ireland and Nikos Kazantzakis of Greece. Every year new archaeological discoveries add to our knowledge of Ulysses and his historical background. In some ways we now know more about the kind of life our proto-Ulysses may have led than even Homer did. In Homer's time, some five hundred years after the Trojan War, the palaces and treasures of the Mycenaean Age were buried in earth and debris. It is only within the last century that archaeologists have fully revealed Mycenaean Troy, Ithaca, Tiryns and Mycenae itself. No palace fit to be accepted as Nestor's Pylos, as mentioned in the *Odyssey*, was identified until 1939.

Clearly, then, with so much new archaeological evidence for the art, life and language of the Mycenaean Age, we can now embark on the historical and archaeological part of our quest with greater confidence than has ever been possible since the Dark Age of early Greece. The questions we shall be asking are chiefly these: to what extent was Ulysses a historical person of the Mycenaean Age? Are the places

Ill. 1. Detail of the centre part of a fresco by Tibaldi in the University of Bologna (formerly the Palazzo Poggi) depicting a finely modelled Ulysses at the palace of Circe. He draws his sword apparently to defend himself against half-animal creatures at the approach to the palace, as suggested in *Odyssey* 10:210–15. (See p. 202 and *Ills. 34, 166, 167.*)

which Homer and the early Greek writers describe in connection with him (especially Ithaca) identifiable with actual places in the Greek world? Are Homer's descriptions of buildings, monuments, works of art, furniture and similar things, based on memories of Mycenaean times? How much factual material is there in Homer's account of Ulysses' wanderings in countries beyond the confines of the Mycenaean world? The only firm basis for answers to questions of this kind is archaeology, since no written histories survive from the periods involved.

The second area of our quest—creative literature and art—presents different problems. The imagination of poets and artists is free to alter or invent in a traditional story—though within the bounds of plausibility. (A cowardly Achilles, for example, or an ugly Paris, or a stupid Ulysses, would hardly be accepted.) These poets and artists have the deluding gift of making their own inventions look like historical fact—sometimes even more so than the facts themselves. Homer in his *Iliad* and *Odyssey* presents a portrait of Ulysses which satisfies us as being essentially 'true' while we are under the spell of his narrative. But when we reconsider it afterwards we see that some of it simply could not have happened. And then we may begin to wonder if any of what Homer tells us happened at all, apart from the elements which are verifiable by archaeology.

Here we are confronted by one of the deepest questions of all human inquiry—What is truth? How 'true' is Hamlet or Pickwick, or Leopold Bloom? Any book that sails out into that sea of speculations may never reach the further shore. For our present purpose it will be better, perhaps, to recognize two kinds of truth, one of history and one of art, which overlap at times, but often obey their own independent laws. Ultimately both strive towards the same end—a better understanding of human life, as it is and as it ought to be.

The literary, artistic and archaeological material for our search is so voluminous that only a much longer work than the present study could do it justice. One earlier publication listed in our bibliography, *The Ulysses Theme*, has already surveyed most of the literary evidence, and included a brief appendix on the Ulysses tradition in the visual arts. The present book contains much more on the archaeological and artistic side, and at times suggests new interpretations of the old facts. One can never reach finality in a quest of this kind. New archaeological discoveries and new artistic characterizations (as this introduction was being written a notable new poem on Ulysses appeared in an English journal) constantly change the total perspective of the Ulysses tradition. This principle of imperfectibility holds, of course, for all major inquiries about eminent figures. But in the quest for Ulysses the double dimension—in history and imagination—presents more complex problems than one would be likely to meet in, say, a quest for Alexander the Great or Julius Caesar, where the historical element is much clearer. Yet in this, too, there is a stimulus for our efforts—'the fascination of what's difficult', as Yeats has called it.

So two trails lie before us, one leading back to Bronze Age Greece, Schliemann's Troy and Blegen's Pylos, the other forward towards the master-writers and artists of our own time and the times to come. But one thing that seems as certain as anything in the future of our civilization can be is that major portraits of Ulysses, such as have come in the past from writers like Homer, Sophocles, Dante, Tennyson and *Ill. 1* Joyce, and from artists like Primaticcio, Tibaldi, Poussin and Rubens, will not end in the twentieth century.

I Ulysses in the early epic tradition—from his birth to the fall of Troy

W. B. Stanford

IN our first two chapters we shall follow the quest for Ulysses through the earliest remains of Greek (and indeed of all European) literature: the *Iliad* and the *Odyssey* of Homer, composed perhaps in the eighth century BC, and also through the epic cycle which supplemented Homer's narrative. As we shall see, their statements and implications do not always coincide. Our task will be to distinguish what seems to be historical fact from what looks like poetic fiction in these narratives and to account for the disagreements in them. In dealing with poetry one can never be quite sure, unless independent evidence exists, how much is historical and how much imaginary. But at least one can suggest probabilities.

Ulysses, Homer tells us, was born and bred near the sea. His island home, Ithaca, lay off the west coast of Greece near the intersection of two major trade routes, north and south, east and west. Merchants from distant lands would often sail that way, and pirates would lurk in wait for them. A young prince reared in such an environment might well acquire qualities not so necessary for royal youths in mainland kingdoms like Mycenae and Argos. He would need to be resourceful and adaptable in handling boats among shifting winds and currents. He would learn to deal warily with merchants and swiftly with pirates. (And perhaps, if the chance came, he might indulge in an occasional act of piracy himself like Drake or Raleigh: he certainly did so later during his Odyssean adventures.) The wide expanse of the sea visible from his island home—'rough but a good nurse of youths' is how he described it (*Odyssey* 9:27)—could set him dreaming of far-away countries which he might someday explore. There was nothing of that kind to stimulate the imagination or sharpen the wits of the young men from Eastern Greece who were to be Ulysses' comrades-in-arms—Agamemnon, Menelaos, Diomedes and the rest. Their neighbouring kingdoms were mostly inland, set in rich, fertile plains and surrounded by high mountain ranges. Their life, in contrast with Ulysses', was opulent, sheltered, secure, and perhaps rather monotonous.

It may well be, then, that when Ulysses went to Sparta as a young man to woo Helen, he felt rather an outsider in the close-knit society

◀ *Ill. 2.* Opposite: it is uncertain what particular incident in Ulysses' career is presented in this vigorous statue in the Doge's Palace, Venice (probably a copy of a work of the fourth century BC—see p. 158). At any rate it expresses the concept of Ulysses as a man of full heroic mould, and not as the contemptible villain that his literary detractors in the fifth century and later described.

of the great dynastic families of that region—something like a Scottish chieftain from the Outer Hebrides among the sophisticated nobility of Edinburgh, or a professor from a small Mid-Western college in the United States on a visit to Harvard or Yale. He would need to compensate with wit and intelligence for what he lacked in status and prestige.

Ill. 3

There was another reason why, in a world that attached great importance to ancestry, Ulysses might have felt socially—but never intellectually—at a disadvantage among the eastern princes. They boasted of long and illustrious lineages. Ulysses' ancestry was briefer, and, unfortunately for him, it contained a distinctly dubious element. In the male line it was respectable enough, though undistinguished. His father, Laërtes, was a rather quiet, unadventurous man, who ruled his Ithacan kingdom without winning anything more than local renown for his exploits. No history would have remembered him, if Ulysses had not been his son. Laërtes' father, Arkeisios, was an even dimmer figure in the early tradition. (Later mythologists tried to brighten up his reputation with a sensational story: relying on an unlikely derivation of 'Arkeisios' from the word *arktos*, a 'she-bear', they alleged that his mother was a bear.) Arkeisios' father, and Ulysses' great-grandfather, was (according to Homer) Zeus—a conventional way of implying 'earlier ancestry unknown but deemed to be illustrious'.

Compared with the pedigrees of heroes like Ajax or Achilles, well endowed with much more famous ancestors, this was a lacklustre lineage. But, worse still, on the female side Ulysses had a distinctly discreditable progenitor. His mother, Antikleia—the name could be understood as meaning 'Counter-fame' or 'She whose reputation is hostile'—was the daughter of Autolykos from Mount Parnassos. Autolykos (a remote literary ancestor of that engaging rascal Autolycus who appears in Shakespeare's *Winter's Tale* as 'a snapper-up of unconsidered trifles') had the reputation of 'surpassing all men in thievery and perjury' (*Odyssey* 19:395, 396), as Homer phrases it, qualities which he inherited from his reputed father, the god Hermes (patron of liars, thieves and tricksters). Autolykos specialized in stealing cattle. He even tried to outwit the supremely cunning Sisyphos of Corinth at this game, but failed. Later versions of the Ulysses legend alleged that Sisyphos seduced Antikleia before her marriage to Laërtes and was the true father of Ulysses. No writer earlier than the fifth century mentions this slur of illegitimacy. Whether Homer knew about it and suppressed it for the sake of his favourite hero's reputation, or knew nothing about it at all, cannot now be determined.

It should be remembered here that such genealogical information may be mainly, or entirely, fictional. But it seems reasonable to deduce from the statements of Homer that Ulysses' ancestors on the male side, Laërtes and Arkeisios, were actual kings in Western Greece, since their names suggest no clear mythological qualities (unless we accept the she-bear fantasy). On the other side Mrs. Counter-fame (Antikleia) and Mr. Very-wolf (Auto-lykos) sound fictional. So, we may be justified in taking this to indicate that the early Greek writers saw the Ulysses tradition as it had come down to them from prehistoric times as being half history and half folklore.

We find a similar discrepancy in the names traditionally used for Ulysses. Two different forms appear in the early tradition. In Eastern Greece and along the Greek coastline of Asia Minor (and, consequently, in the epic poems which emerged from these regions), his name is *Odysseus* or something similar. The Etruscans, who according to tradition came from Asia Minor, used forms probably cognate with this, varying from *Utuse* to *Uthuste*. But Western Greece, together with Sicily and the non-Etruscan parts of Italy, called the Ithacan hero *Olixes* or *Ulixes* (with further variations). Homer, who always calls him *Odysseus* (or *Odyseus*) explains how the newborn prince received that name. When Laërtes' son was born in Ithaca, Autolykos, his grandfather, came to see him. The baby's nurse, Eurykleia, waited until Autolykos had eaten his supper after his arrival. Then in the presence of Laërtes and Antikleia she put the child on Autolykos' knees and asked him to name this 'much-prayed for' son and heir. Autolykos gave a curious reason for his choice:

> Because I have come here after experiencing woeful anger from many people, men and women, throughout the fruitful earth, let his name be *Odysseus*.　　　　　　　(*Odyssey* 19:407–9)

There is a solemn and ominous connection between the Greek words for 'after experiencing woeful anger' (*odyssamenos*, connected with *odyne*, 'pain', as in our word 'anodyne') and *Odysseus*. Apparently Homer meant that Autolykos called his grandson 'Child of woeful wrath' in order to express what he had himself experienced as the result of his thefts and perjuries. (It was common in ancient Greece for children to be named after their grandparents.) But elsewhere in the *Odyssey*, Homer suggests that the name referred to the child's own destiny. Early in the first book the goddess Athena asks Zeus: 'Why are you so angry (*odusao*) with Odysseus?' (*Odyssey* 1:62), and much of Ulysses' suffering while wandering in faraway lands resulted from the anger of Poseidon. It seems, then, that Homer saw the name 'Child of wrath' as one of those 'significant names', as the early Greeks called them, which contain in themselves a prediction of their owner's destiny.

Odysseus, then, was a name-with-meaning like Antikleia and Autolykos. *Ulixes*, on the other hand, has no obvious etymology in Greek. The two are not used interchangeably by any ancient author. Why did these alternatives exist? Perhaps the best explanation is that *Ulixes* goes back to some pre-Greek figure of folklore, who was specially renowned for cunning (like the Polynesian Maui-of-a-thousand-tricks, who has much in common with Ulysses), while

Ill. 3. Bronze statuette of Ulysses from the Roman period (see p. 158). It contrasts with the previous illustration in its pose and expression. The face is apprehensive and strained, the limbs relaxed but ready for swift action. Possibly it depicts Ulysses disguised as a beggar after his return to Ithaca as described in *Odyssey* 13–21. Here we have the Ulysses who has to depend on intelligence to survive in a hostile environment.

13

Odysseus (with its aristocratic final syllable, as in Achilleus and other eminent Homeric names) was given to him by the Greek epic poets.

The only notable incident recorded from Ulysses' childhood involves Autolykos again. Homer relates that the young prince went to visit his grandfather on Mount Parnassos. There he was wounded by a wild boar. His dangerous bleeding was stopped by a magical incantation sung by his uncles, the sons of Autolykos. Here is another 'primitive' element in the background of Ulysses' life. The orthodox Greek heroes at Troy had skilled physicians to attend to their wounds. Here in Autolykos' domain magic was still used: Ulysses' uncles are more like 'medicine men' or 'witch-doctors' than trained medical practitioners. Autolykos himself was credited with magical powers in the later tradition: he could make his stolen goods invisible when necessary—not the kind of thing any near ancestor of Menelaos, say, or Theseus would be accused of doing. So it seems that Autolykos belonged to a kind of society markedly different from that of the other heroes of the Greek epic, a society more akin to the world of folklore.

Another incident in Ulysses' career before he joined the expedition to Troy has a slightly unheroic flavour about it. Homer mentions that Ulysses went on a journey to a place called Ephyre (probably in Thesprotia, on the mainland of Greece north of Ithaca) to get poison for his arrows. No conventional hero in antiquity is said to have possessed poisoned arrows (though their use in hunting was well known). In fact to fight in battle with bow and arrows at all seems to have been regarded with some disdain by the more conventional Greek heroes of the Trojan War. At Troy, Ulysses is stated to have been equipped with a bow only during the perilous spying expedition described in *Iliad* 10, and he boasts in *Odyssey* 8 that he was the best archer among the Greeks at Troy after Philoctetes. He also kept a famous bow among his heirlooms in Ithaca, and used it for killing the Suitors when he returned from his wanderings.

Another journey took him farther afield, and it was for a more honourable purpose. Homer implied, and Hesiod (probably a contemporary of Homer in the eighth century BC) narrated in his poem *The suitors of Helen*, that he went to Sparta as one of the many princes from all over the Greek world who wooed the most beautiful of women. But Ulysses shrewdly guessed from the beginning that he had no chance:

> So he sent no gifts to win the slim-ankled maiden,
> for he knew in his heart that the auburn-haired prince Menelaos
> would win, being far the strongest in wealth and possessions.
>
> (*Fragment* 198)

In Sparta, before the favoured suitor was chosen, Ulysses, according to late writers, advised a fateful precaution. Foreseeing that when the final choice was made by Helen's father, Tyndaros, the unsuccessful suitors might feel insulted and take revenge, Ulysses advised Tyndaros to make all the suitors take an oath that they would accept the decision peacefully, and further, that if anyone should take Helen away by force they would unite to punish him. Hence the Trojan War, when Paris later abducted Helen. This would have been a characteristic example of Ulyssean prudence. (But Hesiod, in contrast with the later tradition, attributes the precaution to Tyndaros alone.)

It was characteristic, too, of Ulysses that he did not return from Sparta without any personal gain. It seems—the early tradition is uncertain here—that before he left Sparta he wooed and won Penelope, daughter of Prince Ikarios, a brother of Tyndaros. Penelope was descended in the male line from the kings of Sparta and, through her grandmother, from the famous Perseus, the gorgon-slayer, founder of the royal line of Tiryns. Though Penelope could not rival Helen in beauty, she was destined to surpass all the women of her time in fidelity to her husband, and as Homer presents her in the *Odyssey* she equalled even Ulysses himself in sheer intelligence. The early tradition never suggests that the marriage was anything but a happy one.

We are told very little about their early married life. Ulysses built their nuptial bedroom with his own hands as an extension to the main palace. In it he constructed and decorated—with gold, silver and ivory—a bed which was attached to the trunk of an olive tree growing on the site. In due course their only child (according to Homer), Telemachos, was born. Ulysses, now king of Ithaca, Laërtes having abdicated, gained a high reputation for piety, justice and generous hospitality, and won the lasting affection of his people. His wealth, especially in herds of cattle on the mainland of West Greece, increased abundantly, helped, no doubt, by the riches which Penelope brought with her from Sparta.

At this moment of Ulysses' career the picture is of a prosperous, contented minor king, ready to disappear from history and live

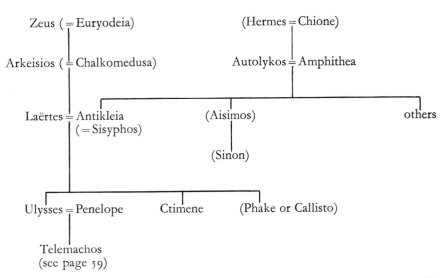

Ill. 4. Genealogy of Ulysses (with post-Homeric additions in brackets). On his father's side his descent from Zeus is less illustriously long than in the pedigrees of other Homeric heroes. On his mother's side there is that enigmatical and not entirely respectable personage Autolykos ('Very-wolf'), who appears much later in Shakespeare's *Winter's Tale*.

15

Ills. 5, 6. Two scenes portraying the different versions of the enlistment of Achilles: the Attic kantharos, sixth century BC, (left) follows Homer and depicts Patroklos and Achilles (in the centre) taking leave of his mother, the goddess Thetis, when Ulysses (second from the left, behind Patroklos) and Menelaos (behind Thetis) went to Peleus' palace to enlist them in the Greek army. In fact, in *Iliad* 11, Nestor relates that it was he who accompanied Ulysses, and not Menelaos. Another discrepancy is the presence of Mnestheus, the leader of the Athenians in the Trojan War (far left, behind Ulysses); perhaps the Attic painter included him for patriotic reasons. The Roman wall-painting from Pompeii, first century AD, (opposite) shows the post-Homeric version of the incident: *Achilles on Skyros*. This is the most celebrated ancient representation of the discovery of Achilles in disguise as a girl among the daughters of King Lykomedes. Achilles has betrayed himself by his interest in the armour cunningly placed by Ulysses, disguised as a merchant, among feminine trinkets. A rather Neronically podgy Achilles is seized by the central figure of a dynamic and intense Ulysses.

happily ever after. Now fate intervened. Paris abducted Helen from Sparta. The oath that bound all her former suitors became operative. According to *Odyssey* 24, Agamemnon and Menelaos went to Ithaca to recruit Ulysses for the campaign to bring Helen back and punish Paris. Ulysses accepted their summons, though an Ithacan prophet predicted that he would be away from home for twenty years and would suffer greatly during his absence. In saying farewell to Penelope, he charged her to take care of his father and mother, and advised her that if he had not returned by the time Telemachos had grown his first beard she should marry again. But the *Cypria*, an early epic poem describing events before the main battles at Troy, gave a different account, which impaired Ulysses' reputation as a hero: Menelaos, Nestor and Palamedes (a hero renowned for unusual sagacity) were the recruiting officers. When they arrived at Ithaca they found Ulysses apparently in a state of lunacy. (Later writers say that he had yoked two oddly-assorted animals to a plough and was ploughing the sands of the sea-shore, sowing salt in the furrows.) Unfortunately for Ulysses, Palamedes was as shrewd as himself. Palamedes, suspecting deceit, advised that the baby Telemachos should be seized and placed

in the path of the plough. Ulysses turned the plough aside to avoid his son. Clearly he was sane. He now had no excuse for avoiding conscription. The implication of this story is clear: a prudent Ulysses, happy in his home life and foreseeing the murderous consequences of a war, would avoid enlisting if he could.

But what about his oath? Ulysses was morally bound by it to join with the other ex-suitors in seeking revenge, though he could have argued that in fact he had not refused to honour that obligation: all he had done was to try to make the recruiters believe that it was not worthwhile to conscript him. But a Ulyssean sophistry of that kind would not impress blunt soldiers. Homer does not refer to the ruse at all, perhaps because he saw that it could be taken as discreditable to Ulysses. Perhaps for the same reason, too, he ignores the following incident.

Ulysses now set out from Ithaca for twenty years, having appointed a friend called Mentor as adviser to his family. Then, according to the *Cypria*, Ulysses' failure in his attempt to evade the horrors of war led to a dastardly deed on his part. He waited for an opportunity to revenge himself on the man who had outwitted him, Palamedes. After the arrival of the Greek army at Troy, Ulysses caused his death, either by drowning him or else by having him executed on a false charge of treachery. This perfidy gave Ulysses his revenge and also relieved him from having a hero of intelligence equal to his own in the Greek army.

The murder of Palamedes is the one example of utter villainy in Ulysses' career as described in early Greek epic poetry. Otherwise his conduct was civilized and co-operative. After he had joined the expedition, he devoted himself to bringing the war to a successful end as soon as possible. Homer tells us that he even became a recruiting officer himself, going with Nestor to the kingdom of Peleus to enlist his son Achilles. As James Joyce put it, 'Once at the war the conscientious objector became a *jusqu'auboutist*'.

A post-Homeric version of the enlistment of Achilles became famous later. It related that Peleus, Achilles' father, having been warned by a prophecy that if Achilles went and fought at Troy he would die there, persuaded his son to go to Skyros to escape recruitment. (Achilles was not bound by oath to fight since he had been too young to be a suitor of Helen.) There he was concealed by being disguised in feminine dress as one of the daughters of King Lykomedes of Skyros. Ulysses was sent to find him. He came to the island dressed as a merchant and was allowed to display his wares to the princesses. Among the dresses and jewellery he had placed military arms. Soon he saw one of the girls, as it seemed, handling the arms in a quite unfeminine way. He guessed it was Achilles and soon persuaded him to join the army.

Post-Homeric writers mention several other actions by Ulysses before the Greeks reached Troy. The most important were his negotiations leading to the sacrifice (or near-sacrifice) of Iphigeneia,

18

Ill. 5

Ill. 6

Ill. 7

Ill. 7. Opposite: another famous Roman wall-painting from Pompeii, AD 63–79: *The Sacrifice of Iphigeneia*, probably based on a lost work by the Greek artist, Timanthes. Agamemnon, shrouded in grief, stands on the left in front of a statue of Artemis to whom his daughter Iphigeneia (the figure lifting her on the left looks like Ulysses) is about to be sacrificed. On the right, full of foreboding, stands Calchas, the prophet of the Greek army. The figures in the sky imply that Artemis will substitute a deer for Iphigeneia at the last moment (as in the Euripidean version of the event).

daughter of Agamemnon, at Aulis (a favourite theme in ancient art), the successful persuasion of Achilles—never an easy task—to heal Telephos, King of the Mysians, who was needed as an ally against the Trojans, and his success in persuading the Greek commanders to maroon Philoctetes on the island of Lemnos when his gangrened foot disgusted the army.

When the Greeks had established a bridgehead in the Troad, an opportunity came for Ulysses to display his talents as a diplomat. The Greeks decided to send an embassy to Priam demanding the return of Helen and her treasures. (Homer mentions this incident briefly in *Iliad* 3. It was more fully described by the author of the *Cypria* and by Bacchylides in a lyrical ode.) Menelaos, as the aggrieved husband, and Ulysses, presumably as the most skilful diplomat among the Greeks, were sent to Troy to demand reparation. When the Greek ambassadors arrived in Troy they were courteously received. They were lodged in the house of Antenor and his wife Theano. In *Iliad* 3, Antenor gives his impressions of Ulysses and Menelaos—our first piece of information about Ulysses' appearance. Whether it is based on historical fact about an actual person or not, one cannot now determine. But at any rate Homer, as will be discussed in a later chapter, could give an accurate description of conditions prevailing in the Mycenaean era, and it is not impossible that memories of distinctive personalities also survived until his time.

Ills. 8, 9

Antenor says that Menelaos was head and shoulders taller than any of the Trojans while all were standing. But when he and Ulysses were seated, Ulysses looked the more impressive. In the debate Menelaos spoke briefly and fluently. When Ulysses stood up to speak, at first he

Ill. 8. This Corinthian column krater (*c.* 560 BC) depicts a scene from the events preceding those described in the *Iliad*, the embassy of Ulysses and Menelaos to demand the return of Helen from the Trojans. Ulysses sits with Menelaos on steps on the left, faced by the herald Talthybios, Theano, wife of Prince Antenor of Troy (who received them hospitably), and two other women.

seemed morose and gauche—'You'd say he was a cross-grained boor, a fool' (*Iliad* 3:220). But as soon as his mighty voice sounded out and his words came thick and fast, then his oratory seemed like a snowstorm, overwhelming all his hearers with its relentless persistence and its accumulating weight. No-one could rival him at that. This is a remarkable tribute to Ulysses' powers of persuasive eloquence. Other heroes were good orators, too: training in eloquence was part of a prince's education in that era. But Ulysses surpassed them all in sheer effectiveness, though this particular mission of his failed. Fate had decreed war.

Ills. 2, 3

In the same part of *Iliad* 3, Priam gives a striking description of Ulysses' physical appearance: he was less tall than Agamemnon by a head, but broader in the shoulders and chest, and when he marched among his troops he was like a sturdy ram among sheep. The comparison suggests a stocky, energetic man, and, taken with Antenor's description of the seated Ulysses, it distinguishes him from the other tall, long-legged Achaean heroes. Possibly there is an indication here that Ulysses differed genetically from the mainland princes: they being pure-blooded descendants of the earlier Greek invaders, he perhaps being (on his mother's side) partly of pre-Greek Aegean stock. On the other hand Homer states that Ulysses had the auburn hair of a typical Achaean prince—a feature presumably inherited from his father Laërtes. Some other personal features are mentioned elsewhere in the Homeric poems. He had fine, darting lively eyes, expressive eyebrows, strong thighs, broad shoulders and chest, and perhaps a dark beard (despite his auburn hair).

The main narrative of the *Iliad* begins in the tenth year of the Trojan War. In the opening scene we learn about two successive crises, the first caused by the wrath of Apollo, and the second by the anger of Achilles. (Apollo was enraged by the fact that Chryseïs, the daughter of his priest Chryses, was held as a captive by Agamemnon. When Agamemnon eventually sent her home, he took Achilles' concubine Briseïs in her place, thereby infuriating the greatest champion in the Greek army.) Ulysses plays a leading part in coping with both crises. In fact from the outset he shows himself to be the most serviceable of the princes at Troy. His motto might have been that of the Prince of Wales—*Ich dien*, 'I serve'. He knew that most of the other Greek leaders surpassed him in pride of ancestry or wealth or military power. Consequently, his best policy was to make himself personally valuable in dealing with difficult situations. Thus, when Agamemnon, in order to avert the plague sent by Apollo, decided to relinquish his captive woman Chryseïs to her father, Ulysses was sent on the delicate mission of bringing her back, a task he performed quietly and *Ill. 174* effectively. Soon afterwards he had a chance to demonstrate his energy and initiative more positively. An ill-judged speech to the army by Agamemnon caused the Greeks to rush to their ships with the intention of sailing home at once. Hera and Athena intervened to stop the stampede. Athena ordered Ulysses to speak to the soldiers 'with his gentle words' and persuade them to remain. He used his own discretion in executing her command. He addressed the princes and officers with gentle words, as directed. But, as Homer tells us,

> whenever Odysseus met a rowdy man-at-arms, he shook the sceptre at him. 'Sit down,' he would shout, 'and await orders. You count for nothing, either as a soldier or a thinker. All Greeks cannot be kings. It is a bad army in which each soldier claims freedom of action: we need a united command, and our leader is Agamemnon, High King and the representative of Zeus, Son of Cronus. Father Zeus, in his inscrutable wisdom, has conferred this sceptre on him, with the right to exact obedience from you.'
> (*Iliad* 2:198–206; Robert Graves' translation)

By these discriminatory methods Ulysses halted the retreat and brought the army back to another council of war.

Then another crisis developed. A private soldier named Thersites—his name later became proverbial for scurrilous demagoguery—stood up, screamed abuse at Agamemnon and urged the men to sail home. Immediately Ulysses, with a fierce scowl, ordered him to be silent, threatening to strip him naked and whip him from the council. As soon as he ended his speech he beat Thersites on his back and shoulders with his staff. Thersites lurched back and burst into tears. The rest of the Greeks laughed at this ludicrous scene and commented:

> Come now: Odysseus has done excellent things by thousands,
> bringing forward good counsels and ordering armed encounters;

Ill. 10. This superb composition on an Attic skyphos (*c.* 490 BC) by the 'Brygos painter' is one of a number of fine vase-paintings by early fifth-century painters on Iliadic themes (see pp. 144–7). Ulysses sits in a relaxed pose and with a rather quizzical expression, looking up at Nestor who perhaps has been delivering one of his customary lengthy harangues.

but now this is far the best thing he ever has accomplished
among the Argives, to keep this thrower of words, this braggart
out of assembly.

(*Iliad* 2:272–5; Richmond Lattimore's translation)

Ulysses was now on the crest of a wave of popularity. Being a skilful tactician, he followed up his success at once with a highly sensible speech to Agamemnon, advising him and the Greeks as a whole to press on with the war. This won tremendous applause. Then Nestor, King of Pylos, a man as wise and eloquent as Ulysses, but precluded from vigorous action by his great age, spoke in support. Agamemnon accepted their advice. The war would go on.

Here for the first time we see Ulysses in a role that he would often play, for good or for evil, in the later tradition—as an adroit and effective politician, quick to speak and act decisively at moments of crisis. Obviously he had no democratic ideas about the equality of all men: nor, indeed, had Homer, as his caricature of Thersites—lame, bandy-legged, hunchbacked, peaky-headed and nearly bald—shows. Homer also states that Ulysses' action won general approval. In fact, by stopping the sudden impetus towards abandoning the war, Ulysses' intervention here was as important for the ultimate capture of Troy as was his later ruse of the Wooden Horse.

In Book 3, Ulysses accompanies Agamemnon in negotiating a truce with the Trojans, and, with Hector, arranges the duel between Menelaos and Paris. Then for a while he remains in the background. A minor incident, however, gives us a glimpse of another aspect of his character and reputation. Agamemnon goes through the Greek encampment rousing the men for battle. He comes to where Ulysses and his detachment are stationed. Agamemnon addresses Ulysses and a companion in half-mocking terms, beginning:

> You with your mind always set on profit and trickery!
> (*Iliad* 4:339–40)

Ulysses replies very sharply, ending

> You are talking windy nonsense. (*Iliad* 4:355)

Agamemnon smiled at the angry retort and apologized. The brief episode is revealing. Ulysses is no lick-spittle. He will not take any disparaging remarks, even from the Commander-in-Chief. And Agamemnon genuinely likes Ulysses. It is made clear that they 'speak the same language' (*Iliad* 4:361). Clearly, too, Ulysses, the prince from the backwoods, so to speak, need feel no social or political inferiority towards the other Greek champions, when the High King has accepted him fully as a congenial comrade.

Shortly afterwards Homer shows us Ulysses going into the front line of battle 'helmeted in gleaming bronze' (*Iliad* 4:495) and slaying a son of Priam. As this and several other forays by Ulysses during the fighting at Troy prove, he was certainly not unwarlike or cowardly, though he was not one of the supremely powerful fighters at Troy— Achilles, Ajax, Diomedes and Agamemnon surpassed him in battle.

Meanwhile Achilles has been angrily keeping out of the fighting, sulking because Agamemnon took away from him the captive woman, Briseïs. The other Greeks, hard-pressed by the Trojans, need him desperately. Agamemnon decides to send delegates, offering him an apology, the return of Briseïs and lavish gifts. Ulysses and Ajax are selected. A brilliantly portrayed encounter follows between the implacable, but nobly courteous Achilles and his two former comrades-in-arms. A much longer analysis than can be undertaken here would be necessary to bring out the nuances of the psychological

Ills. 11, 113, 114

Ill. 11. One of the many notable vase-paintings of the embassy to Achilles (as described in *Iliad* 9) on an Attic hydria by the 'Eucharides painter', *c.* 490 BC (see p. 144). An almost nude Ulysses sits in the centre in a deliberately nonchalant pose facing a muffled-up Achilles (who looks more grief-stricken than angry here). The elderly figure on the left is presumably Phoenix, Achilles' old tutor. The third member of the embassy, Ajax, does not appear (cf. *Ills. 113, 114*).

interplay between these three very disparate war-lords—Achilles, high-spirited, outspoken, aflame with insulted pride, the unrivalled exemplar of reckless heroism; Ulysses, tactful, persuasive, full of practical wisdom and social responsibility; Ajax, massive, silent in the exchange of speeches and finally interrupting the dialogue to say that they might as well go, as obviously Achilles will not relent. Achilles in his reply to Ulysses addresses him courteously and answers his arguments considerately. But he makes one curious remark:

Hateful to me as the gates of Hell is the man who
Speaks one thing with his lips but hides something else in his mind.
(*Iliad* 9:312, 313)

This could be taken as a reason for his own frankness. But spoken to a man with a reputation for wiliness—Achilles calls Ulysses 'resourceful' in the opening words of his reply—it might also imply a certain heroic scorn for devious dealing. In contrast Achilles replies to Ajax in more sympathetic terms. We are given the impression that Ulysses is regarded as something of an outsider by these two illustrious princes. In the end Ulysses' eloquence fails to win Achilles over, as Ajax saw it would.

As if to restore the balance of fortune for Ulysses, Homer portrays him as going on an eminently successful mission almost immediately after this failure. During the night Nestor advises that two warriors should steal into the Trojan encampment and bring back information.

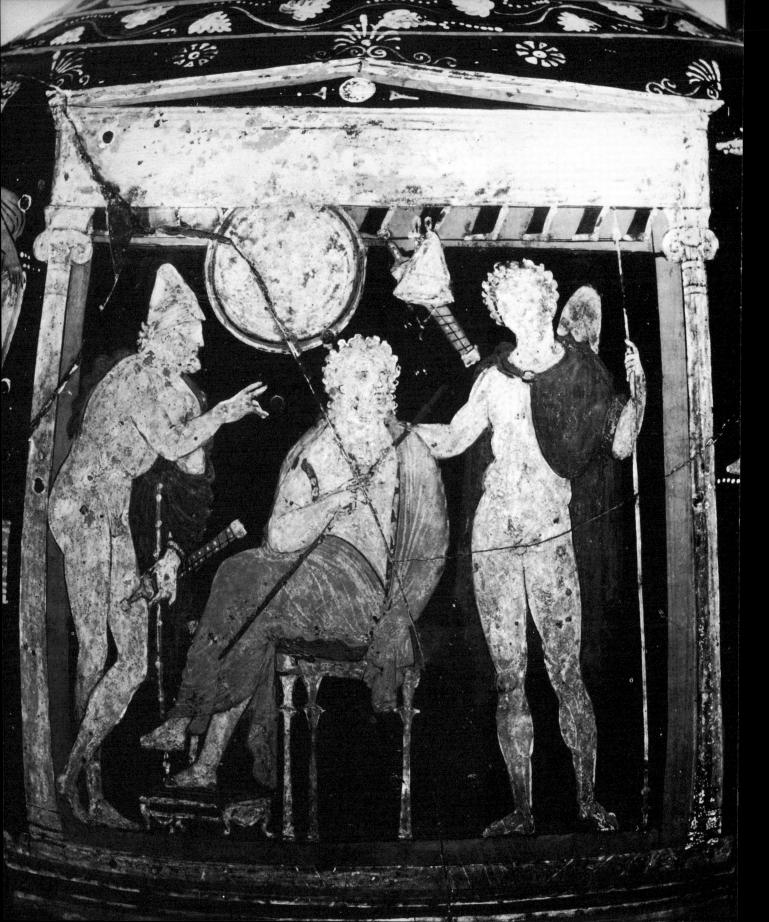

Ills. 12, 13. Two presentations of Ulysses with his frequent companion Diomedes. Opposite: Ulysses on the left tries to catch Agamemnon's attention on some matter but Agamemnon turns to the less urgent Diomedes. From a red-figure funerary amphora. Right: a scene from *Iliad* 10 on a Lucanian calyx krater representing the capture of Dolon (cf. *Ill. 115*) in burlesque vein (possibly an echo of the caricatures of the painter Zeuxis). Ulysses, wearing his pilos at a rather rakish angle, on the left, and Diomedes on the right are about to capture and kill the Trojan spy, Dolon, in their night foray. The talented painter of this and several other notable vases is called the 'Dolon painter' from this piece.

Ill. 12

Ill. 13

Diomedes immediately volunteers to go if someone else will accompany him. Five heroes offer. Given his choice by Agamemnon, Diomedes chooses Ulysses because his 'heart excels in foresight and his spirit in valour for every kind of hardship, and Pallas Athena loves him' (*Iliad* 10:244, 245). During their foray they encounter a Trojan named Dolon, son of Eupeithes (meaning 'Wily-man, son of Good-planner'). But like Palamedes, he met a wilier man in Ulysses, and was tricked and killed.

In a later episode we see the less heroic side of Ulysses again: Achilles has finally decided to resume the fight, because his fury at the death of his dearest friend Patroklos is stronger than his wrath against Agamemnon. He wants the Greeks to rush into battle with him at once. Ulysses objects. The soldiers should eat a meal first. The battle may last a long while. An army (he believes, with Napoleon) marches on its stomach. Agamemnon supports this advice. Achilles' reply is, in brief: 'You go and concern yourselves about food, if you must: I shall not touch a morsel until Patroklos is avenged' (*Iliad* 19:205–14). Ulysses, foreseeing, no doubt, the risk that if Achilles goes without food before fighting the redoubtable Hector, he may fail through physical weakness (though he does not, of course, say this explicitly), emphasizes the danger of fatigue in war and mildly criticizes the view that fasting is a good way for warriors to mourn comrades slain in battle. Obviously he hopes to persuade Achilles to eat, too. But once again he fails to move Achilles' passionate resolve. Later Homer shows that the advice was good and necessary: Athena intervenes to feed Achilles with nectar and ambrosia 'so that joyless hunger should not affect his strength' (*Iliad* 19:354).

The contrast between the heroism *pur sang* of Achilles and the level-headed realism of Ulysses is obvious here. Achilles in fact has the best of both worlds: he holds to his high resolve and at the same time gets fed by divine intervention. Ulysses has to bear contempt for his down-to-earth prudence. Elsewhere, too, Homer, though clearly not sharing in that contempt, hints that Ulysses took a more than average interest in food.

The final appearance of Ulysses in the *Iliad* shows him in a more conventionally heroic role—as a victorious athlete. At the funeral games in honour of Patroklos he won prizes in two events. First he wrestled with the mighty Ajax. In the first bout he threw him by a trick—quite a legitimate one, apparently—to the astonishment of the spectators. The second bout was a draw. Then, before the third bout could begin, Achilles stopped the contest and gave prizes to both. Next came the foot-race. When Ulysses saw that he was losing, he prayed to Athena for help. She strengthened him and also made the leading runner slip and fall. Ulysses won the first prize, an unexpected achievement for a man not renowned elsewhere for swiftness of foot, and described here (rather tactlessly) by one of the younger contestants as

> A man of an older time, of a former generation,
> in the early phase of old age . . . . (*Iliad* 23:790, 791)

In fact Ulysses was probably then in his middle thirties. Perhaps some insult was intended, though the speaker goes on to say that only Achilles could be sure of beating Ulysses in running. However,

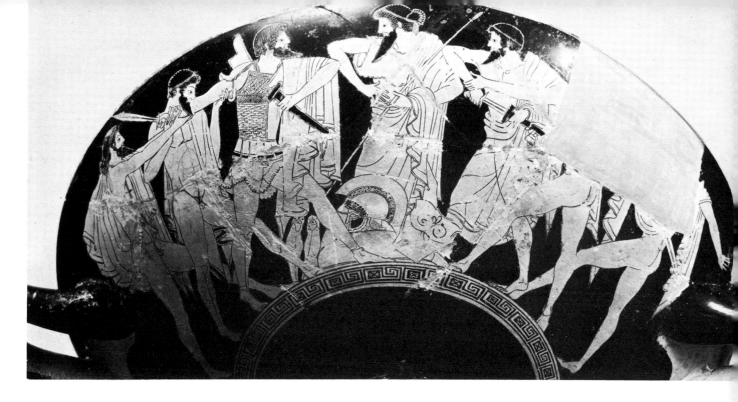

Ills. 14, 15. Two sides of a superb Attic kylix by the master-painter Douris, *c.* 490 BC (see p. 145), depicting the judgement between Ulysses and Ajax for the arms of Achilles (a post-Iliadic incident mentioned in *Odyssey* 11:544–6). Opposite: Athena in the centre watches Greeks casting their votes. Her outstretched right arm proclaims that those in Ulysses' favour are decisive. Above: Greeks restrain Ulysses (on the left of the central figure, probably Agamemnon) and Ajax (on his right) from fighting over Achilles' arms (at their feet).

Ills. 14, 15

Athena's intervention is highly significant. It foreshadows her attitude to Ulysses in the *Odyssey*.

The *Iliad* ends with the death of Hector. Another early epic poem, the *Aithiopis*, describes battles with Amazonian and Ethiopian allies of the Trojans and also how Achilles killed Thersites for abusing him and was purified from the guilt of this deed by Ulysses. Later Achilles was killed by the arrow of Paris with Apollo's help. The Greeks and Trojans fought furiously over his corpse. Eventually Ajax carried it to safety while Ulysses fought valiantly in support (another account reversed their roles). After the obsequies of Achilles, Ulysses and Ajax began to quarrel about which of them was to have his armour.

The next poem in the epic sequence, the *Little Iliad*, described how the Greeks held a trial to decide who among them should be awarded the armour as a prize for heroic excellence. This was the Judgement of Arms which became a favourite theme in later literature and art. In the end the field was reduced to two, Ulysses and Ajax. Many must have expected Ajax to win, for all agreed that he had been next to Achilles in military strength and valour. But by Athena's influence the prize was awarded to Ulysses. The reason for choosing Ulysses for the supreme prize of excellence presumably was that the heroes (and Homer) considered intelligence to be more valuable in winning a war than mere fighting power. In fact Troy in the end was captured not by military force but by a stratagem conceived by Ulysses.

After winning the prize Ulysses performed some useful services for the Greeks. He captured the prophet of the Trojans, Helenos, and learnt from him that the hero Philoctetes would have to join the Greek army before Troy could be captured. Consequently Ulysses (according to the version which Sophocles used in his tragedy on that theme) or Diomedes (according to the *Little Iliad*) went and brought him back from his exile on Lemnos. Next Ulysses sailed to Skyros and enlisted Achilles' son, Neoptolemos (nicknamed Pyrrhos, meaning 'Red'), who later played a leading part in the slaughter of the Trojans. Ulysses gave him his father's armour.

Ill. 16. Ulysses coming from behind a rock on the right approaches Philoctetes on Lemnos. (Perhaps a scene from Sophocles' *Philoctetes* or a later version.) Flies hover over Philoctetes' gangrened foot. A Graeco-Roman sard intaglio (from a cast), see p. 159.

Ulysses also undertook a daring and perilous task, with a touch of Autolykos about it. Disguising himself as a beggar, he entered Troy to spy out conditions there. No one recognized him except Helen. She, because (as she says herself in describing the incident in *Odyssey* 4) her 'heart was already turned towards going home', did not betray him, but treated him kindly and sent him safely back to the Greek camp. Ulysses showed great courage and initiative in this exploit. But again, the more conventional heroes might have felt some disdain for a man who could demean himself by dressing in filthy rags.

Soon afterwards Ulysses dared to enter Troy again, this time in company with Diomedes. Details of their method of entry are lacking. They succeeded in their purpose—to steal the Palladium, the holy statue of Athena on which the fate of Troy was believed to depend. In the *Little Iliad* Ulysses takes the leading part in this exploit, Diomedes acting in a subsidiary role. Later accounts make Diomedes the leader and say that Ulysses tried to kill him in anger or envy, which would have been quite out of character for the Ulysses of the *Iliad*.

Ill. 17

When these necessary preliminaries for victory had been completed, Ulysses produced his master stratagem, the Wooden Horse, famous ever since in European legend. Homer does not explicitly say that Ulysses devised it, presumably because he assumed that everyone knew that already. Certainly the later tradition always gives Ulysses the credit for having planned it. Estimates vary widely about its capacity. Homer names five warriors who hid in it—Ulysses (who was in command and controlled the door), Menelaos, Neoptolemos, Diomedes and an otherwise unknown soldier named Antiklos—but implies that there were others. After the Greek heroes had concealed themselves inside, the other Greeks dragged the Horse up to the walls of Troy in the night and then pretended to withdraw from the Troad. Next day, as Menelaos recounts in *Odyssey* 4, Helen came out to view the strange apparition. Then she did a curious thing. She walked round the Horse three times, feeling it and calling 'the best men of the Greeks' by name in voices that imitated the voices of their wives at home. (Presumably Ulysses had told Helen his intentions about the Wooden Horse when he had encountered her on his spying expedition in Troy.) Diomedes and Menelaos wanted to get up and go out, or at least to answer her from inside. Ulysses quickly stopped them. But Antiklos still wanted to answer. 'Then with mighty hands Ulysses

Ill. 19

Ill. 17. Ulysses, right, faces Diomedes who holds the Palladium (the statue of Athena on which the fate of Troy depends), just captured in a night-raid on Troy. A sard intaglio of the Roman period signed, in Greek, 'Felix' (see p. 159).

Ill. 18. Another fine painting by Douris, on an Attic red-figure kylix, *c.* 490 BC (see p. 145). Ulysses, with a kind look and carrying a shield with a chimaera on it, gives young Neoptolemos, the son of Achilles and a daughter of King Lykomedes of Skyros, the armour of his father before the youth comes to fight for the Greeks at Troy, as described in the *Little Iliad*. Between them are Achilles' greaves.

seized on his jawbone, ruthlessly holding him still, and he kept the Achaeans in safety' (*Odyssey* 4:287, 288). In another brief account of the incident in *Odyssey* 11, Ulysses himself describes the state of extreme nervous tension inside the Horse. He saw, he says, all the other heroes growing pale with anxiety and even weeping with dread, all except Neoptolemos who instead kept grasping his sword and spear in eagerness to get out and attack the enemy.

After Helen's visit another danger arose. It is briefly described by a bard at the court of King Alkinoös of Phaeacia in *Odyssey* 8. The Trojans came crowding round the Horse and debated whether they should pierce it through with spears, hurl it down the steep rocks of their acropolis, or leave it intact as an offering of appeasement to the gods. The third opinion prevailed, despite (according to the post-Homeric epic writers who continue the story) the omen of the two serpents which devoured Laocoön and his two sons when he tried to warn them. Eventually the Horse was taken inside the city walls. Then during the night, while the Trojans feasted in joy at the apparent withdrawal of the Greeks, Sinon the Greek (a cousin of Ulysses, according to a late account), who had been accepted by the Trojans as a deserter, lit a fire-signal to recall the rest of the Greeks from their hiding-place behind the island of Tenedos. Ulysses and his comrades crept out of the Horse, opened the gates, and joined in the slaughter of

the Trojans. After ten long years the war was won. The great city of Priam was sacked and burnt, the men killed, the women and children enslaved. Ulysses, though wounded in the first attack, joined in the carnage. According to the *Sack of Troy* it was he who killed Astyanax, the young son of Hector (but the *Little Iliad* said it was Neoptolemos who hurled him from a high tower). Subsequent writers also blamed him for taking the lead in the killing of the Trojan princess Polyxena. It was also said that when the lesser Ajax (not related to Ulysses' rival, the great champion from Salamis) committed sacrilege against Athena by dragging Cassandra forcibly from her sanctuary, Ulysses encouraged the Greeks to stone him to death (but Ajax escaped), and that as an act of mercy Ulysses spared two sons of Antenor in gratitude for his father's courtesy during the embassy to Troy.

One detail given in *Odyssey* 8 demonstrates how constantly Ulysses kept an eye on the essentials of the matter in hand. The chief motive of the Trojan War was to restore Helen to her husband. Accordingly, Ulysses went with Menelaos straight to the house of Deïphobos, where Helen now lived after the death of Paris. There, after a grim battle, he made sure that Menelaos got Helen back safely. Ulysses owed Helen a debt of gratitude for her help when he entered Troy as a spy. Now it was paid.

Looking back over the career of Ulysses at Troy as presented by Homer and the authors of the other early epics, one can see two main features. First, he says and does things which no other hero says or does, and sometimes, as when he disguised himself as a beggar, he accepts a distinctly unheroic role. Yet apart from two discreditable incidents, which Homer does not mention (the attempt to avoid conscription and the murder of Palamedes), all his efforts were concentrated on winning the war. When he demeaned himself, it was in the public interest.

Secondly, the other Greek princes seem to regard him at times as something of an outsider, a not quite top-flight hero, partly as a result of his unconventional ways of talking and acting, but partly, too, on account of his less exalted home background and ancestry (though Homer, as we have seen, never says in the *Iliad* that Autolykos was his grandfather). Yet Agamemnon and Menelaos clearly liked and admired him, and in the end he was awarded the supreme prize of excellence in preference to the high-born and valiant Ajax. In fact his career at Troy is shown as one of steadily increasing success and prestige; and in the end he was the architect of the final victory.

How, we may ask, did Homer himself regard Ulysses in his Iliadic aspects? It is not Homer's custom to offer personal judgements on his heroes, but a good deal can be deduced from the kind of epithets he applies to them. In the *Iliad* he gives Ulysses most of the conventional epithets of a hero—'most renowned', 'faultless', 'lordly', 'skilled in the art of war', 'god-beloved', 'god-born', 'illustrious', 'famed in spear-fighting', 'noble', 'divine', 'godlike', 'bold', 'mighty', 'famed', 'great-spirited', 'great-hearted', 'sacker of cities', 'glorious'. More significantly, he also gives him several which none of the other heroes had: 'insatiable in wiles and toils', 'wily-minded', 'much-praised' (or 'famous in many stories'), 'of many counsels', 'of many devices', 'of many turns', 'of much intelligence', 'with enduring heart', 'much-enduring', and simply 'enduring'. These unusual epithets clearly emphasize two main qualities: his versatile intelligence and his endurance—qualities not often found in one person. Versatile and clever people tend to be impatient and lacking in pertinacity: but Ulysses, once he had set his mind on some task, carried it through to the end unrelentingly. We shall see this quality of endurance tested to extremes in the *Odyssey*.

Ill. 20. An unusual scene from Ulysses' first adventure after he left Troy. When he sacked Ismaros, the town of the Cicones, he spared the local priest of Apollo, Maron. Maron gave him a skin of wine (with which Ulysses later made the Cyclops drunk). The other two figures depicted here may be the wife and child of Maron. From an Apulian bell krater, *c.* 350 BC.

2 Ulysses in the early epic tradition—his return home and death—and in early Greek art

W. B. Stanford

IN the famous first line of the *Odyssey*,

Tell me, Muse, of the man of many turns,

we are assured of two things: first that, unlike the *Iliad,* in which the theme is the effects of the wrath of Achilles on many people, this poem is more concerned with a single personality; and secondly that the supreme quality to be displayed by him will be versatility, the power to twist and turn and escape from the varied trials and dangers that beset him on his journey home. The next few lines of the poem emphasize the wide experience of cities and men that he acquired, the bitter woes he suffered, and the folly of his Companions, whom he tried to save.

After this brief introduction Homer begins to tell the immortal story in his own masterly way, not beginning at the point when Ulysses sets out from Troy but breaking into the narrative just forty days before the final triumph of Ulysses, when he slays the Suitors and is re-united with Penelope. With consummate boldness, the poet postpones telling us the events of the previous ten years, between the fall of Troy and the eve of his hero's homecoming, until eight books are completed. But for the purposes of our present quest it will be more suitable here to adopt the more humdrum method of the mere chronicler, rearranging the material in chronological order.

As the ashes of Troy cooled, quarrelling broke out between Agamemnon and Menelaos. At first, Homer tells in *Odyssey* 3, Ulysses sided with Menelaos and sailed away with him to Tenedos. Then for some reason not stated, he turned back and joined Agamemnon. After this he set out for home with his twelve ships. A southerly wind carried them to Thrace on the north-west Greek mainland. They landed there and sacked the town of Ismaros, an act of piracy quite normal in the heroic age. But Ulysses, with characteristic piety, spared the family of Maron, a local priest of Apollo. As a reward he received *Ill. 20* the strong wine that would later help him to escape from the Cyclops. After the sack of the town they killed the men, took the women as slaves (we hear nothing more about them) and looted the treasure. Then Ulysses advised an immediate withdrawal. His Companions refused. This was the first of a series of disastrous semi-mutinies on their part. They began feasting on the captured cattle. Soon the local tribe, the Cicones, attacked in force—'as many as the leaves and flowers in spring' (*Odyssey* 9:51) Homer says—and killed six of the crew of each ship. Ulysses and the rest sailed sadly off with a following north wind.

They steered steadily southwards from Thrace, eager to round Cape Maleia, the southernmost tip of the mainland of Greece. There they would turn westwards and reach Ithaca in two or three days. Unfortunately for them, but fortunately for the *Odyssey*'s millions of readers, Zeus sent a hurricane—Homer does not explain why—which ripped the sails to shreds and drove the ships off-course southwards away from Maleia. Then, after passing the island of Cythera, the last clearly identifiable place that Ulysses saw until reaching Ithaca again, they came to the land of the Lotos-eaters. They went ashore for water and a meal. Soon Ulysses, always eager for new information, sent two men and a herald to ask who the people were that could be seen eating food on the beach. The three were kindly received, and given some of 'the honey-sweet fruit' of the lotos to eat. They then lost all desire to return home, wishing only to stay on idly with the Lotos-eaters. Ulysses acted promptly. He drove the would-be 'drop-outs' on to their ships by force, tied them down, as they struggled violently to get back among the Lotos-eaters, and sailed away at once. Perhaps Homer intended this as an allegory of the danger of sloth on Life's Voyage, as later writers took it, perhaps not.

The fleet sails on into the unknown world. They reach the land of the Cyclopes. Beside the shore they find a high cave. Before entering,

Ill. 21. A rather naive presentation of the blinding of Polyphemos on an early South Italian calyx krater (late fifth century BC). Ulysses, wearing the pilos on the right, directs three Companions who are about to thrust the trunk of a tree, no less, into the eye of the drunken Cyclops. The satyr-figure, bottom right, beside the wine-cup and skin, suggests that this is a scene from a satyr-play like Euripides' *Cyclops*.

Ill. 22. An early, highly formalized version of the blinding of Polyphemos on a black-figure Laconian kylix, *c.* 550 BC. It has some non-Homeric features: the Cyclops is seated, not lying down as in *Odyssey* 9:371, and the offering of the wine-cup is simultaneous with the use of the staff for blinding. Ghoulishly, Polyphemos holds the lower legs of a mostly eaten Companion. The snake and the fish are decorative. (Cf. *Ill. 44.*)

Ills. 21–24

Ulysses chooses the twelve best men from among his Companions and takes a goatskin of the strong wine that he had been given by the priest of Apollo at Ismaros. Inside they find lambs and kids, baskets of cheese and buckets of whey.

Something very unusual in Ulysses' career happens now. When his Companions, sensing danger, advise that they should take some of the food and withdraw at once, Ulysses refuses, because with typical curiosity he wants to see what the owner is like. (He sadly admitted his mistake later.) They wait until the Cyclops, Polyphemos, arrives. The sequel is one of the best known stories in the world. More than two hundred versions of it have been collected from many parts of Europe and Asia, with remarkable variations. The original tale may have been composed before the early ancestors of the Indo-European peoples divided into separate tribes and nations. Essentially it is a variation of the Jack-the-giant-killer theme, in which an ogre is defeated by a small, wily opponent.

Polyphemos soon sees the Greeks and questions them. Ulysses in reply asks him for the customary gifts given to strangers, reminding him that strangers are under the special protection of Zeus. Polyphemos replies that Ulysses must be a fool—a touch of irony there—if he thinks that any Cyclops cares about Zeus and his laws. He asks Ulysses where his ship is. Ulysses tells him a protective lie, saying that

it has been wrecked. The Cyclops seizes two of Ulysses' Companions and eats them. Ulysses thinks for a moment whether he should try to kill the monster with his sword. But then, even if he succeeded, they would all die, since the entrance to the cave was now sealed with a great rock which only a Cyclops could move. So he decides to wait.

Next morning Polyphemos devours two more Companions and then goes out to tend his flocks. He blocks the exit from the cave again. Ulysses has plenty of time to prepare a plan. He takes a large staff of olive wood belonging to the Cyclops, hardens one end of it in the fire, hides it, and, having explained to his Companions what he hopes to do, waits for Polyphemos' return. In the evening Polyphemos returns, and when he has looked after the animals, he seizes two more of the Companions and eats them. Then Ulysses begins his plan. He offers the Cyclops some of the strong wine. Polyphemos takes it and likes it greatly. He drinks more and begins to get drunk. Now he asks Ulysses his name and promises him a gift. Ulysses craftily says his name is 'No-man'. Brutally Polyphemos replies:

> I shall eat No-man last among his Companions
> The others I shall eat first. Such is my guest-gift to him.
> (*Odyssey* 9:369, 370)

Then he collapses into a drunken coma. The moment for action has come. Ulysses exhorts his Companions to be brave and heats the point of the staff in the fire. They thrust it into the single eye of the ogre and blind him. He, too late, pulls the staff from his eye, leaps up and shouts for help to the Cyclopes who live nearby. They come to the closed

Ill. 23. Ulysses escaping from the Cyclops under the ram, as described in *Odyssey* 9:444–63. This was a favourite theme in early Greek and Etruscan art (cf. *Ill. 101*). From an Attic krater by the 'Sappho painter', *c.* 510 BC.

38

door of the cave and ask what's wrong. Polyphemos shouts back: 'Friends, No-man is trying to kill me by craft, not by strength' (*Odyssey* 9:408). Mishearing 'No-man' as 'No man' (in the Greek the difference between *oûtis* and *oútis* is one of tonality), they tell him that, if no man is trying to kill him, his affliction must have been sent by the gods: so he'd better pray to his father Poseidon for help. Inside the cave Ulysses laughs in exaltation at the success of his brilliant use of deceptive nomenclature.

A grim bout of blind-man's buff follows, as Polyphemos gropes for his enemies in the cave. Eventually he has to remove the boulder to let his sheep and goats out. He stays inside the opening of the cavern, feeling the back of each animal as it goes out. Ulysses and his companions escape underneath the sheep, reach the ship and row off.

At this point Ulysses again endangers lives by a rash action. Shouting back to the shore, he boasts to Polyphemos that he has punished him for his impiety towards strangers. The Cyclops hurls a great rock in the direction of the voice, and nearly hits the ship. Ulysses, with further astonishing rashness and despite the urgent begging of his crew, shouts at the Cyclops again, revealing that his true name is Ulysses. Polyphemos prays to his father Poseidon to

Ill. 24. Polyphemos hurling a rock at the ship of Ulysses (*Odyssey* 9:481–3, 537–40). A powerfully conceived and executed detail from a wall-painting at Boscotrecase, first century AD. Compare the treatment in Turner's picture (*Ill. 173*).

punish Ulysses, and hurls an even larger rock at the ship. He misses again. The Greeks rejoin the rest of their fleet. Next day they sail on.

This episode presents a puzzling contrast with Ulysses' normal conduct. Why did he twice behave with such uncharacteristic imprudence, first by staying on in the cave until Polyphemos returned, and secondly by shouting back at the furious ogre? Elsewhere it is usually he who has to overcome the foolhardiness of his Companions. Here they are the prudent ones, trying in vain to restrain him. The best explanation offered as yet is that here Homer was using an already well-known tale in which a bold and boastful folklore hero—brash, cocksure and loud-mouthed—outwitted a giant in flamboyant fairytale style. When Homer adapted this story, it is suggested, he found it difficult to prevent Ulysses from retaining something of that folk-hero's character; hence the uncharacteristic rashness and boastfulness. At any rate, whatever the true explanation may be, Ulysses never behaves so imprudently again in the *Odyssey*.

Next they come to the island of Aiolos ('Aeolus' is the Latin form), King of the winds. He receives them hospitably and sends them on towards Ithaca with all the winds, except the favourable west wind, tied up in a bag. They sail on happily and on the tenth day see their homeland. Ulysses, who has been continuously navigating, decides that their homecoming is safely assured now. He snatches some sleep. The Companions, suspecting that treasure is concealed in the mysterious bag, open it. The winds rush out in a terrible storm. Ulysses wakes to see Ithaca receding fast. He thinks for a moment of trying to swim ashore, though he sees that he would certainly die in the attempt—the only time in his career when he considered anything like suicide. But he decides to endure. They are blown back to Aiolos. He drives them away with curses.

This episode throws light on a side of Ulysses' nature which has not previously been emphasized by Homer. It seems that his relations with his comrades were not as frank and open as they could have been. No clear reason is given why he should not have told them that the bag contained the winds, but kept it a secret. They suspected his motives, with lamentable results. Later writers like Fénelon were to praise this gift of dissimulation, which they regarded as a necessary quality in ruling princes. But among the Homeric heroes, as we have seen, it was not admired, and in this case, it was disastrous.

Numerically the greatest loss of the whole voyage occurred in the next episode, the massacre by the Laistrygonians. Apart from some remarkable topographical details, which will be considered in a later chapter, the action is rather brusquely presented. Three men sent ashore as ambassadors by Ulysses meet a girl drawing water. They go with her to Telepylos, 'the lofty citadel of Lamos', and encounter the wife of the local ruler Antiphates:

She was as big as a mountain and they loathed her.

(*Odyssey* 10:113)

Ill. 25. A rare incident in classical art, if the identification is correct: a Companion of Ulysses is untying the bag of the winds (as described in *Odyssey* 10:47), while the bearded head of a wind-god emerges from it. An Etruscan scarab of the late fifth century BC (see p. 159).

Ills. 140, 141

Her ogre husband arrives and, like Polyphemos, seizes and devours one of the Greeks. The other two rush back to the ships. Then the gigantic Laistrygonians come flocking on to the cliffs over the narrow fjord where Ulysses' ships are moored. They smash eleven of the ships, harpoon their crews, and take the bodies home for a cannibalistic feast. Ulysses manages to cut the hawsers of his ship with his sword, and escapes with his personal Companions. But now his fleet is reduced to only one ship.

The next incident is much more fully described. It has remained a favourite theme, often allegorically interpreted, in poetry and legend ever since Homer's time. The single surviving ship reaches the island of Circe, daughter of the Sun. Ulysses and his Companions land and lie for two days in a state of inertia after the shock of the Laistrygonian massacre. On the third day Ulysses goes off to explore. He sees smoke in the distance, but he postpones further search until he and the others have had a meal (which he augments by killing a splendid stag on his way back). Then he divides his men into two bands. He heads one, and a Companion named Eurylokhos the other. Lots are drawn to see which band should go and explore further. Eurylokhos and his men have to go. They meet strange fawning animals before they come to Circe's palace. There Circe turns them by her enchantment into pigs,

Ill. 26. Ulysses and his Companions at the house of Circe are depicted on an Attic red-figure krater, *c.* 440 BC. On the top band, Ulysses threatens Circe with his sword as in *Odyssey* 10:321–2. She runs away. (In the *Odyssey* she runs under the sword and supplicates his knees.) Behind Ulysses a Companion, semi-metamorphosized into a pig, stretches out his arms in appeal to Ulysses.

except Eurylokhos who prudently stayed outside. When none of his men comes out again, he suspects harm, and returns to tell Ulysses. Ulysses at once buckles on his sword and sets out to the rescue. On his way the god Hermes meets him, and warns him about Circe's baneful enchantments. As a counter-charm Hermes plucks and gives him a plant called *Moly*. (There has been much speculation about its botanical and allegorical nature: all Homer says is that it had a milk-white flower, a black root, and was dangerous for mortals to dig up.)

Protected by this, Ulysses goes on to meet Circe. She, when her enchanted cup fails to turn him into an animal, recognizes him from a prediction about his coming. She immediately invites him to come to bed with her. Hermes had told Ulysses that he must do this. But first, acting on Hermes' advice, he makes her 'swear a great oath' that she will not try to harm him any more. After their intercourse, attendants provide lavish food and furnishings. Ulysses refuses to eat and Circe asks why. Ulysses says he wants first to have his comrades turned back into men. Circe goes to the pigsties and transforms them, making them, as a compensation for their agonizing experience, younger, handsomer, and stronger than they had been before. Then, at Circe's request, Ulysses goes back to his ship and brings the remaining Companions to a feast.   *Ill. 26*

Circe apparently likes having them about the place, as a change from the company of the lions, wolves and pigs. She suggests to Ulysses that they should stay on with her until they have regained their strength and spirit after their many catastrophes. A whole year elapses. Ulysses seems to have forgotten his desire to reach home. Under Circe's influence he has become a kind of lotos-eater himself. Eventually it is his comrades who have to come and ask him to resume their voyage. He tells Circe he wants to go. She coolly says that she certainly won't keep him against his will—and then adds the shattering statement: 'But you'll have to visit Hades before you go home'. She gives the reason: only in the Land of Departed Spirits can Ulysses consult the ghost of Teiresias, that renowned prophet of Thebes, who has essential information to give him for his future safety. Ulysses is appalled by this terrifying prospect. He writhes on the bed in an agony of lamentation. (Homer's men were not inhibited about bursting into tears: in fact Dryden called them, in contrast with Britishers, 'St. Swithin's Day heroes'.) But he pulls himself together; since there is no alternative if he wants to reach Ithaca safely, he resolves to go to Hades. After a fatal accident to the youngest of his comrades, Elpenor (whose ghost will reach Hades faster than any ship could travel), the Greeks sail away towards the dark regions where the Land of Ghosts lies.

When Ulysses has reached Hades and has performed the necessary rites of propitiation and evocation, ghosts appear. First comes a vividly described crowd of nameless women, youths, maidens, old men, and warriors: then Elpenor (Ulysses promises to give him a   *Ill. 27*

Ill. 27. A masterly piece on an Attic red-figure pelike, *c.* 450–40 BC, by the 'Lykaon painter' (see p. 147). Ulysses, accompanied by Hermes, has just sacrificed animals to the ghosts in Hades. Unexpectedly (*Odyssey* 11:51–6) the ghost of a Companion, Elpenor, appears first. The melancholy, disturbed expression on Ulysses' large-eyed face, together with the arresting contrast between his right hand supporting his chin in an attitude of contemplative grief and his left firmly holding his sword in readiness for attack or defence, make this a most moving conception of the scene (perhaps influenced by Polygnotos—see p. 152).

hero's burial), and then the ghost of Antikleia, his mother. Rather ruthlessly Ulysses does not allow her to address him until Teiresias has come and given him the information that is vital for his safe return. Teiresias tells Ulysses what he needs, adding a mysterious prophecy about events that will take place after Ulysses has returned to Ithaca (which will have sequels in later literature). Then Ulysses talks with his mother, the daughter of Autolykos, as Homer reminds us here. She speaks to him with deep affection. The final moment, when Ulysses tries to embrace Antikleia lovingly but finds his arms passing through empty air, is unforgettable.

After this a rather irrelevant, but mythologically very remarkable, episode follows. The ghosts of famous Greek women from earlier times appear, and then the ghosts of dead Greek commanders of the army of Troy. The appearance of the first of these, Agamemnon, shocked Ulysses, for he did not know that he had been brutally murdered by his wife and her paramour in Mycenae. Agamemnon tells how he died, and sadly contrasts his fate with the good fortune of

Ulysses, who will be welcomed home by Penelope and Telemachos. Then come the ghosts of Achilles, Patroklos, Antilokhos and Ajax. Ulysses first converses with Achilles. When Achilles has told him how he hates being dead, Ulysses comforts him with news of his son Neoptolemos. But when Ulysses speaks to the ghost of Ajax, saying how sorry he was that he had committed suicide in chagrin at losing the prize for valour, Ajax makes no reply. Instead he turns silently away into the darkness—a majestic gesture which for a moment makes all Ulysses' eloquence seem trivial.

After further experiences in Hades, Ulysses returns to Circe. He gives Elpenor a hero's funeral. Afterwards Circe refreshes Ulysses and his Companions with a banquet and tells Ulysses about further

Ills. 28, 29. Contrasting treatments of the ever-favourite scene of Ulysses and his Companions sailing past the Sirens. The drawing from a Corinthian aryballos, *c.* 570 BC, (above) is an early version, with the primitive, half-bird Sirens apparently assisted by large birds which attack the ship. No music or song is indicated. The Campanian terracotta relief (below) is some seven hundred years more recent (first century AD). Ulysses, tied to the mast, seems to be gesturing to his Companions to release him (cf. *Odyssey* 12:192–4).

adventures that he will encounter before he reaches Ithaca, warning him especially against eating the Cattle of the Sun. Next morning they set sail for home. Soon they approached the island of the Sirens. Ulysses remembered Circe's warning about the fate of anyone who was lured by the magic of their song—there was a great heap of corpses 'rotting on their bones' beside them, she said—and took precautions in a characteristic way. He decided to stuff the ears of his Companions with wax so that they would not hear the fatal incantation, and arranged that they should bind him tightly to the ship's mast so that he himself could hear the song and yet be prevented from being drawn to his destruction. In other words he made it possible for himself to satisfy his typically Ulyssean curiosity and, with equally Ulyssean prudence, ensured that he and his men would not suffer any harm. So his crew rowed steadily past unable to hear anything, while he listened raptly to the song that no man before had heard in safety.

Ills. 28, 29, 33

Apparently the Sirens varied their temptations to suit the character of their victims. If Ulysses had been essentially a sensual man, they would no doubt have offered him voluptuous delights, music, or delicious food, or sexual pleasures, as in the later tradition. Instead, divining his insatiable desire for knowledge, they offered him the equivalent of 'a global news-service' or, in Homeric language, information about 'whatever comes to pass throughout the fertile earth'. Eager to hear what the Sirens had to tell him, Ulysses struggled

Ill. 30. An unusual presentation of the monster Skylla in a decorative relief on a Roman bronze cup from Boscoreale, near Pompeii, first century AD. Homer describes Skylla in *Odyssey* 12:85–92 as having six long necks and twelve hanging limbs. The artist has avoided these horrors, following a later description that attached dogs' heads to her lower body. Here they are seen seizing some of the Companions.

45

to escape from his bonds. His Companions, as he had instructed them, tied him tighter, and rowed on in safety. Later writers were to allegorize this incident elaborately, and pictorial artists to revel in it.

More dangers lay ahead. The ship, passing the Wandering Rocks without disaster, approached the strait where Charybdis and Skylla lurked to seize unwary voyagers. Charybdis ('The Swallower') could suck whole ships down to what Homer calls the 'dark-blue' sands of the sea-floor. Skylla ('the Gnawer') with a voice like a yelping cur, had twelve legs, six long necks, and six hideous heads filled with three rows of thick-set, deadly teeth. She lurked in a cave above the waterway and snatched sailors from ships below. Ulysses had a tragic choice *Ill. 30* here. There was no question of sailing safely between the two. The channel was too narrow. He had to sail within reach of one monster or the other. Naturally he chose the lesser evil, Skylla. She seized six of his Companions from the ship and dragged them, piteously calling to

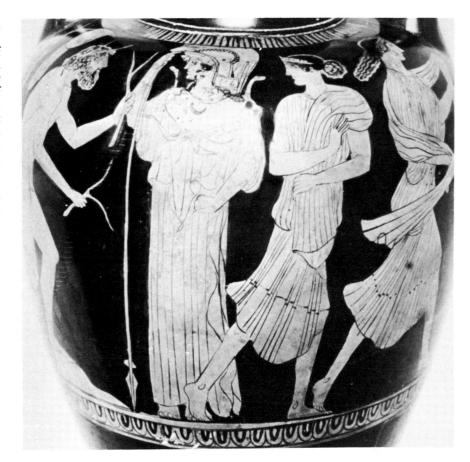

Ill. 32. Here, on an Attic red-figure amphora from *c.* 450–40 BC (see pp. 148, 149), we have a lively version of the meeting of Ulysses with Nausikaä on the sea-shore of Phaeacia (*Odyssey* 6:127–36), though the figure of Athena in the centre is not from Homer's narrative. Ulysses on the left symbolically conceals his nakedness with a branch while Nausikaä does not stand her ground bravely, as in Homer, but seems inclined to flee. However, unlike her handmaiden, who runs away, she looks over her shoulder at the stranger, as though about to turn towards him.

Ill. 34

Ill. 31. Opposite: this intimate and genial scene on a Tanagra terracotta (see p. 159) captures the mood of Homer's descriptions in *Odyssey* 5. Ulysses, looking rather sad, is apparently saying farewell to a more cheerful Calypso, while a cupid flutters between them. The ship's prow beside Ulysses is non-Homeric: in the *Odyssey* he departed on a raft.

Ulysses for help, into her butchering cave. Ulysses could only watch helplessly—'the most pitiful sight in all my exploring voyage through the paths of the sea', he called it (*Odyssey* 12:257, 258).

The Companions who escaped did not survive for long. They landed on Thrinakia where the Cattle of the Sun grazed. Despite Ulysses' solemn warning, they eventually killed and ate some of these animals when continuous adverse winds had kept them ashore for a month. The Sun-god, enraged by the sacrilege, demanded punishment from Zeus. When Ulysses' ship set sail again, a storm wrecked it. All the Companions perished. Ulysses, clinging to the keel, drifted to the lonely, but lovely, island of Calypso, Ogygia. She, a kind and motherly person, cherished him there for seven years, in her langorously beautiful island—a faraway paradise like Gauguin's Tahiti. Then, on the initiative of Athena, Zeus sent Hermes to tell Calypso to send Ulysses home. The parting scenes between the demi-goddess and Ulysses are full of deep feeling. She loves him dearly and tries to persuade him to remain with her. She warns him of further dangers in his path and offers him immortality if he will stay with her. Ulysses refuses. He has long been yearning, with many tears, for his wife and homeland. He builds a makeshift boat and sails steadily homewards, steering by the stars at night.

47

After seventeen days he saw land in the distance. But Poseidon, still angry at the blinding of his son Polyphemos, sent a sudden storm which wrecked Ulysses' boat and would have drowned him if a sea-nymph, Ino Leukothea ('the White Goddess'), had not intervened to keep him afloat with her magical head-veil. After two more days of struggling through the waves, Ulysses reached land and sank exhausted into a deep sleep near the sea-shore.

Ill. 167

He had come to Scheria, the land of the Phaeacians, the last place he was to visit before returning to Ithaca. Next day he was awakened by the voices of young women. They were Nausikaä, princess of Scheria, and her girl companions. Nausikaä is one of Homer's most vivid and memorable creations: beautiful as Artemis, sympathetic, outspoken and lively, she is just on the border between girlhood and womanhood, and is thinking about married life. When Ulysses suddenly appears before her, naked except for a leafy branch broken off as a covering, and ill-kept from his struggles in the sea, she stands her ground bravely, listens to his request for help, replies with poise and humanity, treats him kindly, and eventually guides him to her father's palace. The encounter between the grizzled seafarer—Ulysses' first speech to her is one of the most adroit and tactful he ever had to make—and the naively charming girl is presented by the poet with superb delicacy and insight. Scholars have suggested that Homer is using here the folktale motif of the unknown stranger who defeats local champions in competitions (as Ulysses later does in Scheria) and marries the native princess. This may be right: Nausikaä in fact does say that Ulysses (after he has been magically beautified by Athena) is the kind of man she would like to marry. But Ulysses, as Homer portrayed him, was not a figure of romance to marry *la princesse lointaine*: he was determined to return to the family and the home that he had never wanted to leave.

Ill. 32

When Ulysses arrives at the palace of King Alkinoös and Queen Arete, he is received with kindness and hospitality. They entertain him with the delights of their luxurious society—feasting, dancing, athletics, poetry, and song. Keeping to the etiquette prescribed for receiving strangers in the era described by Homer, they do not ask him who he is, or where he comes from, until a whole day has elapsed. In the evening, after a banquet, he dramatically reveals his identity:

> I am Odysseus, son of Laërtes. All men take account of my wiles and my fame has reached high heaven. My home is in Ithaca, fair in the evening light.
>
> (*Odyssey* 9:19–21)

Then, in one of the most spellbinding and most celebrated after-dinner speeches ever made, he relates his adventures during the ten years since the fall of Troy (as already described in this chapter).

Next morning King Alkinoös offers a sacrifice to Zeus and sends Ulysses homewards with rich gifts in one of the magically swift ships of the Phaeacians. Ulysses falls into a deep sleep on the way and is still

Ill. 33. Opposite: this famous red-figure Attic stamnos, *c.* 475 BC, from Vulci presents a dramatic version of the Sirens episode (see p. 148). Ulysses stands stiffly bound to the mast while his unheeding Companions (he has stuffed their ears with wax) row steadily on. Two bird-Sirens call to the ship from rocks on either side while a third rather unconvincingly plunges down towards it (Homer, in *Odyssey* 12:167, implies that there were only two).

Ill. 34. *Ill. 34.* Opposite: a macabre illustration of the fateful eating of the forbidden Cattle of the Sun (*Odyssey* 12: 353 ff.), as conceived by Tibaldi in what was formerly the Palazzo Poggi in Bologna and is now the University (see p. 202 and *Ills. 1, 166, 167*). The artist has caught the atmosphere of uncanny eeriness implied in Homer's description by putting an unforgettably apprehensive look in the eyes both of the Companion on the left and of the ox or cow (Homer says they were cows) on the right, suggesting all the horror of the events soon to come.

sleeping when the Phaeacian seamen put him ashore with his gifts on Ithaca and sail back to Scheria. When Ulysses awakes he fails to recognize his Ithaca, after so long an absence. Despairingly he thinks that the Phaeacians have deceived him and marooned him on another hostile island. He counts his gifts to make sure that none has been stolen. Athena, disguised as a shepherd, approaches. She assures him that he is in Ithaca. Cautiously and cunningly Ulysses proceeds to tell a fictitious tale about himself—that he is a refugee from Crete, brought here to Western Greece by Phoenician strangers. Athena, amused by his incorrigible craftiness, smiles, reveals her identity and in a bantering tone commends him not only for his inexhaustible powers of deception, but also for his clever resourcefulness, his unrivalled eloquence and his practical wisdom, qualities in which she herself excels among the gods.

Convinced now that he has at last come back to his Ithaca, Ulysses kisses the ground with joy. At Athena's suggestion he hides his gifts in a cave of the Nymphs nearby. Then the two of them, goddess and hero, sit down together at the base of a sacred olive tree and plan how Ulysses can kill the Suitors of Penelope in his home. It is an idyllic moment of peace before the final struggle begins.

Here we must go back to the opening books of the *Odyssey* for knowledge of the state of affairs in the palace of Odysseus at this time. During the first ten years of Ulysses' absence at Troy, Penelope's status was secure enough. It was assumed that her husband would return to his kingdom as soon as the war ended. But after the fall of Troy became known in Ithaca, and when Ulysses failed to return year after year, eligible young men from Ithaca and its neighbourhood— one hundred and eight in all, Homer says—came to woo Penelope, who was now assumed by most people to be a widow. She, never losing hope that her husband would return, delayed their wooing by various ruses worthy of Ulysses' own wiliness. The most celebrated was her pretence that she would be willing to make a decision when she had finished weaving a large robe as a shroud for Ulysses' father when he died. She wove it ostentatiously during the day, and unwove it surreptitiously during the night. Disloyal maidservants betrayed her secret to the Suitors, and they began to press her hard. At the time when the *Odyssey* begins (which is thirty-four days before Ulysses lands on Ithaca), she has almost reached desperation. The Suitors have now occupied the public rooms of the palace and are spending their days there more and more insolently.

Ill. 35

Her son Telemachos is now about twenty years old. He has gone, at Athena's prompting, to seek news about his father from Nestor in Pylos. On the day when Ulysses returns to Ithaca, Telemachos is still away from home. The Suitors, alarmed and angered at his recent show of manly independence, have laid an ambush for him near the home port in Ithaca, intending to kill him on his way back. Penelope now

has no member of the family to support her in the palace. Ulysses' father, Laërtes, has gone to live a sad and lonely life on a distant farm. (We are not told why. Perhaps Homer intends us to understand that he could not endure the arrogance of the Suitors; or perhaps it was the custom for kings who abdicated to leave the royal palace.)

To return to Ulysses: Athena, after warning him of the trials that lie ahead, disguises him as an old beggar and tells him to go first to the swineherd Eumaios, who has remained staunchly loyal to him. She then sets out for Sparta to recall Telemachos, while Ulysses climbs up the rough path towards the Raven's Crag where Eumaios lives. Eumaios, formerly a prince, now a slave and a keeper of pigs, receives the apparent beggar hospitably. They talk about the Ulysses whom Eumaios believes to be dead. Eumaios affectionately recalls his kindness and consideration. In reply, Ulysses predicts that the absent king will return very soon, and goes on to tell an elaborate tissue of lies about himself, narrating a kind of counter-*Odyssey* of fictitious adventures on voyages from Crete to Troy, Egypt, Phoenicia, Thesprotia (where he claims to have heard news of Ulysses), and finally to Ithaca. Ulysses' powers of imaginative deceitfulness are never better displayed than in this highly circumstantial piece of fiction. In further conversations Ulysses takes the opportunity of finding out about the state of affairs in Ithaca.

Ills. 35–37. Three scenes from Roman art connected with the return of Ulysses to Ithaca after his wanderings. On the terracotta relief (opposite), Penelope mourns (presumably for her absent husband) in a conventional pose, with Eurykleia behind her and two women-servants in front. On the sarcophagus relief of the second century AD (top right), Ulysses, dressed as a beggar, is recognized by his dog, Argos, in the poignant scene described in *Odyssey* 17:291 ff., a favourite in Roman art. On the Campanian terracotta relief of the first century AD (bottom right), Ulysses grabs Eurykleia by the mouth to prevent her revealing that she has recognized him by noticing the tell-tale scar on his leg as she washed it (*Odyssey* 19: 480).

Meanwhile Athena has gone to Sparta to fetch Telemachos home. He avoids the ambush set by the Suitors (Athena has forewarned him), lands on Ithaca and makes his way, as instructed by Athena, to Eumaios' farm. There, after some preliminaries, he recognizes Ulysses, and they make plans for killing the Suitors. Next morning they set out separately for the palace.

Homer, a master in the art of suspense, now delays the great climax of his narrative, the slaughter of the Suitors, by many ingenious episodes. These also serve to deepen our understanding of Ulysses' character and to display the doomed arrogance of the Suitors (though among them Homer presents some who are less culpable than the rest). Ulysses, that 'much-enduring man', has to submit to insults and ill-treatment from the worst of the Suitors. He fights and defeats a local beggar called Iros. He observes the disloyalty and immorality of some of the palace manservants and maidservants, and is insulted by them. He finds that he can rely for help on only two besides his son—Eumaios and a cowherd called Philoitios.

Ulysses tries to avoid being recognized by Penelope or any other than those just mentioned, but does not entirely succeed. First, there is an incident that was to be frequently remembered and re-enacted in later literature and art: as he comes near his home he sees his favourite dog, Argos, now decrepit with age, lying uncared for in the dirt of the *Ill. 36* courtyard. The dog recognizes its master after twenty years' absence. It feebly wags its tail and lowers its ears to welcome him—and dies. Luckily no enemy notices. Later another unintended recognition nearly betrays him, too. Penelope orders Ulysses' old nurse Eurykleia to wash Ulysses' feet. Eurykleia, as she washes them, recognizes the scar of the wound that Ulysses had received on his visit to Autolykos. *Ill. 37* Instantly she guesses who he is. Ulysses grabs her by the throat and commands her not to betray him. Athena takes care that Penelope, though sitting nearby (the Suitors had gone away to their homes for the night), should not notice anything unusual. Just before this *Ill. 38* incident Ulysses had been conversing with Penelope. He had found it bitterly hard not to reveal himself as she talked so sadly about her loneliness. But, firm of purpose as ever, and convinced that it was best for the success of his plan, he told her lies about having met Ulysses in Crete.

After several such episodes in which Ulysses' cunning and endurance are tested very fully, the plot begins to move faster towards its crisis. Athena directs Penelope to propose the Trial of the Bow. In the store-chamber of the palace at Ithaca there was a mighty bow, which Ulysses had been given by another famous archer and had kept as a precious heirloom in his treasury. It was so massive that only a hero of Ulysses' strength and skill could string it. Penelope has it brought in among the Suitors and announces that she will marry the person who can string the bow and shoot an arrow through a row of axe-heads set in a straight line by Telemachos. When two of the Suitors have failed

Ill. 38. Ulysses, disguised as a beggar after his return to Ithaca, talking to Penelope, who is grieving for her absent husband. From the naive but expressive set of terracotta reliefs from Melos, 460–50 BC (see p. 157 and *Ills. 123, 124*). This pose of Penelope recurs frequently in later representations of this favourite episode.

to string it, Ulysses gets possession of the bow. Then comes the
great moment: he gives a signal to Eurykleia to go out and lock the
doors of the Great Hall. He strings the bow, shoots an arrow through
the axe-heads, exults in triumph, and then, with the help of his son and
the two loyal servants, he slays the Suitors pitilessly.

Ills. 39–41

This book of the *Odyssey*, the twenty-second, with its scenes of
violence and carnage, was a favourite among later Greeks. But despite
the ruthless slaughter it is not entirely a saga of heroic vengeance.
Homer relieves its savagery by touches of compassion. Most
significantly for the characterization of Ulysses, when Eurykleia begins
to raise a shout of savage exultation at the sight of the dead malefac-
tors, he restrains her because, he says, 'It is not pious to glory over
slain men' (*Odyssey* 22:412). How different is this attitude to that of
Achilles, for example, when he has killed Hector! Here we are in the
presence of a man who does not revel in revenge, but sees death and
destruction as the inescapable results of evil-doing.

At this point a poet of less mastery than Homer would probably
have made Penelope rush in and recognize Ulysses with passionate
affection. But Homer knew what twenty years of separation from her
husband could do to a loving wife's heart. Moreover, Penelope, he
saw, deserved a moment of triumph too. So when Penelope comes in
and sees Ulysses she does not—or pretends that she does not—

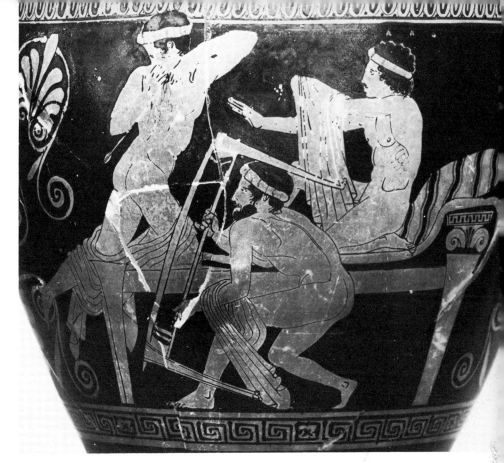

Ills. 39, 40. Two sides of an Attic red-figure skyphos by the 'Penelope painter' (see p. 149) showing the slaughter of the Suitors by Ulysses (*Odyssey* 22) after he has strung his bow and shot the arrow through the axe-heads as described in Book 21. The defensive attitudes of the three Suitors are vigorously conceived (right). The two female figures behind Ulysses (opposite) do not appear in Homer's version of the episode.

recognize him at first, to Telemachos' indignant surprise. Ulysses, smilingly tolerant of her diffidence, is willing to wait, confident that when he has had a bath and looks like his kingly self again, she will recognize him. But he is wrong: even then she holds off. He, rather vexed now, orders a servant to prepare their accustomed bed for him to go and sleep. Penelope intervenes to tell the servant to move the bed out of their nuptial bedroom. This is a trap for Ulysses, for he knows that the bed is fixed to the floor and cannot be moved.

Ulysses is caught by her wifely wile. Indignantly, he exclaims that she knows perfectly well this bed can't be moved out! Penelope, accepting this as a final proof of Ulysses' identity, bursts into tears and throws her arms about his neck, asking him not to be angry at her ruse, and telling all her joy at his return. In this way, Homer has shown us that she can outwit even Ulysses when she wants to, and also that she is too wise and too loving to triumph at the success of her wiliness. Penelope deserved this moment. Ulysses had been taking her love and loyalty too much for granted. Now he has had to woo her again before their reunion. In other words she is not just a simple-minded, unimaginative, patient, *hausfrau*—but a woman of spirit, courage, and intelligence, a true partner for Ulysses.

Some scholars in antiquity and many more in modern times believed that Homer's *Odyssey* ended with the lines in Book Twenty-three

which describe how Penelope and Ulysses are united in love again in their marital bed. But though such a happy reunion could seem a most fitting conclusion to critics attuned to the romanticized domesticity of Alexandria under the Ptolemies (or of Western Europe after the return of romanticism), it hardly accords with what Homer tells us about Ulysses in the *Odyssey*. Undoubtedly he loved Penelope deeply and faithfully (except when the demi-goddesses Circe and Calypso demanded his love). Yet Homer makes it equally clear that he also loved his son, father, kingdom and home. To end the *Odyssey* with Laërtes still on a lonely farm mourning his son's unending absence, and with Ulysses' palace and kingdom under the threat of vengeance from the multitudinous relatives of the slain Suitors, would hardly have satisfied an early Greek audience. So the remaining book and a half of the *Odyssey*, despite stylistic anomalies, is needed to establish Ulysses' victory on a lasting basis.

After an interlude in which the ghosts of the Suitors meet the ghosts of heroes slain during or after the Trojan campaign, Ulysses sets out for the farm where his father is living in lonely sadness. Having first tested Laërtes' mood with another characteristic piece of deception, Ulysses makes himself known. Later the relatives of the dead Suitors arrive in battle dress to take vengeance on Ulysses. He, together with Telemachos and Laërtes, prepares to fight them. (This is a truly heroic reunion for the three—grandfather, father, and son arrayed in pride of battle against their foes.) Old Laërtes, made valiant and strong again by Athena, has the joy of striking one enemy down with his spear. Then Athena breaks in to turn the others back. Ulysses leaps after them in fierce pursuit. A thunderbolt hurled in his path by Zeus checks him. Athena makes both sides pledge themselves to peace. She has the last word. She has established her favourite hero securely in his kingdom once more. There the poem fittingly ends.

But post-Homeric epic writers and later mythologists were not content to let the story end there. They remembered the mysterious

Ill. 41. Another version of the slaying of the Suitors, from the limestone relief of the frieze on the west wall of the Heroon at Gjölbaschi-Trysa in Lycia (beginning of the fourth century BC—see p. 158). On the left are Telemachos and Ulysses, with his left arm outstretched to hold his lethal bow.

order given to Ulysses by the prophet Teiresias in Hades that when he had killed the Suitors he must make a pilgrimage to a land 'where men do not eat food mixed with salt, and know nothing of scarlet-cheeked ships or well-made oars' (*Odyssey* 11:123-5), and offer there a rich sacrifice to Poseidon. After that, Teiresias said, Ulysses would die 'in sleek old age, with his people happy and prosperous round him' (*Odyssey* 11:136, 137). Teiresias described Ulysses' death as being 'off the sea' (*ex halos*, in the Greek, which could mean a death 'away from the sea' or else a death 'coming from the sea').

Prompted by this ambiguous prophecy, various writers sent Ulysses on further travels to Elis, Thesprotia, Aetolia, Arcadia and to Italy. There he fathered sons who became the mythical ancestors of local princes. Further children by Penelope, Circe and Calypso were also invented. (The accompanying genealogy gives the full list.) A son of his by Circe, Telegonos, according to one legend killed Ulysses unawares. Others devised stranger deaths for him. His grandchildren by Telemachos were said to include Homer.

Ill. 42

Possibly, as we shall see in a later chapter, some grains of historical truth can be extracted from these post-Homeric writers on the Ulysses theme, especially in the references to visits by him to Thesprotia and Epiros in North-west Greece. But in so far as these writers suggest that Ulysses was the kind of person who, after his return from his Odyssean wanderings, could not bear to live on in little Ithaca quietly to the end of his life, they run contrary to the whole tone of the *Odyssey*. Homer's portrait of Ulysses is of a man whose

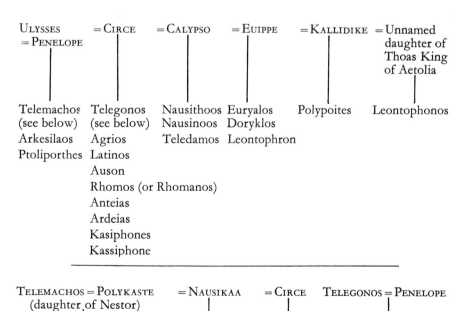

Ill. 42. The sons (above) and grandsons (below) of Ulysses. Out of this prolific progeny only one son, Telemachos, is mentioned by Homer. The rest were probably supplements by post-Homeric writers, interested either in producing illustrious genealogies for local magnates or else in devising gossipy details of the private lives of famous heroes. We may note the varying accounts of Homer's alleged descent from Ulysses.

ULYSSES = PENELOPE	= CIRCE	= CALYPSO	= EUIPPE	= KALLIDIKE	= Unnamed daughter of Thoas King of Aetolia
Telemachos (see below) Arkesilaos Ptoliporthes	Telegonos (see below) Agrios Latinos Auson Rhomos (or Rhomanos) Anteias Ardeias Kasiphones Kassiphone	Nausithoos Nausinoos Teledamos	Euryalos Doryklos Leontophron	Polypoites	Leontophonos

TELEMACHOS = POLYKASTE (daughter of Nestor)	= NAUSIKAA	= CIRCE	TELEGONOS = PENELOPE
Perseptolis Homer	Perseptolis Homer	Latinos Rhome (Roma)	Italos

chief desire was to live at home in Ithaca. In fact he makes Ulysses plainly assert that in his opinion

> There is nothing worse for mortal man than wandering,
> (*Odyssey* 15:343)

and

> Nothing is sweeter than one's own native land.
> (*Odyssey* 9:28)

Literature is not the only source of information about Ulysses in the period when these epics were being written. The visual arts also showed a growing interest in his achievements. The first Ulyssean scene that can be identified with any certainty dates from about 700 BC. (Attempts to find examples in earlier artefacts have not won general acceptance.) It appears on a fragmentary bronze fibula from Thebes. On it one can see the hind legs of a horse (with wheels attached to them) and a part of its body with rectangular trap-doors or hatches. In view of its resemblances to the next piece to be described, this must be the Trojan Horse. The other side shows five warriors who cannot be individually identified.

Shortly after 700 BC unmistakably Ulyssean scenes begin to occur on vases (and on other artefacts to be noticed later). There is a very striking, though naive, representation of the Horse on the impressive relief pithos found in Mykonos in 1961 and dated at about 675 BC. The front of the vessel is decorated with several scenes from the Sack of Troy. The Wooden Horse is modelled above these, on the neck. It shows a distinct resemblance to the fibula from Thebes, with similar wheels and trapdoors. Its bigger scale allowed the artist to show the heads of warriors inside the hatches together with their weapons. Lower on this pithos are several metope-like sections portraying warriors threatening or killing women or else killing children in the presence of women. One of these probably represents the death of Astyanax, the killer being either Ulysses or Neoptolemos. The emphasis here on the cruelty of the Greek victors anticipates the mood of Euripidean tragedy.

In none of these works of art can Ulysses himself be identified, though he is presumably among the Greek figures in the representations of the Wooden Horse. He may also be a member of the impressive group of Achaean kings accompanying Menelaos (who alone is named) on a Proto-Attic vase (before 650 BC). At any rate, Ulysses is the prominent figure in a series of vase-paintings representing events described in the *Odyssey* which date probably from the middle of the seventh century. The blinding of the Cyclops Polyphemos appears three times: on a fragment of an Argive krater; on a large Proto-Attic amphora from Eleusis; and on the krater from Caere (now in Rome) signed by Aristonothos. On the Eleusis

Ill. 43. Opposite: a forceful, unsophisticated presentation of the Trojan Horse, modelled on the neck of a relief pithos in Mykonos, dated *c.* 675 BC. The rectangular hatches with wide-eyed warriors' heads inside recall a feature found elsewhere in early versions (cf. *Ill. 19*). The armed warriors on the outside may be threatening Trojans or else Greeks (with perhaps Ulysses and Neoptolemos leading), or perhaps the two warriors below the Horse are Trojans advancing to resist the Greeks above (a variation from the literary accounts). There is a similar presentation on a Gandhara relief (see p. 174).

Ill. 43

Ill. 44

60

amphora the giant holds a wine-cup, which implies that Ulysses has made him drunk as in the *Odyssey*. In the Aristonothos picture one can see a wicker cheese-basket and a milk-pail (as described in *Odyssey* 9). Limitations of space and artistic conventions prevented the painters of these pictures from making a great difference in size between the humans and the giant, though the Argive krater clearly suggests it. Also no attempt is evident to characterize Ulysses as distinct from his Companions, except that on the Eleusis amphora his body is light-coloured in contrast with the black bodies of his single Companion and the Cyclops. In no case can one be quite certain that Homer's account in the *Odyssey* was the model for the artist, although the pastoral details in the picture by Aristonothos make it possible. It could be that the artists had local Attic, Argive or other versions of the story in mind. The blinding of Polyphemos also recurs on sixth-century vases. Another incident in Ulysses' encounter with the Cyclops is a favourite in early Greek and Etruscan art—the escape from the cave of Polyphemos. Fragments of an Attic oinochoë from Aegina (dated about 660 BC) show two men—apparently there was a third on a piece now lost—each hanging under the belly of a sheep. The subject recurs on several other seventh-century works of art, and remained popular on Greek and Etruscan pottery until the end of the sixth century.

A bronze tripod-leg in Delphi, dating from the last quarter of the seventh century, contains a relief depicting the mission of Ulysses and Ajax to the wrathful Achilles, a theme very popular later. Ulysses is distinguished by wearing his customary conical cap, the *pilos*. His other features are conventional. At the end of the seventh century a rather badly blurred Corinthian krater shows Ulysses with Diomedes finding Ajax impaled suicidally on his own sword.

These early pictorial representations of Ulysses and his adventures serve to prove that the events narrated in the epic poems (and perhaps also current in folk-tales now lost) were becoming popular as subjects for art as early as the eighth century BC. But they do not add anything of importance to what is known about Ulysses in the literary tradition. Ulysses is presented as a highly stylized figure to suit the formalistic conventions of the period, and without any distinctive characteristics of his own. Even the sophisticated sixth-century vase-painters failed to create a Ulysses who stands out as an impressive personality. But they did introduce some noteworthy variations on the literary tradition. On a Corinthian olpé (*c.* 550 BC), which shows the comforting of Achilles by his mother Thetis after the death of Patroklos, Ulysses stands behind Thetis—a variation on the narrative in *Iliad* 19 where Ulysses does not take part in the episode at all. Another divergence from the literary tradition is implied on the famous François vase by the painter Kleitias (*c.* 570 BC). The name of Ulysses is written over the victor in a chariot race (unfortunately the figure itself is missing) as he reaches the winning post where Athena waits to welcome him. This has no parallel in the *Iliad* or in the epic cycle. Also

Ill. 45. Opposite: the François ▶ vase—a krater made by Ergotimos and painted by Kleitias, *c.* 570 BC. The second band from the top depicts the chariot race which was part of the funeral games held in honour of Patroklos by Achilles (*Iliad* 23 : 262 ff.). Contrary to Homer's account, in which Ulysses does not compete in this event, the name of Ulysses (the figure is lost) stands over the victorious chariot here as it reaches the winning post where Athena, his patron, awaits him.

Ill. 44. The blinding of Polyphemos, a favourite early theme, on a Proto-Attic amphora (*c.* 675–50 BC) found at Eleusis (with a sitting Cyclops as in *Ill. 22*). Ulysses, in front, carefully directs the stake towards the Cyclops' eye. The relative scale fails to suggest the hugeness of the giant (contrast *Ill. 166*).

Ill. 46. A man, presumed to be Ulysses, on the back of a turtle (on a sixth-century skyphos from Palermo). Apparently there was a Sicilian or South Italian variation on Homer's account of Ulysses' escape from Charybdis the second time (*Odyssey* 12:431 ff.), in which he passed through the straits on a turtle's back (cf. *Ill. 129*).

one scene from the *Odyssey* is, perhaps, given a new feature on a late sixth-century skyphos from Palermo. It shows a man riding on the back of a swimming turtle with a fig-tree in the background, as in *Odyssey* 12:432. (There is a similar composition on a metope at Paestum to be described later, and it recurs on three Etruscan pieces of bronze-work and on several late gems.) If, as has been suggested, this is Ulysses going through the straits of Skylla and Charybdis with the help of a turtle, it differs from Homer's account in which Ulysses floats on timber from his wrecked ship. Another early vase deserves mention as depicting an episode rarely, if ever, found elsewhere in Greek art— a Corinthian column krater (*c.* 560 BC) which illustrates the Greek ambassadors, including Ulysses, demanding the return of Helen before the beginning of the Trojan War (see p. 20).

Ill. 46

Ill. 8

The encounter with the Cyclops remained a favourite theme in sixth-century vase-painting, as, for example (with variations from the account in *Odyssey* 9), on a well-preserved Laconian cup (about 550 BC) and on a fine Chalcidian black-figure amphora (about 520 BC). A skilfully stylized version of Ulysses' escape under the ram decorates a column krater (about 510 BC) perhaps by the 'Sappho painter'. Ulysses holds a sword in his right hand and clings to the ram with his left in an unrealistic but visually pleasing pose. In contrast with this elegant composition, a slightly later Attic oinochoë pays chief attention to an almost comic, satyrlike figure of Polyphemos.

Ill. 23

Ill. 101

Probably these surviving examples of earlier Greek art represent only a small fraction of the total production of the time. As they stand, their portraiture of Ulysses is very scanty in comparison with that of the contemporary literature. Nor have they reached anything like the subtlety and maturity of characterization that we have found in the epic tradition. We have to wait until the classical period of Greek art before we can find anything to equal this.

3   The world of Ulysses

J. V. Luce

Ill. 48

Ill. 51

*The Catalogue is the list of the Greek contingents at Troy as given in the *Iliad* 2:494-759.

Ill. 47. A rock-crystal bowl from a woman's grave in Circle B at Mycenae, sixteenth century BC. The type is Egyptian; the workmanship may be Minoan. Its translucent walls (3–4 mm. thick) and the sensitive carving of the duck's head make it an outstanding example of lapidary art.

BETWEEN Ithaca and Troy stretched a world shaped by the creative achievement of Greek-speaking peoples over many centuries. To understand Ulysses and his age, one must view them against the background of Greek civilization as it developed through the Late Bronze Age from about 1600 to 1150 BC. The heartland of 'Greece' in this period lay in the Peloponnese, but a common culture extended northwards through Attica and Boeotia to Thessaly. After 1400 BC the power and influence of mainland Greece spread out over the Aegean to embrace the Cyclades, Crete and Rhodes, and was felt as far east as Cyprus and the Levant. Westwards the same culture expanded into Zakynthos, Kephallinia and Ithaca, islands that were later to form part of the kingdom of Ulysses as defined in the Homeric Catalogue.*

The basic evidence for the history of the period is archaeological, but the legends preserved in later Greek tradition must also be taken into account. This tradition included the Homeric poems as one very important ingredient, but comprised also much non-Homeric epic poetry, genealogies, local folk memories, and the legends of cult-places. Some contemporary written documents are also available from Greece itself (the Linear B tablets), and from the Near East (Hittite records and Egyptian inscriptions).

The first archaeological evidence of major opulence on the Greek mainland was found by Schliemann in 1876 in Shaft Grave Circle A at Mycenae. A similar Grave Circle, B, discovered in 1952, goes back to a somewhat earlier period, with graves not quite so magnificently furnished as the major graves in Circle A. Between them the Circles span a period from before 1600 to after 1500 BC. They indicate a remarkable expansion of the power, wealth and overseas connections of the rulers of Mycenae. The astonishing richness of the grave goods ensured the widest publicity for Schliemann's discovery, and the acceptance of the name 'Mycenaean' for the culture they represented. Nothing as early and as rich has been found on any other Greek site, so Mycenae holds priority for regal development in Greece. But in the fifteenth century BC many other centres of power and wealth were to be found on the Greek mainland. This is shown by the distribution of the vaulted tombs of well-cut masonry known as *tholos* tombs. The

65

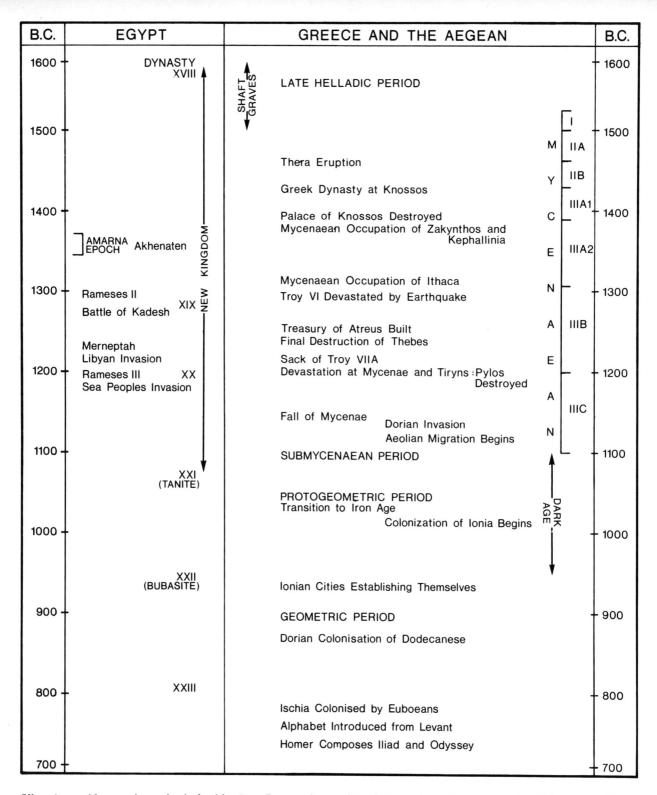

B.C.	EGYPT	GREECE AND THE AEGEAN			B.C.

The table contents:

EGYPT column:
- 1600 — DYNASTY XVIII
- AMARNA EPOCH — Akhenaten
- NEW KINGDOM
- 1300 — Rameses II, Battle of Kadesh — XIX
- Merneptah, Libyan Invasion
- 1200 — Rameses III — XX, Sea Peoples Invasion
- XXI (TANITE)
- XXII (BUBASITE)
- 800 — XXIII

GREECE AND THE AEGEAN column:
- LATE HELLADIC PERIOD
- SHAFT GRAVES
- Thera Eruption
- Greek Dynasty at Knossos
- Palace of Knossos Destroyed
- Mycenaean Occupation of Zakynthos and Kephallinia
- Mycenaean Occupation of Ithaca
- Troy VI Devastated by Earthquake
- Treasury of Atreus Built
- Final Destruction of Thebes
- Sack of Troy VIIA
- Devastation at Mycenae and Tiryns : Pylos Destroyed
- Fall of Mycenae — Dorian Invasion — Aeolian Migration Begins
- SUBMYCENAEAN PERIOD
- PROTOGEOMETRIC PERIOD — Transition to Iron Age
- Colonization of Ionia Begins
- DARK AGE
- Ionian Cities Establishing Themselves
- GEOMETRIC PERIOD
- Dorian Colonisation of Dodecanese
- Ischia Colonised by Euboeans
- Alphabet Introduced from Levant
- Homer Composes Iliad and Odyssey

MYCENAEAN (right-hand vertical labels):
- M Y C E N A E A N
- I
- IIA
- IIB
- IIIA1
- IIIA2
- IIIB
- IIIC

B.C. scale: 1600, 1500, 1400, 1300, 1200, 1100, 1000, 900, 800, 700

Ills. 48, 49. Above: chronological table: Late Bronze Age and Early Iron Age. Opposite: a detail from a gold cup from the tholos tomb at Vapheio in Laconia, *c.* 1500–1450 BC. Of exquisite Minoan workmanship, the embossed decoration on the cup depicts stages in the capture of wild bulls in a rocky landscape. Here, a bull is being hobbled by the left hind leg.

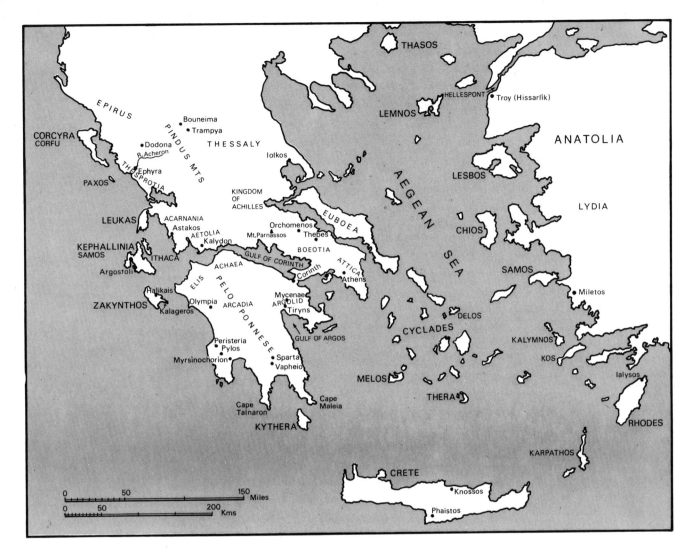

Ills. 50, 51. Opposite: a gold death mask from Grave Circle A at Mycenae. At first taken by Schliemann to be the 'face of Agamemnon', the mask is a portrait of a much earlier ruler, *c.* 1550 BC. Above: map of the Mycenaean world in the Late Bronze Age.

Ill. 49

Ills. 50, 58

Ill. 55

finest specimens are at Mycenae, where they follow on from the Shaft Graves, but other notable examples were built elsewhere in the Peloponnese, for example, at Vapheio, Peristeria, Myrsinochorion, and north of the isthmus in Attica and at Orchomenos. They were such conspicuous monuments that almost all were plundered. The very few exceptions show why they came to be called 'treasuries'. The Vapheio tomb robbers overlooked a grave pit under the chamber floor which contained the famous gold cups decorated with bull hunting scenes. Also in the pit were rings, gems, an amethyst necklace, alabaster vases, amber beads, a gold-plated dagger, perfume vases, and numerous weapons including a rapier, nine knives and a pair of axes.

The rapid spread and standardized form of the *tholoi* probably indicate the establishment of a network of kingdoms ruled by an ambitious aristocracy of warrior princes. Their dominance was due to their martial prowess, their fine bronze weapons, and, above all, to their use of chariots—a comparatively new piece of equipment in the

Ills. *52–54*. Views of the citadel at Mycenae. Left: the main entrance, the famous Lion Gate. The 'relieving triangle' over the lintel is faced with a sculptured slab of limestone. Two lions flank a pillar which stands on a pair of Minoan-type altars. The device may be a dynastic emblem. Below: Grave Circle A, discovered by Schliemann in 1876. The Circle, originally a tumulus, was later enclosed by a double row of standing slabs roofed to give the appearance of a solid parapet. The entrance is visible to back and right. In the centre may be seen the rectangular mouth of one of the six grave shafts. Opposite: an aerial view of the citadel with the palace at its summit (furthest from the viewer).

Near East.* They raised themselves to power on the base of the agriculture and the competent, but not very advanced, technology of the Middle Helladic villagers. Their enterprise can be seen in the distribution of early Mycenaean sherds from Syria to the Lipari islands. Remote trading connections are also reflected in the amazing variety of the places of origin of materials found in their sepulchres: ostrich eggs from Nubia, lapis lazuli from Mesopotamia, alabaster and faïence from Crete, ivory from Syria, silver from Anatolia and amber from the Baltic. It seems unlikely that the Middle Helladic population of Greece could on its own have so suddenly achieved the advances that mark the early Mycenaean period. The influence of invaders and conquerors seems the most likely hypothesis to explain the rapid growth of military power and regal wealth that we can trace in the archaeological record.

The heyday of Mycenae fell in the period from 1400 to 1250 BC, and the end of this period probably saw the culminating architectural achievement of the Treasury of Atreus, a magnificent royal tomb whose corbelled vault was not surpassed in span until the building of the Pantheon at Rome. Homer remembered a time when the king of Mycenae was 'ruler of all Argos and many islands'. We may legitimately regard the rulers of Mycenae in this golden period as the most powerful in Greece. But there were other kings too with luxurious palaces and well-furnished treasuries, notably at Pylos in the Peloponnese and at Thebes and Orchomenos north of the isthmus.

Later Greek tradition remembered a long and bitter struggle between the Argolid and Thebes, with an earlier expedition, the Seven against Thebes, which was unsuccessful, and a later attack by the Epigoni in which the Theban Kadmeion was sacked. Archaeological evidence indicates that a 'first palace' was burnt about 1300 BC, and that a 'second palace' suffered a like fate some fifty years later. Thebes sent no contingent to fight at Troy. She had ceased to exist as a

*A type of Mycenaean chariot with a quadrant-shaped body appears for the first time in sixteenth-century representations, e.g. on an engraved gem from Knossos, and it is interesting to note that some Hittite chariots of the early thirteenth century, as depicted on the Abu Simbel reliefs of the battle of Kadesh, show the same structural feature.

Ills. 52–54

Ill. 56

kingdom by then, but not, on Homer's evidence, very long before, since some of the warriors who sacked Thebes fought also at Troy (*Iliad* 4:406). It is plausible to locate an increasingly greedy and aggressive Mycenae at the heart of these traditions.

About 1300 BC, so the hypothesis would run, the Mycenaeans of the Argolid enter upon a prolonged struggle with Thebes, which does not finally fall until, say, 1240 BC. The rulers of Mycenae are satisfied for a decade or two with the resultant access of power and plunder. Then the urge for more conquest renews itself. Across the Aegean the western principalities of Anatolia are restive, shifting their allegiances and jockeying for position as the hold of the Hittite empire begins to weaken. The Mycenaeans have ancient trade connections with Troy and know it to be a citadel of great wealth with an important strategic position at the mouth of the Hellespont. They know also that earthquake damage a generation or so earlier caused a severe set-back to its power and prosperity. They sense an opportunity for new expansion and fresh plunder. Paris' abduction of Helen provides an opportune excuse. The king of Mycenae espouses his brother's quarrel with the Trojans and uses all his influence to muster forces from the Achaean kingdoms throughout Greece.

Ill. 57

Ill. 59

The expedition was directed against an ancient and powerful stronghold on the hill of Hissarlik in the north-west corner of Asia

1. The Perseids and Pelopids of Mycenae

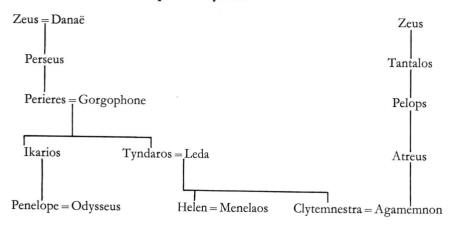

Ill. 57. Genealogical tables of the principal Achaean families—the product of later Greek literary tradition based initially on orally transmitted legend and myth.

2. The Neleids of Pylos

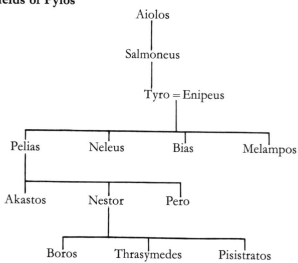

3. The Aeacids

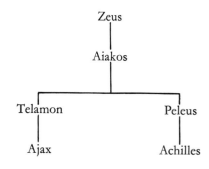

74

Ill. 60

Ill. 62

Ill. 61

Minor. Excavation has revealed a succession of cities there dating far back into the third millennium. One of these cities, Troy VI, was surrounded by an exceptionally powerful system of walls and towers, portions of which are still standing to a considerable height. After many centuries of dominance, Troy VI and its fortifications were seriously damaged in an earthquake at a date not far from 1300 BC. The damage was repaired, and life continued without serious interruption into a successor city, Troy VIIA. But the city now gives an impression of overcrowding, with mean, hastily-built houses covering what had formerly been wide open spaces inside the citadel. Sunk into the floors of many of these houses are great storage jars for oil and grain. It is hard to resist the conclusion that the old security of Troy VI had gone, and that the inhabitants of Troy VIIA felt themselves under threat of attack. Their fears proved well founded, for their city eventually perished in a great conflagration. Enemy action is indicated by the finding of some fragments of human skulls and an arrowhead of mainland Greek type in the streets of the city. The archaeological evidence is entirely consistent with Greek traditions about the Trojan War, and it is now widely accepted that Priam's Troy is to be identified with city VIIA at Hissarlik.

There is, however, continuing controversy about the date of the destruction. The dispute turns largely on the classification and dating of the meagre fragments of Greek pottery found in the ruins, and will not be settled until the experts reach a measure of agreement on this factual evidence. Pending such agreement, one can only record that Carl Blegen (who directed the 1932–38 excavations) first put the date at about 1240 BC and then tended to revise it upwards to even as early as 1270 BC. (It is interesting that Herodotus dated the fall of Troy '800 years before my time', i.e. *c.* 1250 BC.) Others (for example, Hammond and Desborough in the revised edition of the *Cambridge Ancient History*) bring the date down much nearer to 1200 BC, close in fact to the date of 1184 BC calculated by Eratosthenes. It might seem that fifty years is not a very significant divergence as we look back to such a remote epoch. But in fact it will make a considerable difference in our conception of Ulysses' world if we put his Trojan exploits at 1250 rather than 1200 BC. At the earlier date conditions in the Mycenaean world, and in the Near East generally, seem to have been more stable and prosperous than fifty years later. About 1200 BC, there was extensive destruction on a number of Greek sites, including Mycenae. Mycenae recovered, but other places, notably Pylos, were destroyed and never reoccupied. In the Near East the fabric of Bronze Age civilization was being shaken by the onslaught of the 'Sea Peoples' on Egypt and the Levant. Soon after 1180 BC the Hittite empire collapsed, and other ancient cities and states like Ugarit and Alalakh disappear from history. A Hittite tablet from the closing years of the empire mentions a certain Mukshush, and there is a reference to the 'house of Mukshush', *c.* 800 BC, in a bilingual inscription (Hittite and Phoeni-

Ill. 58. A perforated bead of amethyst (9 mm. in diameter) from Grave Gamma (Circle B), Mycenae. The intaglio carving shows a bearded head, with long hair and no moustache. The physiognomy (thin lips and nose, large ear, heavy brows) should be compared with the grave mask from Circle A (*Ill. 50*). The resemblance encourages belief that we have here a portrait of a Mycenaean ruler done by a Minoan gem-carver.

cian) from Karatepe in Cilicia. It seems likely that Mukshush founded a dynasty in Cilicia *c.* 1200 BC. Many authorities agree that Mukshush is to be identified with the hero Mopsus, who, according to Greek tradition, settled in Cilicia *about the time of the fall of Troy*. This identification, if correct, tells strongly in favour of the later date for the destruction of Troy VIIA.

The Achaean sack of Troy led to no permanent settlement in the Troad. The Greeks withdrew with their plunder, and some Trojans crept back to re-occupy their looted citadel for a generation or two before succumbing to barbarian invaders from Thrace. The Achaean world seems to have overstrained its resources, and such unity as had made the Trojan expedition possible was lost and never regained.

Thucydides speaks of the war leaders returning to face revolutions at home. The Argolid, the power centre with the greatest prestige, suffered the greatest disruption. By contrast, peripheral regions like Attica and the Dodecanese seem to have enjoyed increased prosperity for a time. Grave goods found in these areas show evidence of vigorous trading, and their IIIC pottery is inventive in design, and departs markedly from the conformity of IIIB ware. An increase of population is also apparent in the area later known as Achaea, doubtless due to an influx from the Argolid, and this wave of refugees also seems to have reached Kephallinia.

Ulysses' followers at Troy were 'great-hearted Kephallinians' from three islands: Ithaca, Zakynthos and Samos, and from parts of the adjacent mainland. Assuming that Samos was the old name for Kephallinia, his realm centred on the three large islands which form a group off the mouth of the Corinthian Gulf. It is now time to discuss the possible relationship of such a kingdom to the Mycenaean world that we have been describing.

If one stands on the citadel of Mycenae, one's eye is inevitably drawn eastwards across the plain to the sheltered waters of the Gulf of Argos, a natural terminus for shipping from Crete and the Levant. To the west and north the site seems hemmed in by mountains. In fact a major route slips through the folds of the hills and leads on to the isthmus of Corinth. There, at the head of another long sheltered gulf, is the terminus of an ancient sea-route to Italy and the Adriatic. It is an interesting fact that in the Catalogue, Agamemnon's kingdom extends

Ills. 59, 61. Opposite: the hill of Hissarlik viewed from the plain bordering the River Dumbrek (ancient Simoeis). The defensive strength of the citadel of 'beetling Troy' is most apparent from this northerly aspect. Above: a bronze arrowhead of mainland Greek type found by Blegen in a street of Troy VIIA.

Ills. 60, 62. Opposite: one of the best-preserved sections of the great circuit wall of Troy VI. In the foreground are the remains of a projecting tower designed to protect the approaches to one of the gates. The lower portion of the wall has a marked batter; it would have been surmounted by a parapet of smaller stones or mud-brick. Right: a room of one of the houses of Troy VIIA backing on to the wall (opposite), with storage jars sunk below the floor.

much farther to the north and west of Mycenae than it does to the east. In particular it reaches far along the southern shore of the Corinthian Gulf. On the north side of the Gulf lay Aetolia, listed in the Catalogue as a Mycenaean kingdom, and now known to have substantial Mycenaean remains on a number of sites. A scarab of Amenophis III (1417–1379 BC) has been found on the suggested site of Homeric Olenos. Outside the Gulf, on Zakynthos, four Late Bronze Age sites have been identified. One of these, at Halikais, shows the remains of a *tholos* tomb and a Mycenaean house. Another, at Kalogeros, occupies a typical site—an easily defensible promontory at the extreme south-eastern tip of the island. Pottery from these sites (including quite numerous finds from a well) is representative of standard Mycenaean IIIA and IIIB styles, and indicates occupation during the fourteenth and thirteenth centuries BC.

Kephallinia, separated from Zakynthos by a ten-mile strait, is a much larger island, with mountains rising impressively to between five and six thousand feet, and some good but scattered stretches of arable land. At least a dozen Mycenaean sites are known, the bulk of them lying not far from Argostoli, where the museum now houses an extensive collection of Mycenaean pottery.

Ulysses' own island of Ithaca is much the smallest of the group, but its rugged hills contain some pockets of good land, and it was inhabited from the Early Helladic period on. Its main asset was its central position in the sea-routes of the area. It is well placed to control coastwise shipping among the archipelago of small islands to the east of it, and also to dominate the sea passages that divide it from Kephallinia and Leukas. Ithaca lay right in the path of shipping heading north for the Adriatic and the short sea-crossing to Italy. The trade-conscious Mycenaean world could not afford to neglect it, and excavation (described more fully in Chapter 4) has shown that there was a Mycenaean occupation of the island from *c.* 1300 to 1100 BC.

Ill. 64

The results of field surveys and excavation corroborate the Homeric tradition that the three islands formed part of the Mycenaean world towards the close of the Bronze Age. For Homer they constituted a single principality, an island fief with the Achaean Ulysses of Ithaca as overlord. Legend would have been unlikely to attribute the kingship to the smallest island had not this been the historical situation. In this area, broad acres were less important than personality and naval resources. One might compare the hegemony of Grace O'Malley over the coasts and islands of Mayo in the time of Elizabeth I. Grace's headquarters were on Clare island, which is smaller and less fertile than Achill immediately to the north or Inishboffin to the south. Yet she dominated the whole area by strength of character, the prestige of her clan, and by a small but efficient squadron of ships. The basis of Ulysses' rule was probably not dissimilar.

Apart from the Ulysses saga, the Ionian islands are not rich in legends. In Ulysses' family neither his father Laërtes, nor his paternal

Ill. 63. A plastic vase from the Mycenaean settlement at Ialysos on Rhodes, twelfth century BC. The circular object on the side represents a pilgrim flask, part of the pack-horse's load. The lively design of the vase, and the gay painting, attest the vigour of the art of peripheral regions in the last century of the Mycenaean era.

grandfather Arkeisios, has much pretension to heroic stature. On his mother's side, the main legendary connection is with Corinth through Sisyphos, and with the area round Parnassos through Autolykos. These traditions may reflect the historical fact of an Achaean family moving westwards with their retainers to acquire a stake in a recently founded Mycenaean kingdom in Ithaca. There are vestiges of a tradition of an earlier dynasty on the island represented by Ithakos, Neritos and Polyktor, who built a stone fountain near the royal palace (*Odyssey* 17:207). Ithakos and Neritos (a name now certified as Mycenaean by the Pylos tablets) were said to have crossed from Kephallinia to found the city of Ithaca, and the detail about the fountain rings true as a mark of Mycenaean expansion. In the pottery recovered from sites in the north of Ithaca, the earliest examples of Mycenaean ware (IIIB, i.e. thirteenth century BC) coexist with large quantities of a cruder local ware representing a long tradition but a low standard of ceramic work. Building in cut stone would probably have been beyond the resources of pre-Mycenaean culture in the western islands, and the construction of a fountain basin with good masonry surrounds might have been remembered as one of the novel public works of the first Mycenaean rulers. The cut stone *tholos* tombs on Zakynthos and Kephallinia would be the product of a similar colonizing movement which reached these larger islands at a somewhat earlier date.

A list of three or four kings before Ulysses fits the chronology indicated by the pottery, particularly if his *floruit* is to be put towards the end of the thirteenth century BC. He inherited a kingdom much inferior in wealth and resources to the older and more opulent Mycenaean states. No rich graves have been found in the islands, and no palaces. A piece of gold leaf and a small gold disc from Pilikata are the only indications of ruler wealth. But we may suppose that Ulysses made good use of his strategic position in the western trade routes of the Mycenaean world. He is once described as an outstandingly knowledgeable merchant (*Odyssey* 19:283–6). The *Odyssey* also contains some interesting details of his relations with neighbouring areas, especially Thesprotia.

Thesprotia included in its territory the river Acheron and the famous oracle of Zeus at Dodona. In recent years important Mycenaean remains have been found near the mouth of the Acheron (see below, pp. 129, 130), and the district must now be regarded as part of the Mycenaean world. Penelope describes the Thesprotians as good friends of the Ithacans, and Ulysses had good relations with a Thesprotian king called Pheidon (*Odyssey* 16:427, and 14:316). He is even described as negotiating unsuccessfully for arrow poison with a man named Ilos of Ephyra (*Odyssey* 1:259 ff.), probably the Thesprotian Ephyra, which is to be identified with the Mycenaean settlement at the junction of the Acheron and Cocytus. Trading by ship is carried on between Thesprotia and Doulichion 'rich in wheat' (*Odyssey* 14:335). (The problem of the identification of Doulichion is discussed on p. 90.) In the later epic tradition represented by the *Telegony* of Eugammon, Ulysses commanded Thesprotians in a war against the Brygi, a migratory tribe which later settled in Pelagonia. This campaign is dated after his return from Troy, and fits in well with the archaeological evidence that northern invaders introduced new cultural elements into northern Epirus between 1200 and 1150 BC. He was also said to have founded Bouneima near Trampya, where an oracle bearing his name was later established. These places were associated with the command of Teiresias that he make a pilgrimage to 'men ignorant of the sea who eat their food unmixed with salt' (*Odyssey* 11:119 ff.). Hammond suggests that these were 'pastoral peoples of the Pindus range, where men can live on meat and milk without the use of salt'.

From these and other legendary tales of life in North-west Greece we can construct a picture that agrees well with the archaeological

Ill. 64. The view northwards from Mt. Aetos on the central isthmus of 'rugged' Ithaca. To left, the Ithaca channel, with the northern tip of Kephallinia and the southern promontory of Leukas bounding the horizon. To right, the inmost portion of the Gulf of Molo. Mt. Anogi dominates the skyline, with the road from Vathi to Stavros winding along its western flank, and the rounded outline of Mt. Exogi beyond.

evidence. In the thirteenth century, Achaean princes are in control of the islands as far north as Ithaca, and have occupied territory near the mouth of the Acheron in Thesprotia. This marks the limit of the Mycenaean world, though not necessarily of Greek-speaking tribes. In this region is the island kingdom of the Taphians who raid for slaves as far as the Syrian coast. In the uplands of Epirus are pastoral tribes soon to emerge in Greek history as the invading Dorians. Also in the hinterland of Epirus or Acarnania lurk savage rulers like Echetus, who does not hesitate to maim and mutilate strangers that stray into his domain.

Conditions in the outlying areas of North-west Greece had not altered much by the fifth century BC, as Thucydides noted. He compares life in the Aetolia and Acarnania of his day with what he took to be the general state of affairs throughout Greece at the time of the Trojan War. Piracy was common, and not unrespectable; so was armed robbery on land. People carried arms as a matter of course. Communications were unsafe. Yet, combined with this insecurity and marauding was a certain measure of organization, with attempts being made to control piracy in the interests of trade, and with stronger powers fortifying their cities and offering protection to the weaker and less wealthy (*Thucydides* 1:5, 8).

The figure of Ulysses slips easily into this general picture. As an Achaean king he holds sway over Kephallinians scattered through various islands and coastlands. His rule is regarded as kindly and just. He maintains good relations with Achaeans and non-Achaeans to the north along the trade route that most concerns him, and is pictured as wealthy and successful in commerce. He assists the Thesprotians to hold back migratory tribes, and his reputation extends inland to Dodona and the Pindus. Yet on the high seas he has no compunction about turning pirate and freebooter. His foray on the Cicones was ruthless and destructive (see p. 35). When posing as a Cretan he describes a similar incident, a passage which seems to preserve a genuine memory of a typical Achaean plunder raid on the Egyptian delta:

> The spirit moved me to make an expedition to Egypt with my illustrious comrades. I fitted out nine ships and there was a rush of men to fill them. For six days my trusty comrades feasted with me, and I provided many animals for sacrifices and banquets. On the seventh day we set sail from Crete, speeding on easily as if down stream with the strong and steady North wind behind us. The ships suffered no harm and we sat there unscathed and in good health as wind and helmsman guided our course. On the fifth day we reached broad Nile, and there I anchored my curved ships. Then I ordered my noble comrades to wait by the ships and guard them while scouts went out to survey the country. But they were unruly and confident in their prowess, and began at once to plunder the very rich fields of the Egyptians, killing the men and driving off the women and children. The alarm was soon raised in the city, and at dawn they came upon us in force, and the whole plain was filled with soldiers and horses and the flash of bronze.
>
> (*Odyssey* 14:246 ff.)

The raid ended in disaster for the Achaeans with many being killed and others taken prisoner.

Inscriptions from Egypt dating from the reigns of Merneptah and Ramesses III give us a vivid picture of how such raids appeared to the Egyptians. Merneptah records an incursion into the western delta by hostile 'Sea Peoples' in alliance with Libyans in the fifth year of his reign, 1233 BC on the current chronology. Among the raiders were Akaiwasha (or Ekwesh), plausibly identified as Achaeans; Lukka (from Lycia); Sherden (who had fought for Ramesses II at the battle of Kadesh, 1286 BC) and Shekelesh, marauders and mercenaries, who later settled in, and gave their names to, Sardinia and Sicily; Tjekker (Teucrians from Cyprus?) and Tursha (proto-Etruscans from Lydia?). The raiders were repulsed with the loss of over three thousand men.

In the eighth year of Ramesses III, 1191 BC, the Egyptians had to face an even more serious threat coming this time from the direction of Palestine. The Egyptian records speak of the northern isles as restless and disturbed, and describe how a great confederate host of free-booters and marauders moving on by land and sea wreaked destruction in Cyprus, Cilicia and Syria. 'No land stood before them'; 'they were fighting to fill their bellies daily' are some of the graphic phrases used in the Ramesses inscription at Medinet Habu. A decisive naval battle was fought not far from the eastern delta, and the Egyptian fleet managed to surround and destroy most of the Sea Peoples' ships. The raiders, who included Danuna (Danaans?) and Pulesati (Philistines), were beaten back and dispersed.

Ills. 65, 66. Top: outline drawing of a ship on a stirrup jar from the island of Skyros, twelfth century BC. Bottom: one of the ships used by the Sea Peoples who invaded Egypt in 1191 BC. The repulse of the invaders is depicted in a series of reliefs on the walls of the Mortuary Temple of Ramesses III at Medinet Habu. The similarity between the two ships is an indication that the Sea Peoples included raiders from the Aegean.

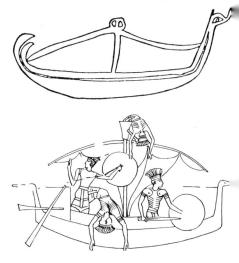

The Sea Peoples were not a homogeneous group or a single race. They should rather be viewed as a product of the increasing turmoil and insecurity in the Late Bronze Age. Emily Vermeule describes them as 'tribes shaken loose from their provincial village lives into piratical or mercenary careers'. The Egyptian records make it clear that they came from the islands and coasts of Greece and also from the western and southern coasts of Asia Minor. The destruction and burning of ancient cities like Enkomi and Ugarit, which occurred *c.* 1200 BC, may plausibly be attributed to them. The pressures they generated disrupted old political patterns and led to mass migration, either in search of plunder, or simply to escape from famine and desolation in the homeland. It was both a heroic and a desperate age, and it saw the decline and collapse of centuries of Bronze Age civilization over large areas of the Near East.

Greek tradition mirrors the turmoil and instability of this era. It knows of adventurers and emigrants before as well as after the Trojan War: Bellerophon, for example, who campaigned for the king of Lycia, and Tlepolemos, son of a Thesprotian princess, who led 'much people' to the Dodecanese. Trojans as well as Achaeans were involved in the adventuring, if we are right to equate the Dardana of the Egyptian records with Homer's Dardanians. We find Dardana fighting on the Hittite side at Kadesh, doubtless contributing to the chariot strength of the Hittite army. There is also a tradition preserved by Pindar (*Pythian Odes* 5, 82 ff.) that the Trojan sons of Antenor migrated to Libya after the sack of Troy and were well received because of their prowess in chariot fighting. This tradition finds interesting confirmation in the Egyptian records in which the Libyan tribes of Retenu and Tehenu become increasingly associated with the Sea Peoples. The exploits of Paris fit well into this general picture. We see him sailing with his ships round the Peloponnese, calling as a guest-friend on Menelaos, and departing with a valuable item of plunder. From Sparta he makes for Egypt, and spends some time there with Helen before eventually returning to Troy.

The careers of many of the Greek leaders after the Trojan War conform to the same pattern. Agamemnon was murdered in his hour of triumph, and his son Orestes, after avenging his death, wandered all over the Aegean. Diomedes found a usurper in power at Tiryns, and migrated to Libya and southern Italy. Neoptolemos went across from Thessaly to Epirus, and founded the Molossian royal house. Menelaos spent a long time in Egypt before finally reaching home. But the most protracted wanderings were those of Ulysses. He was pirate, explorer and castaway by turns, and there is poetic justice in the legend that he met his death at the hands of Telegonos (his son by Circe), who landed to plunder Ithaca and slew his father unknowingly.

The world of Ulysses stands on the dividing line between the more prosperous and stable era of the hegemony of Mycenae and the increasingly lawless epoch of the Sea Peoples. It is significant that

exports of Mycenaean pottery to the Levant cease abruptly at the end of the IIIB period, which is also the probable date of the Trojan War. Ulysses joined an expedition which was a great joint enterprise of many Achaean states. Behind it lay wealth procured by enterprising trade, force based on well-designed weaponry and mobility by sea, and a spirit of aggression nourished by generations of successful military expansion. Success at Troy was slow to come and cost many noble Achaean lives. The victors returned to a disrupted Greece. In the words of Thucydides, 'the return of the Greeks from Troy took a long time, and brought many innovations. Civil wars occurred in most cities, and the exiles went off to found new cities.' City sacking brought its appropriate nemesis. The palace at Pylos was sacked and burnt at a date near 1200 BC. The citadel at Mycenae lasted on for perhaps another fifty years, and then it too was destroyed. At Tiryns, as Hood has described it, 'the skeletons of some of the last defenders, fallen or thrown from the battlements, were found lying beneath piles of burnt debris at the foot of the walls'. By 1100 BC the Mycenaean world was fading away, and Greece was entering a darker and more impoverished age than it had known for more than a thousand years.

But the exploits of Greeks in the Late Bronze Age were not forgotten by their descendants. A rich legacy of legend was transmitted orally through the Dark Age, and survived to form the basis, not only of Homeric poetry, but also of the complex and detailed picture of the Heroic Age assembled by later poets and historians. To the classical Greeks the tales of Ulysses and the other heroes were not fiction or romance, but a real and inspiring part of their past history. For us, the progress of archaeological discovery over the last hundred years has made it increasingly difficult to be sceptical about the historicity of the heroic legends. Their picture of the world of Ulysses rings true and is consistent with what can be independently known about Mediterranean peoples in the Late Bronze Age.

Ill. 67. Portion of the great circuit wall on the western side of the citadel of Tiryns. Pausanias considered that these walls bore comparison with the pyramids of Egypt. On the left is a massive semi-circular bastion thrown out to guard the 'postern-gate' access to the citadel. The walls, which have been extensively restored, are 730 metres long, and originally had an estimated height of over 20 metres. They date from the final Mycenaean phase, thirteenth century BC, and represent the culmination of Mycenaean military science. The figure on the skyline gives some impression of the massive scale of contruction. Some of the blocks weigh about 14 tons.

4

Ithaca

J. V. Luce

HOMER describes Ithaca with a wealth of detail, naming its chief mountains, districts, harbours and springs, and picturing its landscape so vividly that it has long been held that he must himself have visited the island. But his picture has also excited much controversy. Critics ancient and modern have found some aspects of it inconsistent with the topography of the island now called Itháki (or Thiáki), and have been driven to seek Homeric Ithaca in a different location, or else have maintained that the poet worked on secondhand information, which he did not fully understand. This chapter is written in the firm belief that Itháki was indeed the home of Ulysses, and that one should not look for him in Leukas, or Corfu, or the Trapani region of Sicily. It will also be argued that every detail in Homer can be matched with the topography of the island and interpreted in conformity with the evidence of excavation.

Ill. 68

Ulysses' own description is the most geographically detailed, and also the most disputed, of the relevant passages. He tells the Phaeacians:

*Comparison with *Odyssey* 13:234 indicates that the meaning is 'clearly defined' i.e., an island, not a peninsula.

> My home is in *clear-seen* Ithaca.* In it is a mountain, Neriton, well-wooded and conspicuous. Around lie numerous inhabited islands, very close to one another, [including] Doulichion and Samê and wooded Zakynthos. Ithaca itself is *low*, and lies in the sea *furthest out* [or *very high up*] towards the *dark quarter*.* The other islands are well away to the east and south.* It is a rugged land, but rears its children well.

*i.e., west to north-west, where the sun hides beneath the earth.
*literally, 'to the dawn and the sun'.

> (*Odyssey* 9:21–27)

The Greek words corresponding to those italicized have been discussed *ad nauseam*, but no consensus about their interpretation has been reached. In my translation I have selected meanings that are in accord with normal Homeric usage. Some scholars would hold that the resulting picture does not agree with the realities of modern Itháki. In my opinion the picture does fit, and fits well, provided one makes two assumptions about the poet's intentions. First, one should allow that Homer has designed his picture to include a series of contrasts, almost contradictions. Ithaca is rough, but kindly; it

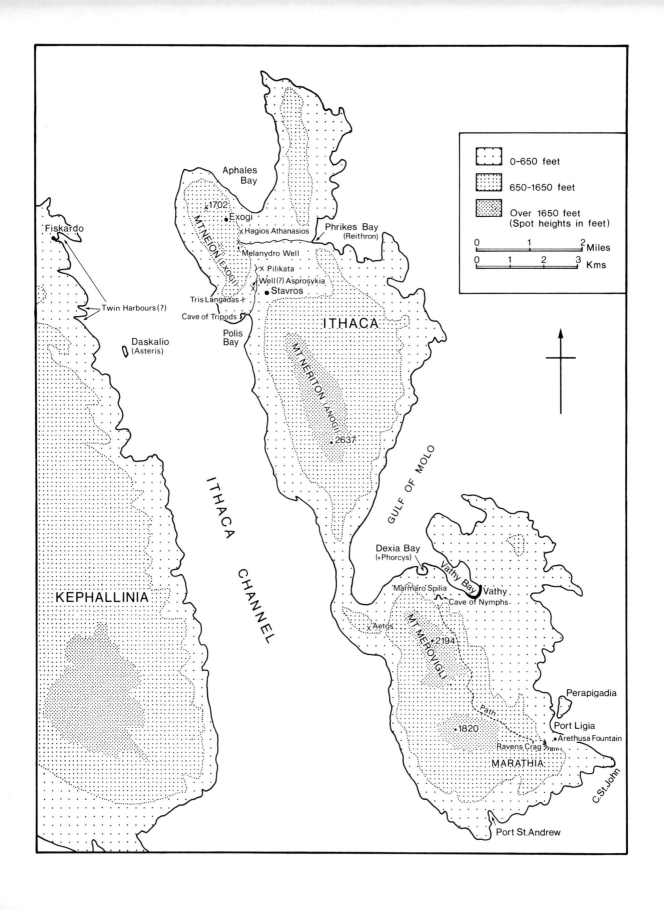

Fiskardo

Twin Harbours (?)

Daskalio
(Asteris)

KEPHALLINIA

ITHACA CHANNEL

Aphales
Bay

•1702

MT NEION (EXOGI)

•Exogi
× Hagios Athanasios
Melanydro Well
× Pilikata
Well (?) Asprosykia
Tris Langadas +
Cave of Tripods
Polis
Bay

Phrikes Bay
(Reithron)

•Stavros

ITHACA

MT NERITON (ANOGI)

•2637

GULF OF MOLO

Dexia Bay
(=Phorcys)

Marmaro Spilia
Cave of Nymphs
× Aetos

Vathy Bay

•Vathy

MT MEROVIGLI
•2194

Path

•1820

Perapigadia

Port Ligia
•Arethusa Fountain
Ravens Crag

MARATHIA

C.St.John

Port St.Andrew

0-650 feet

650-1650 feet

Over 1650 feet
(Spot heights in feet)

0   1   2 Miles

0   1   2   3 Kms

Ills. 68, 69. Opposite: map of Ithaca. All the sites where Mycenaean remains have been found lie in the northern plain bounded by Mt. Exogi (Homeric Neion) and Mt. Anogi (Homeric Neriton). The identification of the Raven's Crag and the Fountain of Arethusa with natural features in the south-east corner of the island is crucial for the understanding of Homer's account of the movements of Ulysses and Telemachos. Above: Aphales Bay and the northern promontory of Ithaca. The mountains of Leukas are visible in the distance.

Ill. 69

contains a conspicuous mountain, but is (in part at least) low-lying; the neighbouring islands lie close about it, yet they are well away to the east and south. Many commentators have seen in these 'inconsistencies' a proof that Homer had only a hazy conception of Ithaca and its surroundings. But this could be a *non sequitur*. When describing places that they know well, people often balance one aspect against another, correcting each emphasis by a counter-emphasis. Secondly, one should allow, as has often been urged, for a sailor's viewpoint in the description. Such a viewpoint seems implicit in the phrase 'lies in the sea furthest out' (or 'very high up'). Ithaca is being viewed on the horizon from a distance. The direction of the view is indicated by 'towards the dark quarter'.

If Homer had gone to visit Ithaca, he would probably have sailed from the isthmus of Corinth. On leaving the Gulf he would have sailed close to the archipelago of islands stretching north from the mouth of the river Acheloös. These islands answer well to the 'numerous inhabited islands very close to one another' of the Homeric description. Ithaca itself would then have come into view across an expanse of twenty miles of sea to the west. It would have appeared long and 'low' against the great mountainous mass of Kephallinia, which extends well to the south of Ithaca and rises in Mt. Aenos to a summit more than twice as high as Ithaca's highest peak. Later, after Homer had landed at Polis Bay, and climbed the populous slopes of the northern part of the island, he would have noted how this part of Ithaca seems to point to the quarter of sunset, with the peaks of Leukas receding to the north-east, and the main bulk of Kephallinia well to the south. Ithaca does indeed give the impression of lying on the extreme north-west perimeter of the island world.

87

A second description of Ithaca, put into the mouth of Athena, concentrates on the island itself:

> I grant that it is rugged and unfit for driving horses, yet narrow though it may be it is very far from poor. It grows abundant corn and wine in plenty. The rains and fresh dews are never lacking; and it has excellent pasturage for goats and cattle, timber of all kinds and watering places that never fail.
>
> (*Odyssey* 13:242–7; E. V. Rieu's translation)

Much here is quite general, and would fit any of the Ionian islands, but Ithaca is certainly much more 'narrow' than Zakynthos or Kephallinia, and also less suited for horses. Nowadays it has few trees, apart from olive groves, but as recently as the sixteenth century it was noted for its export of oak-apples. Undoubtedly it will have been much richer in timber in ancient times, and Neriton may well have been tree-clad up to the summit (Mt. Aenos in Kephallinia still has extensive pine forests). Extensive denudation of soil is confirmed by a rock-cut grave near Pilikata, which must have been below ground level in the Bronze Age, but now stands four or five feet above the surface. But despite this erosion Ithaca still gives an impression of fertility, and even pastures some cattle.

A third description is brief, but pinpoints the essentials:

> Tracks slanting across the slopes, harbours always fit for mooring in, naked rocks and flourishing trees. (*Odyssey* 13:195–6)

Sharp contrasts are again implicit here—the inadequacy of land communications contrasted with the wealth of well-sheltered harbours, and the prosperous orchards alternating with barren beds of bare rock. In the Greek, each phrase taken separately is a stock one, but together they picture Ithaca to the life.

It is on record that a hundred years ago there were no roads at all in Ithaca. Even today they are few in number, and the best route from one village to another is often by a cobbled path winding up through the olive terraces—Homer's 'rocky road'—or by goat track across the open slopes. There is virtually no level ground and in many places one needs the agility of a goat to cross the tracts of fissured limestone that make Ithaca indeed a 'rocky' and 'rugged' island. Yet here and there, notably around the head of Vathy Bay and on the well-terraced slopes that circle Stavros, there are stretches of good soil where little vineyards alternate with olive groves, and the fruit trees in autumn are heavy with pear and pomegranate, apple and fig. Even today, with a much diminished population, Ithaca still exports oil and raisins. For all its ruggedness it is by no means a poor island.

There is little to be said in favour of Dörpfeld's theory that Homeric Ithaca lay in what is now Leukas, and much to be said against it. In Homeric times, one would not have said jokingly to a visitor in Leukas (as one did in Ithaca): 'Tell me what ship brought you, for I

Ill. 70. A cist grave cut into the rock in the Late Bronze Age. At that date soil must have covered the rock, whose top is now four or five feet above ground level. These data provide a measure of soil erosion in Ithaca during the past three millenniums. The site is just to the north of the crest of Pilikata.

Ill. 71

don't suppose you came on foot'. The joke would lose all point on a peninsula as Leukas then was. There are many other objections to Dörpfeld's hypothesis. Leukas would be a peninsula but for the modern ship canal; it was never a 'clearly defined' island; nor is it surrounded by other islands; nor is there a 'strait' between it and another island. Nor does it agree with Telemachos' description of his island as notably unsuited for horses (*Odyssey* 4: 600 ff.), for there are quite extensive plains, especially round Nidri, where Dörpfeld concentrated his excavations. These excavations showed that Nidri was an important settlement in the Middle Helladic period, but only two or three fragments of painted Mycenaean pottery were found. Mycenaean pottery has been discovered in two other areas in Leukas, but the total amount is very small in comparison with what has been found on Itháki. The British excavations in Itháki in the 1930s showed that Greek occupation of the island lasted *without a break* from Mycenaean times on. In the classical period the island was known as Ithaca, and there is every reason to suppose that it bore the same name in the age of Ulysses. Dörpfeld never produced any argument from archaeology or Greek tradition to corroborate his supposition that the name migrated from Leukas after the Trojan War. Nor have his detailed identifications of Ithacan features on Leukas won any lasting support. Engel, after visiting Leukas, roundly declared: 'Not a single feature of the Homeric description of Ithaca corresponds with Leukadian actuality.'

We may be content to believe that the fame acquired by Ithaca during the Trojan War never faded and that the Greeks always remembered its correct location. Where, then, are we to place Samê, Zakynthos, and Doulichion? If the 'channel between Ithaca and rocky

Ill. 71. 'Rocky Ithaca': a typical landscape with well-spaced olive trees interspersed with outcrops of jagged limestone. The picture was taken in the area to the south of Marathia.

Sam[os]' is the Ithaca channel (see below, p. 98), then Samê-Samos must be Kephallinia. The name survives in the modern town of Sami, the terminus of the Itháki-Kephallinia ferry. As for Zakynthos, there is unanimous agreement that modern Zakynthos (commonly called Zante) is to be identified with Homeric Zakynthos.

The identification of Doulichion is more problematical. The Homeric clues (*Iliad* 2:625; *Odyssey* 14:335 ff.; 16:247, 396) are that it is 'rich in wheat' and 'grassy', that it furnished the most Suitors for Penelope, that it is grouped with the Echinades islands, and that a ship coming to it from Thesprotia broke its journey near the hut of Eumaios (i.e. in the south-east corner of Ithaca, see below, pp. 92, 94). None of the proposed locations fully satisfies all these indications, but Leukas probably comes closest to doing so. Leukas could be reached on foot from the mainland, and that may explain why it did not form part of the kingdom of Ulysses. But being virtually surrounded by water it could be called an 'island' by Greek usage, and as such it can be admitted to the quartet of major named islands grouped together by Homer.

We may now proceed to consider Homer's descriptions of particular places on Ithaca. The longest and most striking is that of the Bay of Phorcys and the cave of the Nymphs:

> In that island is a cove named after Phorcys, the old man of the sea, with two bold headlands squatting at its mouth so as to protect it from the heavy swell raised by rough weather in the open and allow large ships to ride inside without so much as tying up, once within mooring distance of the shore. At the head of the cove grows a long-leaved olive-tree and nearby is a cavern that offers welcome shade and is sacred to the Nymphs whom we call Naiads. This cave contains a number of stone basins and two-handled jars, which are used by bees as their hives; also great looms of stone where the Nymphs weave marvellous fabrics of sea-purple; and there are springs whose water never fails. It has two mouths. The one that looks north is the way down for men. The other, facing south, is meant for the gods; and as immortals come in by this way it is not used by men at all.
>
> (*Odyssey* 13:96–112; E. V. Rieu's translation)

Caverns are of course ubiquitous in the limestone hills of Greece, but it so happens that a cave answering very well to the above description is to be found on a hillside about two miles north-west of Vathy. Called Marmarospilia, it possesses two entrances as described by Homer. The 'human' entrance is quite small, and it would have been easy to seal it with a large stone as Athena does after secreting Ulysses' treasure inside the cave (*Odyssey* 13:370). Moreover it faces north. On squeezing through, one finds oneself on a 'landing' some twenty feet long by six feet broad at a higher level than the main body of the cave. At the far end of this landing is a broad rocky ledge like an

Ill. 72. North-facing entrance to a cave at Marmarospilia which shows many features in common with the Homeric cave of the Nymphs. Here, in the *Odyssey*, Ulysses stowed his treasures on his return to Ithaca. The entrance is about five feet high, and could easily be blocked with a large stone, as described by Homer. Within, the cave opens out into a substantial vaulted chamber with a vent at the apex corresponding to Homer's 'divine' entrance (see *Ill. 82*). The entrance shown here is the 'human' entrance.

offering-table with semi-circular depressions answering to Homer's 'stone basins' (although not at present occupied by bees). Rough-cut steps lead down to the main chamber about fifteen feet below—'the way *down* for men'. After descending, and when one's eyes have become accustomed to the gloom, one sees that the cave is roughly circular, about sixty feet in diameter, with a large recess opening off to the south. Above, the roof narrows on all sides like a corbelled vault (the 'broad and vaulted cave'—*Odyssey* 13:349) and at the apex there is a narrow vent admitting a thin shaft of light, surely the 'divine' entrance which no mortal could use without falling to his death on the rocky floor of the cavern. At many places round the walls the slow drip and seepage of water has fashioned fluted columns of stone in 'organ-pipe' formation. In them, and in one free-standing fretted stalactite pillar, one can visualize the 'great looms of stone' where the Nymphs wove their immortal fabrics.

Ill. 82

If one accepts that Marmarospilia supplied the pattern for the Homeric cave of the Nymphs, then the Bay of Phorcys must be sought in the cove now called Dexia (because it lies 'to the right' as one enters Vathy Bay from the Gulf of Molo). The cove is quite small, and well sheltered from the squally north-west wind, a wind which I saw raise waves three feet high on the sea-front at Vathy. It faces across to Mt. Neriton (*Odyssey* 13:351), and at its mouth stand bluff headlands sloping back to the beach. The inner part of the cove is shallow and sandy, unlike most of the harbours of Ithaca, and here the Phaeacian ship could safely have grounded half her length (*Odyssey* 13:113–15). From the beach a little valley runs steeply up to the cave about six hundred feet above sea level. Homer states that the cave was 'away from the road' (*Odyssey* 13:123), which then, as now, must have run close to the shore. The cave is at the 'head' of the harbour in the sense that there the valley leading up from the beach loses itself in the ridge of hills running southwards.

Ill. 73

Having stowed his goods in the cave, Ulysses 'turned his back on the harbour and followed a rough track leading up into the woods and through the hills to the house of Eumaios the swineherd' (*Odyssey* 14:1 ff.). His probable route is marked on the map, and it will be seen that it avoids the lowlands round the head of Vathy Bay and traverses the undulating flanks of the Merovigli ridge at a fairly constant height of about a thousand feet until it emerges on the Marathia plateau.

Eumaios' house is placed by Homer 'close to the Raven's Crag and the Fountain of Arethusa' (*Odyssey* 13:408). The Raven's Crag is the most striking natural feature in the south of the island. A rough gorge runs steeply up from the sea and culminates in a sheer limestone cliff about two hundred feet high. The cliff swings round the head of the gorge in a gentle curve for six hundred yards or so, and as I was contemplating it, a goatherd approached, pointed to it, and said: '*Stefani tou Korakou*'. I found out later that *stefani* is an Ithacan dialect word for 'crag', so here was Homer's 'Raven's Crag'—still known as such to Eumaios' descendants. There were ravens in plenty. At one moment I saw ten fly over in a straggling line, and every now and then one would see a bird swing out from the cliff, and hear its harsh croak as it went gliding and tumbling down towards the sea far below. And there, well down the gorge, lay the 'Fountain of Arethusa'. Even in mid-September I was able to quench my thirst from a spring-fed pool in a cleft of rock. Such a perennial source was clearly a valuable asset in the rocky wilds of the south of the island. It was easy to imagine generations of herdsmen pasturing their swine and goats under the oak-trees and through the scrub of the gorge, and watering them at the spring. Even as I was speaking to 'my' Eumaios, he began urging a small herd of goats down into the gorge past the cliff, driving them with shouts and stones away from the well-cultivated plateau to the rough pasturage below.

We parted, and I walked slowly along the edge of the cliff enjoying the splendid panorama of sea and islands and coastline all the way from Leukas in the north to Zakynthos forty miles to the south. It was indeed as Homer called it, 'a place with a view' (*Odyssey* 14:6). And then I saw the goatherd's cottage, a simple rectangular building of rough stone with a sloping tile roof, one of the very few houses in this part of Ithaca. Homer describes Eumaios' house as fronted by an enclosure which he had made for the swine out of 'field stones topped off with wild pear' (*Odyssey* 14:10). It was with something of a 'wild surmise' that I saw in front of this isolated steading an oval enclosure about twenty yards long surrounded by a rough stone wall topped off with an assortment of spiny and prickly bushes. I cannot be certain that they included 'wild pear'. The finer shrub on top is definitely not the species now known as 'wild pear', but some of the coarser branches below may be. But what is certain is that here, close to the Raven's Crag, was an isolated farmstead with an enclosure for animals in front of it conforming closely to the Homeric description of Eumaios'

Ill. 74

Ill. 83

Ill. 76

Ill. 74. The Raven's Crag near the ▶ south-east cape of Ithaca is the most striking natural feature on the island (opposite). A semi-circle of limestone cliffs tops a wooded gorge running steeply down to the sea (see *Ill. 77*). The cliffs still house a large colony of ravens.

92

house and surrounds. It seems that the pattern of life here has altered little down the centuries. If Homer had visited the spot he would have seen the fountain, the ravens, the cliff, the view, and possibly the same type of enclosure in front of a lonely cottage. He would also have seen at the base of the cliff some south-facing caverns in the rock—the shelters where he makes Eumaios spend the night in dutiful proximity to his herds. (*Odyssey* 14:532–3).

Eumaios' house was visited by Telemachos on his return from Pylos. He had been advised by Athena to hug the coast of Elis (*Odyssey* 15:33), and he had then cut north across the mouth of the Gulf of Corinth to the 'sharp' islands (*Odyssey* 15:299). The promontory of Kutsilaris just south of the Acheloös' delta is pyramidal in shape, over thirteen hundred feet high, and may then have been an island. Just to the west of it lies an island still called Oxeia, the 'sharp island', whose fretted outline makes it a conspicuous landmark. By following this course Telemachos avoided detection by the ambush placed to intercept him on his return to Polis Bay. From their lookout near Fiskardo (see p. 98), the Suitors' men had an uninterrupted view down the Ithaca channel to the extreme southern tip of Kephallinia and the open sea beyond. Had Telemachos returned by the most direct route from Pylos he would have been visible when still a long way south of Polis Bay. But by heading in for the 'sharp' islands he placed the southern portion of Ithaca between himself and his enemies. Athena further advised him to make for the 'first cape' of Ithaca (*Odyssey* 15:36), and there his crew furled sail and rowed the ship into harbour. This landfall must have been close to Eumaios' hut, either at Port Ligia below the Fountain of Arethusa, or else at Port St. Andrew, the only good harbour on the south coast of Ithaca.

Telemachos then made haste to reach the hut of Eumaios where he found the faithful swineherd and his father (*Odyssey* 15:555). After the recognitions had been effected, it was decided that Eumaios should go to the palace to tell Penelope of Telemachos' safe return. Eumaios leaves soon after breakfast, and does not get back until nightfall. Homer emphasizes that he wasted no time on his mission (*Odyssey* 16:452–67). If we take this datum as a fairly precise indication of distance, it follows that the palace must have lain in the northern part of the island. Gell and Schliemann and many others looked for the site of the palace on the central isthmus at Aetos, where local tradition placed a 'castle of Ulysses'. But this site is little more than two hours' walk from the Raven's Crag. If we locate the palace in the Stavros area, a reasonable suggestion on other grounds, we impose on Eumaios a round trip of about thirty miles, a feasible day's journey for a hardy swineherd.

I picture the route as running along the eastern slopes of Merovigli, and then following much the same line as the modern road round the head of the Gulf of Molo and along the western flank of Mt. Neriton. If so, the path in its final stage would pass close to Polis Bay, the only

Ill. 76. Opposite: a lonely cottage on Marathia plateau, Ithaca. The indications of the *Odyssey* place Eumaios' cottage in this area. This homestead, like the one in Homer, is surrounded by a dry stone wall topped off with a parapet of thorny shrubs.

Ill. 78

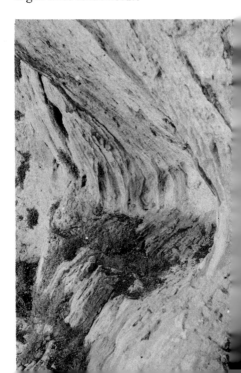

Ill. 75. A natural rock shelter at the base of the Raven's Crag, similar to that described in *Odyssey* 14:532–3, where Eumaios could have spent the night close to his herds.

*Other possible survivals of Homeric place names include Nidri for Neriton and Cape Krokali, reminiscent of the district Krokuleia. Continuity of habitation is sometimes denied on the basis of a Venetian report describing Ithaca as *dishabitata*, *c.* AD 1500. But this may mean no more than 'with diminished population', and in any case not much more than twenty years elapsed between the Turkish invasion in AD 1479 and the Venetian resettlement from Kephallinia soon after 1500.

*Probably the 'ridge of Hermes' mentioned in *Odyssey* 16:471.

really good harbour on the west coast of Ithaca. Polis, the 'city', is surprisingly rare as a place name in modern Greece, and its survival here in Ithaca is a direct link with antiquity. The name was used for the chief city of this part of the island in the classical period, and may well go back even further to the main focus of settlement in Mycenaean times.* Excavation has confirmed that the area from Polis Bay northwards was the main inhabited area in the Late Bronze Age. Evidence of Mycenaean occupation has been found at no less than six sites from the shore of Polis Bay up to the neighbourhood of the modern village of Exogi.

Where, then, was the palace of Ulysses located? No certain answer to this question has yet been found. W. A. Heurtley, the field-director of the British School excavations in the 1930s, was convinced that he had found the site at Pilikata, at the highest point of the long hog-backed ridge running north from Stavros.* He certainly proved that there had been habitation here for a long period in the Bronze Age. From six excavated areas and numerous trial pits he recovered many fine examples of Early Helladic pottery, and some striking pieces of Minyan ware from the Middle Helladic period. But his finds of Late Helladic (Mycenaean) were comparatively few, and all concentrated in one area. Also, he found no remains of a major building *in situ,* though he was able to argue that building blocks incorporated in later structures could have come from a Mycenaean building. He did find traces of a defensive wall ringing the summit. The site is well supplied with water, and affords good views in all directions. From it one can

Ill. 77. A view down the gorge from the Raven's Crag to Ligia Bay. Telemachos may have landed here on his return from Pylos.

see Aphales Bay to the north, an exposed anchorage, and two good harbours, Phrikes Bay to the east and Polis Bay to the south-west.

Phrikes Bay is almost certainly Homer's 'haven of Reithron below wooded Neion' (*Odyssey* 1:186). 'Reithron' means 'torrent', and the longest stream in Ithaca reaches the sea at Phrikes Bay, flowing in its final stages through the middle of Phrikes village. If Reithron is Phrikes, 'wooded Neion' will be Mt. Exogi. 'Neion' implies a 'ship-like' outline, and Mt. Exogi, with its two summits separated by a col, looks from the east like a great ship with high prow and stern. The *city* of Ithaca (as distinct from the island) is once described as lying

Ill. 78. A view of Polis Bay. Mt. Exogi (Homeric Neion) rises behind. The name Polis (= city) may preserve a memory of the location nearby of the chief town of Ithaca in Mycenaean, and again in classical, times. The bay is deep and provides an excellent sheltered anchorage for small craft. It is the only really good harbour on the west coast of the island. The site of the tripod cave (see pp. 99, 100) lies half-way along the far shore.

'below Neion' (*Odyssey* 3:81), and this would be a reasonable designation of the Pilikata ridge and its adjoining slopes.

Homer envisages the palace as situated not far from a well which he describes in considerable detail. The description comes at the dramatic moment when Ulysses at last approaches the home he has not seen for twenty years:

> They followed a rocky path, and were close to the city, and had reached the well-made fair-flowing source from which the townsfolk used to draw water. Ithakos and Neritos and Polyktor had made it. All round in a circle grew a thicket of alders nourished by the moisture, and the cool water flowed down from above from a rock. An altar for the nymphs had been fashioned above it where all passers-by used to make their offerings.
>
> (*Odyssey* 17: 204 ff.)

In the valley to the west of the Pilikata ridge runs a brook which was still flowing quite strongly when I saw it in early May. A water source of this quality is very good by Ithacan standards and one would expect a settlement to grow up nearby. At a point immediately below Stavros church, where paths converge from Stavros, Tris Langadas and Polis Bay, the stream cascades down over rocks into a tangled thicket of reeds and bushes. This would have been a suitable place for the first Mycenaean rulers of Ithaca to have constructed a public fountain by trapping the stream in an artificial basin. No traces of such a work survive to view, but at nearby Asprosykia some Mycenaean sherds were found. The fountain would have been conveniently placed for the inhabitants of the 'city' on the surrounding slopes, and would not have been more than about a quarter of a mile from a palace at the crest of the Pilikata ridge.

Thus the Homeric indications are not inconsistent with Heurtley's hypothesis. Pilikata is somewhat lacking in natural strength, but does command good prospects over all the cultivable areas and harbours of northern Ithaca.* On the whole it appears to be the most likely site for Ulysses' palace, though the quantity of Mycenaean pottery recovered there remains disappointingly small.

If Pilikata is not accepted, one should probably follow Lord Rennell of Rodd, the patron and prime mover of the British Expedition, in looking for the palace somewhat higher up the slopes of Mt. Exogi. There is a possible site at Hagios Athanasios where the hillside levels out into a small plateau. At the point known as Homer's School, the jutting brow of the plateau still carries the massive lower courses of an ancient guard tower dating back to the fourth century BC. The tower stands over a small cliff with an ancient rock-cut shrine at its base. About one hundred and fifty yards to the north-east, Vollgraff excavated some substantial walls surrounding what was clearly a sacred enclosure. The British team also made some soundings near the tower, and a few Mycenaean sherds were found. I suspect that the

*Homer implies that two harbours are visible from the vicinity of the palace. For 'our harbour' = Polis Bay, see *Odyssey* 16:351–2 and 472–3. For the 'haven of Reithron' Phrikes Bay (see above, p. 96) see *Odyssey* 1:185–6.

whole area has very ancient religious associations, and believe it would repay further investigation. It may have been a Mycenaean shrine which became a place of refuge during the Dark Age, and the association with Homer might conceivably have a history going back to the archaic period. Three hundred yards to the south-west the perennial spring now known as Melanydro provides a good water supply.

The next problem to be considered is the location of the ambush set to intercept Telemachos on his return from Pylos. The Suitors are described as patrolling the channel between Ithaca and Samos from a base with 'twin harbours':

> A rocky island lies in mid-channel between Ithaca and rocky Samos, Asteris by name, not a large island, and there are twin harbours in it offering a safe anchorage for ships. There the Achaeans waited in ambush for Telemachos. (*Odyssey* 4:844–7)

In the Ithaca channel directly opposite Polis Bay lies a small rocky island now called Daskalio. Daskalio is the only island in the channel, and is to be identified with Homer's Asteris. But the placing there of twin harbours generates a topographical problem, for Daskalio is nothing but a ledge of rock about two hundred yards long by thirty wide. It could never have afforded a safe anchorage for Homeric galleys. But if one looks across from the islet to the nearby shore of Kephallinia one sees two coves side by side which might well be described as 'twin harbours'. And if one goes a mile north to Fiskardo* one finds a well-sheltered harbour with 'twin' basins at its head where a long ship could lie up in complete security ready to intercept any ship coming up the Ithaca channel. The Suitors' base must have been at the northern end of Kephallinia, and this is confirmed by the routine of the patrol as described by Antinoös:

> By day a string of sentries kept watch from the windy heights; and at sunset we never slept on shore, but kept sailing the sea in our swift ship, waiting for the dawn. (*Odyssey* 16:365–8)

Daskalio–Asteris can never have provided a suitable observation post for it rises only about ten feet from the water. The 'windy heights' must be sought on the promontories to north and south of Fiskardo. These promontories provide splendid vantage points for surveying the whole length of the Ithaca channel. An ingenious solution to the difficulty was suggested by Bérard. He proposed to alter the text to read 'there are twin harbours *near* it', a change of a single letter in the Greek (*epi* for *eni*). If this neat emendation is not acceptable, two courses seem open to us. We can admit that for once Homer is less than precise in his Ithacan topography. We must take it that he is designating the general area of the ambush at the northern end of the channel by reference to Asteris as a distinctive landmark, and we must further suppose that to avoid confusing his hearers, he says that the twin harbours are *in* Asteris, though he knew that they were really 'in

*The Norman dynast Robert Guiscard (whose name survives in 'Fiskardo') recognized the strategic importance of the site, and built a church on the promontory where the lighthouse still stands. During the Second World War the Germans had gun emplacements here.

Ill. 80

98

Ill. 79. Perennial sources of water are rare on Ithaca. This well called Melanydro ('dark water') traps the waters of a small brook in a 'made' basin (opposite). It is close to the site of Hagios Athanasios.

its neighbourhood'. Or alternatively, we may use this passage as a proof that all his topographical information was based on hearsay, and argue that in this instance he did not fully appreciate the relation of the Kephallinia anchorage to Daskalio.

For a local memory of Ulysses himself, we may now turn to an important site not so far mentioned. This is a cave or grotto sacred to the Nymphs. The cave used to stand close to the sea on the north shore of Polis Bay, but its roof collapsed at some date after the first century AD, and the sea rose to the level of its floor. The site was forgotten until the owner of the land, Loizos by name, dug up certain interesting objects there in 1868 and 1873. His finds included a bronze sword and spear, and a bronze tripod-cauldron. Mycenaean pottery was found by Vollgraff in 1904, the first to be discovered on Ithaca, but no thorough exploration was made until 1930. Between then and 1932 Miss Benton carried out a scientific excavation which yielded a large amount of stratified pottery and votive offerings. These had been dedicated at the shrine over a very long period from the Bronze Age down to the first century AD. Inscriptions on some of the sherds proved the cult of the Nymphs at the cave. Also recovered was a small triangular fragment of a terracotta mask with the legend *ΕΥΧΗΝ ΟΔΥΣΣΕΙ*, 'a prayer to Odysseus'. The fragment, dating from the first or second century BC, indicates that there was a cult of Ulysses associated with the cave at this period. It is gratifying to have Ulysses' name turn up in this way within a mile or two of the conjectured site of his palace and city.

The cave yielded other treasures too. Working under great difficulties, caused by the sea-water which kept flooding the diggings, Miss Benton and her team recovered the remains of twelve magnificent bronze tripod-cauldrons. These massive vessels consisted of a circular basin supported on legs about three feet in length. Some of them ran on wheels, and had circular handles surmounted by figurines of dogs

Ill. 80. Daskalio, the only island in the Ithaca channel. A small chapel and a ruined watch-tower straddle its rocky spine. It is probably to be identified with Homeric Asteris. In the early morning its white rocks catch the sunlight and make it gleam like a 'star' in the dark waters of the channel.

or horses. Legs and handles were handsomely chased with linked spirals and other geometric motifs. Of outstandingly fine workmanship, these objects are assigned to the ninth or eighth centuries BC. They are therefore considerably later than the age of Ulysses, but they testify to the continued importance of the shrine which goes back to his time, and which was later to be explicitly associated with his name. Today they may be seen in the museum at Stavros.

The treasure of gifts that Ulysses brought back from Phaeacia included thirteen bronze tripods and cauldrons that Alkinoös and his twelve peers gave him (*Odyssey* 8:390–1 and 13:13f.). If we add to the twelve excavated by Miss Benton the one originally recovered by Loizos we reach precisely the same number. This exact coincidence encourages the belief that Homer had either seen, or heard of, the notable dedication of tripod-cauldrons in the Polis Bay cave. They were important works of art dedicated about 800 BC in a place that must have been much frequented by passing sailors.

The *Odyssey* has been described as the first novel, and if this is a valid description, then Homer must be regarded as something of a historical novelist. Any conscientious historical novelist will study the sources for the period that he intends to treat, and will also take what steps he can to familiarize himself with the places in which his story is set. In Homer's case his sources were given in the complex oral epic tradition that he knew so well. Once he had decided to make a full-length poem about Ulysses and Ithaca it would have been natural for him to try to gather 'local colour' about the island and its immediate surroundings. Some information could have been gleaned from sailors: for instance the fact that a vessel sailing from the 'sharp' islands to the south of Ithaca would not be visible from the north end of the Ithaca channel. But when one goes on to consider the background to movements within the island, the hypothesis of second-hand information becomes harder to sustain. These movements are an integral part of the story. Ulysses, after landing, must be able to stow his goods in a safe place and proceed quickly, and by a secluded route, to Eumaios' hut. Telemachos, after his dawn landing, must be able to reach the hut quickly and confer with Ulysses before going on to the palace. Eumaios must be able to walk to the palace and back between early morning and dusk. All these events, and many more, happen within a topographical setting which is consistently presented in a series of interlocking descriptions and allusions, and which corresponds with the physical facts of Ithaca.

Homer, I believe, must at the very least have had in his mind a picture of Ithaca based on information from someone who knew the island well. Many modern topographers of Ithaca have gone even further than this. They have asserted with conviction that Homer himself must have visited the island. On balance I am inclined to agree that the evidence supports this contention. If one had a good visual imagination and were a persistent questioner, one *might* gather from

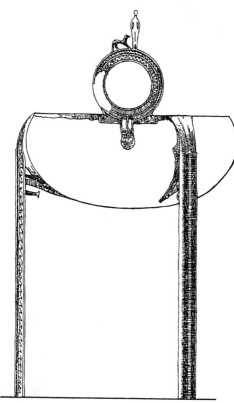

Ill. 81. Drawing of a tripod-cauldron of the Geometric period (*c.* 800 BC) recovered from a cave shrine of the Nymphs on the north shore of Polis Bay, Ithaca. The elaborate chasing of legs and handle, and the figurines of man and hound make it a notable example of early Greek bronze work. It formed part of a dedication of thirteen such tripods, the remains of which are in the museum at Stavros.

Ill. 82. Opposite: the interior of the ▶ cave of the Nymphs near Dexia Bay, Ithaca (see *Ill. 72*). The stalactite formations suit the Homeric description of the 'great looms of stone where the Nymphs weave marvellous fabrics of sea-purple'. Unlike the tripod cave in Polis Bay, no evidence of an ancient cult has been found here.

an informant that there was a lonely cottage near the Raven's Crag, that it commanded a wide prospect, and that a path led from it down the side of the cliff to a cave shelter facing south. Similarly one *might* visualize from a description the relationship between Mt. Neriton, Dexia Bay, the Marmarospilia cave and the path south to Marathia, and one might embody all this correctly in one's story. One *might* describe at second-hand the Asprosykia fountain. One *might* even imagine correctly the intersection at the palace forecourt of sight-lines from two widely separated havens. One *might* get all this right, and say nothing incorrect about Ithaca, never having seen the island. But the more accurate and detailed and self-interlocking Homer's descriptions are proved to be, the less likely it becomes that he did not see it all for himself.

Here, of course, the sceptic will urge the difficulties in the overall picture of Ithaca given by Ulysses to the Phaeacians, and also the problem of the twin harbours on Asteris. I do not underestimate these difficulties, and I freely allow that the easiest (though not the only) way to solve them is to regard them as inaccurate descriptions based on misunderstood information. But they must be weighed against the many other places where Homer gets his picture remarkably right. On balance I consider that Homer's successes in topographical description are so numerous, so varied, and so striking, that they can most reasonably be explained by his having visited Ithaca. One must then try to explain the awkward passages along the lines attempted earlier in the chapter.

The entire hypothesis is in obvious conflict with the tradition that Homer was blind. The ancients must have noted this difficulty, for one of the 'Lives' of Homer makes him go blind *after* his visit to Ithaca. But another 'Life' makes no mention of any blindness. In fact, there is no reliable tradition either way, and the whole story may be no more than an inference based on Homer's portrayal of the bard Demodokos as blind. We might with greater plausibility infer from Homer's similes that he was gifted with unusually acute powers of observation.

I have tried to show that Homer's description of Ithaca corresponds closely with the natural features of the island now called Itháki, and also with what has been discovered about Mycenaean habitation there. I have also pointed out that excavation has demonstrated continuity of Greek habitation from Late Mycenaean times through to the classical period. All this may serve to strengthen our belief in the general soundness of the Homeric tradition about Ulysses, and may help us to assert with more reasoned confidence that Ithaca really was the home of an Achaean chieftain who played a prominent part in the Trojan War.

5

Archaeology and the Homeric palaces

J. V. Luce

MUCH of the action in the *Odyssey* takes place in palaces, and so the archaeology of such buildings must figure largely in any consideration of the material background of the story. In the Late Bronze Age the chief palaces of Greece were complex and costly establishments, with outer walls of finely cut masonry and splendid interior furnishings and decoration. Much has been discovered about the layout and appearance of their component buildings from excavations at Mycenae, Tiryns and Ano Englianos. They provided accommodation, not only for the royal family, but also for craftsmen, scribes and household slaves. Focal points of power and sophisticated living for large areas, they did not survive the disruptions of the Greek Dark Age, and nothing like them was to be found in Homer's Ionia. Yet Homer is able to picture them in considerable detail, thanks to a set of descriptive phrases which he inherited with the epic tradition. In what follows we shall be comparing Homer's account of the palaces with the relevant archaeological data. Much of the discussion will be about the findings at Ano Englianos, the probable site of Nestor's palace. The other palaces of the *Odyssey* can only be treated in a general way, since their sites have not been identified.

THE PALACE OF NESTOR

In the narrative of the *Odyssey,* Pylos is prominent as the first place visited by Telemachos in his personal quest for his absent father, and as the site of Nestor's palace. There is no tradition that Ulysses himself visited Pylos, but he once mentions it as a possible port of call (*Odyssey* 13 : 274), and as a young man he went to Pherai to collect reparation for a Messenian raid on Ithaca, a trip which would have taken him close to Pylian territory (*Odyssey* 21 : 11 ff.).

During the past thirty-five years, a series of important discoveries in the south-west Peloponnese have transformed our knowledge of conditions there during the Mycenaean age. It has become clear that the area was thickly settled and more prosperous than it was ever again to be in antiquity. From 1200 BC onwards many sites were destroyed and abandoned, yet later Greek tradition preserved many details of the history and geography of the region before the Dorian invasion. The

◀ *Ill. 84.* Opposite: a gold cup (about 5 in. high) found by Schliemann in Shaft Grave IV at Mycenae. Because of its unusual shape, and the dove ornament, Schliemann had no hesitation in identifying it with the Cup of Nestor described in *Iliad* 11:632–7. Despite some discrepancies—the Homeric vessel is envisaged as very massive and has four handles, not two—it is probable that this Dove Cup is the type of vessel from which the Homeric description is ultimately derived. The doves may lend it some religious significance as a ceremonial chalice or 'loving-cup'.

LINE 1   Two tripod-cauldrons of Cretan workmanship, of *ai-ke-u* type; one tripod-cauldron with a *single* handle *on* one foot; one tripod-cauldron of Cretan workmanship, burnt away at the legs, *useless*.

LINE 2   three *wine-jars*; one larger-sized *goblet* with four handles; two larger-sized *goblets* with three handles; one smaller-sized *goblet* with four handles.

LINE 3   one smaller-sized *goblet* with three handles; one smaller-sized *goblet* without a handle.

progress of archaeological discovery enables us to assess the reliability of the tradition and in general it emerges from the assessment with credit. Our primary witness, Homer, can be seen to have inherited a reasonably authentic picture of what life must have been like in Nestor's Pylos. He may not have been quite sure of the location of that Pylos—no later Greek was—but he was aware of its very important status in the Mycenaean world, and this must tend to enhance our confidence in his general testimony to the life and times of Ulysses.

To the late Professor Carl Blegen of the University of Cincinnati belongs much of the credit for the large extension of our knowledge of the Pylian kingdom in the Late Bronze Age. On 4 April 1939, he sank an exploratory trench into a Messenian hillside, and by mid-morning, as he has written, 'even the rosiest expectations had been surpassed'. Substantial stone walls, decorated plaster fragments, and five tablets inscribed in the Linear B script (the first to be found in mainland Greece) had been unearthed. No other excavation, one supposes, has ever achieved such success so quickly. But this was much more than a lucky strike. The joint Hellenic-American expedition formed some years before had done its preliminary surveys well. Its leaders had noted a concentration of Mycenaean tombs to the north of the Bay of Navarino, and the hill of Ano Englianos had been selected as the most promising of a number of possible sites for the 'hypothetical palace that was the first object of the expedition's search'. As more trenches were dug and over six hundred tablets recovered, it became clear that a palace had indeed been found. Because of the Second World War and its aftermath, excavation could not be resumed until 1952. However, photographs of all the tablets found in the first season were being studied in Cincinnati from 1940 onwards, and the publication of a preliminary transcript by Bennett in 1951 led directly to the decipherment of the Linear B script by Michael Ventris in 1952.

The Pylos tablets constitute one of the two main groups of Linear B documents so far recovered, the other group coming from the palace of Knossos in Crete. The tablets are of clay and owe their preservation to the baking they received in the conflagrations which marked the end of the palaces where they were found. They represent the

Ill. 85. Linear B tablet (Ta 641) from Pylos (length *c.* 10 in.). This tablet was found by Blegen *after* Ventris had promulgated his system of decipherment, and went far in convincing scholars of its correctness. The ideograms showed that the tablet was a list of tripods and pots. Ventris' system gave appropriate sign-groups the values of ti-ri-po (tripod) and di-pa (Homeric *depas* = vessel). Furthermore, the form ti-ri-po-de (line 1) is the Greek plural, and the corresponding ideogram with numeral showed that *two* tripods were being listed. Most striking of all were the words qe-to-ro-we and ti-ri-o-we (line 2) and a-no-we (line 3). These should mean 'with four ears', 'with three ears', 'with no ears', and the corresponding ideograms showed vessels with four, three, and no lugs, respectively. The complete translation by Ventris and Chadwick is given below the tablet. Some doubt still attaches to a few words (italicized), but the general sense is clear.

Ill. 86. Opposite: map of the western ▶ Greek islands and the Peloponnese.

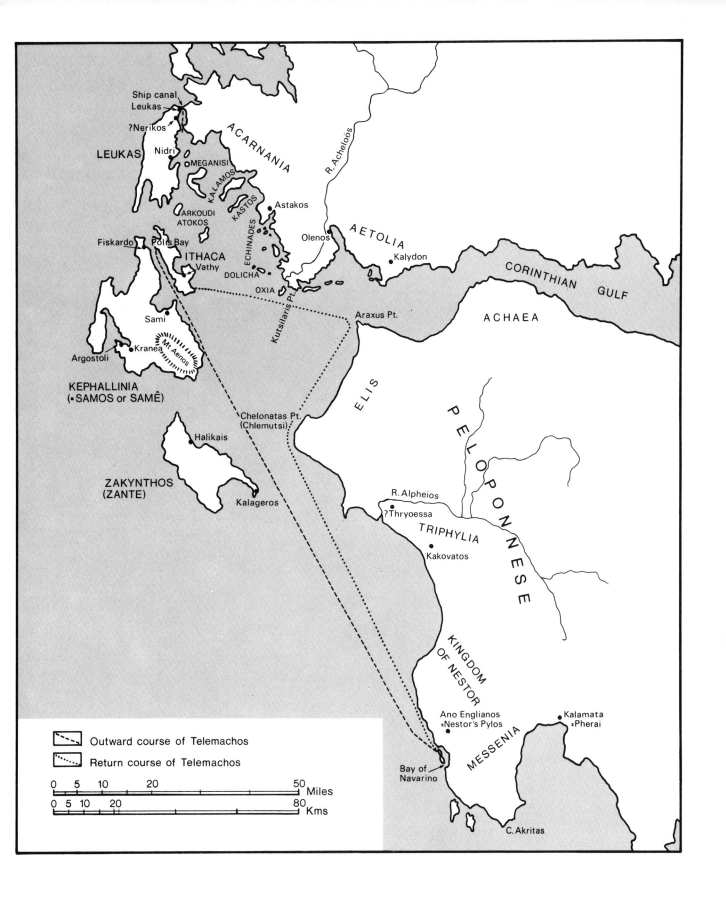

Ship canal,
Leukas

?Nerikos

LEUKAS
Nidri
MEGANISI
KALAMOS
ACARNANIA
R. Acheloös

ARKOUDI
ATOKOS
KASTOS
Astakos
Fiskardo
Polis Bay
ITHACA
Vathy
ECHINADES
Olenos
AETOLIA
Kalydon
DOLICHA
OXIA
Kutsilaris Pt.
Araxus Pt.
CORINTHIAN GULF
ACHAEA

Sami
Mt. Aenos
Argostoli
Kranea
KEPHALLINIA
(=SAMOS or SAMÊ)
ELIS
PELOPONNESE

Chelonatas Pt.
(Chlemutsi)
Halikais
ZAKYNTHOS
(ZANTE)
Kalageros
R. Alpheios
?Thryoessa
TRIPHYLIA
Kakovatos

KINGDOM
OF
NESTOR

Ano Englianos
=Nestor's Pylos
Kalamata
=Pherai

Bay of
Navarino
MESSENIA

C. Akritas

☐╌╌ Outward course of Telemachos

☐┈┈ Return course of Telemachos

0 5 10   20   50 Miles
0 5 10   20   80 Kms

archives for the last few months of the palaces' existence. They have been intensively studied, and most scholars now accept that they contain at least a form of Greek. But for various reasons—the ambiguity inherent in the spelling conventions, the large incidence of proper names, the comparatively restricted subject-matter, and the laconic style of the book-keeping—much in them still remains obscure or totally opaque. The bulk of them consists of inventories or receipts. Items listed include male and female slaves, livestock, corn, oil, wool, tripods, inlaid furniture, chariots, horses and weapons. Transactions documented comprise the issue of rations, the issue of measures of seed corn and the apportionment of lands. Weights and measures and numerical totals abound. Some of the records may represent receipts for produce delivered to the palace, others may be invoices of raw materials issued to craftsmen, or census lists of the resources of towns and villages. The general impression is bureaucratic, not heroic. We see literate scribes keeping close tally of the details of agricultural and manufacturing operations. The whole economy of large areas is clearly palace-centred and palace-directed—an Oriental rather than a Greek trait.

In general the tablets illuminate the social rather than the political history of their times: they are chiefly valuable for the light they throw on the social structure, the conditions of land tenure and the religion of the Mycenaean kingdoms. They confirm the antiquity of many Homeric words and phrases, and tend to corroborate the general reliability of Homer's picture of a network of kingdoms centred on great palaces and dominated by a warlike aristocracy. But they also reveal a world of commerce and sophisticated accountancy of which Homer gives little hint.

Blegen found much besides the tablets. The full extent and complexity of the palace buildings, and something of the surrounding city, were revealed in the thirteen campaigns between 1952 and the ending of the excavations in 1964. The results are available for study in the magnificent volumes of *The Palace of Nestor at Pylos in Western Messenia*.

The title embodies the authors' conviction that the location of Homeric Pylos has been fixed beyond question, though some scholars would still have reservations about this. The problem was much discussed in the ancient world, and its complexities were expressed in the proverb: 'A Pylos before Pylos, and always another Pylos', a jingle which neatly touches on those perennial stumbling-blocks of topography—the migration and duplication of names. Strabo argued that Nestor's Pylos was in Triphylia, well to the north of the Messenian peninsula. When Dörpfeld in 1907 discovered three *tholos* tombs and the remains of a substantial building in this area, he concluded that Strabo's solution was correct, and that his site, Kakovatos, must be Nestor's Pylos. Many scholars agreed with Dörpfeld until Blegen's discoveries threw a completely new light on the problem.

Ill. 86

Ill. 87. Part of the Battle fresco from the north-east wall of Hall 64 in the palace at Pylos. Members of the Pylian infantry armed with helmets and swords are engaging in hand-to-hand conflict with less well-equipped fighters. The variegated background is typical of Minoan fresco technique, but no scenes of actual fighting have ever been found in Crete. In the *Iliad* (11:670 ff.) Nestor recalls frontier skirmishes with the Eleians when 'the rustic folk fled in terror'. This fresco could be an illustration of some such incident.

The palace complex at Ano Englianos is just as large as the great establishments at Mycenae and Tiryns, and its floor decorations and frescoes are similar in style to those found at the other great centres of Mycenaean power. The tablets reveal that it administered a 'hither' province with nine major towns and a 'further' province with seven major towns. These were probably districts lying respectively west and east of Mt. Aigaleon. The exact limits of the kingdom are arguable, but the authority of the ruler probably extended at least as far north as the river Neda and as far east as the river Pamisos. Moreover, it is a large and inescapable fact that the name Pu-ro, i.e. Pylos, occurs on more than fifty of the tablets, and that it is by far the commonest place name on them. It is hard to resist the conclusion that the Pylian kingdom of heroic legend was in fact centred at Englianos in the thirteenth century BC. Field surveys of the south-west Peloponnese have shown that the major concentration of Mycenaean sites rings Englianos, and that the whole area of Messenia was one of the most populous in the Mycenaean world. By comparison, Dörpfeld's site at Kakovatos appears to have been no more than the chief town of a fertile but limited district. Kakovatos enjoyed prosperity for several centuries, but there is no indication that it ever headed a kingdom comparable to that administered from Englianos.

The palace at Englianos was destroyed by fire about 1200 BC, and the site was never reoccupied. When Greece revived after its Dark Age, no one knew for certain where Nestor's Pylos had been located. It is possible that Homer or one of his predecessors believed it to have lain near the river Alpheios, and that this belief has distorted the geography of the tradition, notably in Nestor's reminiscences about the campaigns of his youth (*Iliad* 7:132–56, and 11:670–761). But in other respects the tradition was tenacious of past realities, particularly in regard to the populousness of Nestor's realm—his contingent was the second largest at Troy—and the nine cities of the 'hither' province (*Iliad* 2:591–602; *Odyssey* 3:7).

Ill. 87

A brief description of the palace will show that it was indeed, as Homer calls it, a 'noble and notable building' (*Odyssey* 3:387–8). It stood on a jutting plateau roughly two hundred yards long and one hundred broad, with a commanding view of the surrounding countryside. The ground falls away sharply into deep ravines except on the north-east, and even there the edge of the plateau is marked by a steep bank. Pylos, like Troy, was a 'sheer citadel' (*Odyssey* 3:485). But in marked contrast to Troy, and also to Tiryns and Mycenae, all of which were ringed with massive walls in the thirteenth century BC, no fortifications of this date were found at Englianos. The central palace building embodied a magnificent hall, forty-two by thirty-seven feet, with a throne placed midway along one wall and a large raised hearth in the centre surrounded by four fluted wooden columns on stone bases. This Throne Room was approached from an interior courtyard through a large portico and vestibule, each with a sentry-stand beside their doorways. Round this impressive core ran long corridors giving access to numerous store-rooms. One room called the 'kylix pantry' contained nearly three thousand tall-stemmed drinking cups stacked on wooden shelves. Two magazines at the rear of the

Ill. 88

Ill. 89

Ills. 90, 91

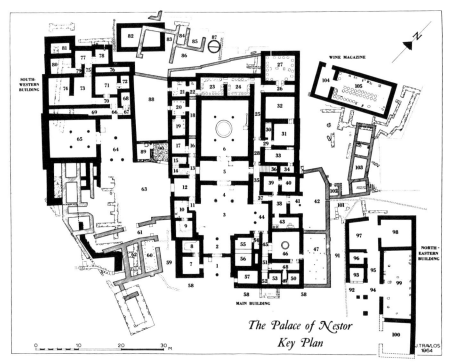

The Palace of Nestor
Key Plan

Ill. 88. Ground plan of the palace of Nestor at Pylos in the thirteenth century BC. Key (numbers not mentioned designate rooms and areas the specific use of which has not been determined): 1–2, Propylon; 3, 42, 47, 58, 63, 88, 92, Courts; 4, Portico; 5, Vestibule; 6, Throne Room; 7, 8, Archives Room; 9, 18-22, 60, 67, 68, Pantries; 10, Waiting Room; 11, 29, 38, 66, 75, 79, Lobbies; 12, Possible South-west Entrance; 13, 26, 37, 48, 49, 61, 70, 95, Corridors; 14–15, South-west Stairway; 23, 24, 32, Oil Magazines; 25, 28, 35, North-east Corridor; 27, North Magazine; 36, North-east Stairway; 41, North-east Gateway; 43, Bathroom; 44, North-east Stoa; 45, 51, 52, South-east Corridor; 46, Queen's Hall; 54, South-east Stairway; 59, 91, Open Ramps; 64, Entrance Hall; 65, Hall; 69, Stairway; 76, Light-well; 93, Shrine; 94, Colonnade; 101, Street; 102, Reservoir; 104–105, Wine Magazine.

Ills. 89–91. Above: the Throne Room in Nestor's palace (no. 6 on plan). The central hearth is surrounded by four pillar bases. The throne stood against the wall on the left. Behind, the vestibule, portico, and court (nos. 5, 4, 3,). In the foreground oil magazines (nos. 23, 24). Below: tall-stemmed drinking cup from Pylos. Right: one of the palace pantries (no. 19). The room once had wooden shelving all round and, when uncovered, it contained the shattered remains of 2,853 cups.

Throne Room had large jars for the storage of olive oil. In the south-east corner a complex of rooms opening on to two walled courtyards may have constituted the private apartments of the royal family. One elegant room here with a central hearth has been named the Queen's Hall. Another room had a painted terracotta bath-tub set against one wall, with a stand in the corner for two large jars, perhaps to hold water and oil. Smaller cups and basins found in the jars and the bath were probably for pouring water over the bather. At several points, flights of stone steps led to an upper story. The principal rooms were lavishly decorated, with painted floors and frescoed walls. The woodwork of the columns, ceilings, and balconies was also no doubt painted in bright colours. Fragments of gold, silver and ivory objects, and scraps of gold foil, were found in many of the rooms.

Ill. 92

Extensive subsidiary buildings flanked the main palace, particularly on the south-west. Remains of a large vestibule and of a stately room with four pillars here perhaps indicate where the banquet hall was situated. To the north-east lay another block of rooms of various shapes and sizes. One of the small rooms is thought to have been a shrine with an open-air altar close by. A tablet found in this area mentions a goddess called 'Lady of the horses'. The largest room was probably a workshop for the repair of chariots.

The complex was completed by a solidly-built wine magazine, consisting of an ante-room and a very large store with rows of capacious jars down the centre and round the walls. Over sixty clay sealings were found here, some of them inscribed with the Linear B sign for wine. Lumps of clay had been wrapped around string securing the lids of the jars, and then stamped, and the inscriptions may have indicated the provenance or age of the wine.

Ill. 93

All this is in keeping with the atmosphere of refined and regal opulence deftly suggested by Homer's account of a palace where guests can expect to 'sleep softly', and where a sacrificial ox has its horns covered in gold leaf personally donated by Nestor (*Odyssey* 3:350-1 and 436-8). It is at least a happy coincidence that Blegen found a building well-appointed with bathroom and wine store, and that Homer should make a point of describing the bathing and anointing of Telemachos by the princess Polykaste, and the broaching of wine that had been in cask for over ten years—one of the few precise references to vintage wine in Greek literature (*Odyssey* 3:464-8 and 390-2). When Telemachos is given a bed in the 'echoing portico' (*Odyssey* 3:399), and when Nestor retires to rest in the 'inmost recesses of the lofty building' (*Odyssey* 3:402), we can visualize them in a ground-floor loggia and an upstairs bedroom. When we read that the king sat on his throne and poured a libation (*Odyssey* 3:389, 394), it is at least interesting to know that in the floor immediately to the right of the throne in the Englianos palace were two basin-like hollows six and a half feet apart, connected by a narrow runnel along which liquid could flow from one to the other.

Ill. 92. A decorated terracotta bath found *in situ* in a bathroom in Nestor's palace (no. 43). An attendant drew water from two large jars on a stand in the corner of the room and poured it over the bather, as described in the Homeric account of Telemachos' bath at Pylos (*Odyssey* 3:464-8).

Ill. 93. The wine magazine (nos. 104, 105) of the palace at Pylos. This is a separate and extensive building, with many capacious jars still in position. About sixty clay sealings were found here, some bearing the Linear B sign for wine. Homer tells how Nestor served Telemachos with wine which the butler broached 'in its eleventh year' (*Odyssey* 3 : 390–2).

A final coincidence calls for rather more extended treatment. Blegen found a rectangle of limestone blocks, with a fill of hard greenish-white earth, jutting out from the front wall of the main building near the entrance. He conjectured that this structure might have been a 'rostrum' or 'reviewing stand'. It is tempting to relate this unusual feature to the scene where Homer describes Nestor coming out of the palace and taking his seat, sceptre in hand, on the 'polished blocks of stone before his lofty portals' (*Odyssey* 3 : 406 ff.). The formal and ceremonial nature of the action is emphasized by the detail that Neleus used to sit there before him. The stones are described in an unusual phrase as 'white, with an oily sheen'. Editors usually envisage a *marble* bench, and discuss whether it was literally polished with oil, or merely looked 'oily'. In fact, the excavators found very little marble at Englianos. Marble seems to have been a scarce and semi-precious material, used for ornaments, or (in one case) for a variegated and inlaid table top. But there was a stone dado in the portico to the Throne Room 'faced with a veneer of limestone almost like marble, 0.045 m. thick, with a smoothly finished surface'. It seems possible that Homer's description of the Neleid rostrum may have originated from some such device for enhancing the appearance of cut limestone blocks.

In short, there is no detail in Homer's account of life at Nestor's Pylos which cannot be illustrated from the Englianos excavation. This might be mere coincidence, or at most might be explained by a general folk memory of Mycenaean palace life. But some of the details, notably the nine-fold division of the Pylians and the rostrum outside the palace, are quite specific. It should not be forgotten that Homer's Ionia had a link with Pylos through the Neleid refugees who came through Athens to found Miletus. On the evidence reviewed above, one cannot exclude the possibility that some authentic memories of the

Mycenaean kingdom ruled from the Englianos palace were preserved by this special connection.

THE PALACE OF MENELAOS

> Look round this echoing hall, my dear Peisistratus. The whole place gleams with copper and gold, amber and silver and ivory. What an amazing collection of treasures! I can't help thinking that the court of Zeus on Olympus must be like this inside. The sight of it overwhelms me.
>
> (*Odyssey* 4:71–5; E. V. Rieu's translation)

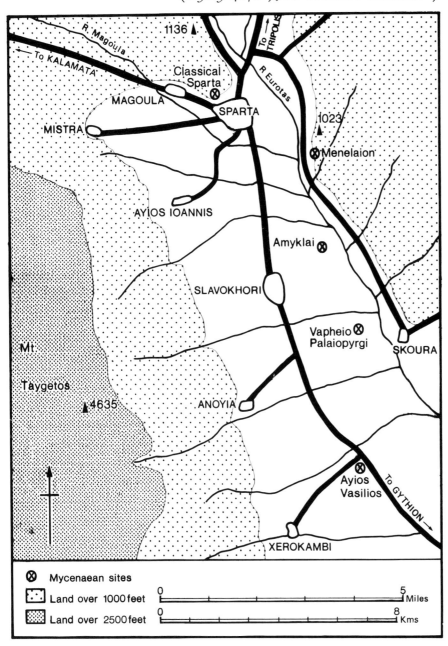

Ill. 94. Map of Sparta and adjacent villages. Note the long valley surrounded by mountains to east and west, and the herring-bone pattern of streams joining the River Eurotas. The plain of Sparta is rich and well-watered.

Ill. 95. The former city area of ancient Sparta seen from the low acropolis to the north-east. In the background, the range of Taygetos bounding the plain of 'hollow' Lakedaimon on the west.

Telemachos' amazement is naively expressed, but the facts may have warranted it. Greek tradition remembered a strong Achaean kingdom in the south-east of the Peloponnese, and there is every reason to suppose that it centred on a palace of great opulence. But so far no building comparable to the Englianos palace has been found, though there has been much exploration and excavation in Laconia since Tsountas' discoveries at Vapheio in 1888 (see above, p. 69). Cut stone had been looted from part of the site at Englianos, and a Laconian palace could have been totally despoiled in the course of centuries. But one may still be discovered, and Homer indicates that it is to be sought *Ill. 95* in the fertile rolling plain near modern Sparta. This region, watered by the Eurotas and hemmed in by hills or mountain ranges on all sides, has always been the focus of the south-east Peloponnese. Here, surely, was 'hollow' Lakedaimon, the legendary home of Helen and Menelaos.

Evidence of Mycenaean habitation has been found at four sites *Ill. 94* within a radius of five miles of Sparta. One of these sites underlies the ruins of classical Sparta just to the north of the modern town, but its remains are scanty in comparison with the other sites in the vicinity. The second site is on the escarpment immediately to the east of the Eurotas where stood the later shrine of Menelaos and Helen. This was the district of Therapnai, associated by Pindar with Helen's family the Tyndarids. The third site is close to the later shrine of Apollo Amyklaios about three miles south of Sparta, and the fourth lies a little further south again in the neighbourhood of Vapheio. The hill called Palaiopyrgi here is the highest point in the chain of low hills south of Sparta and forms a conspicuous landmark. Late Mycenaean sherds are scattered on the surface over an area of about two hundred thousand square yards, making it much the largest Mycenaean site yet noted in the whole of Laconia.

The Homeric tradition which brings Telemachos to the palace of Menelaos *at Sparta* (*Odyssey* 4:10) has good general support from the findings of archaeology. But the precise siting of the Mycenaean capital is still a matter of debate. Greek legends about Therapnai, and the siting of the Menelaion there, with a cult attested back to the eighth century BC, favour the site to the east of the Eurotas. On the other hand, the considerably greater spread of habitation at Palaio-pyrgi, and the evidence from the nearby Vapheio tomb of great ruler wealth there as early as 1400 BC, favour a site not far south of the Amyklaion.

Like Nestor's palace, the great house of Menelaos is pictured with courtyard, portico and main hall, and its amenities include 'polished' baths, a 'scented' bedroom and a store-room for treasure. But there are also some distinctive touches in the description. In a brief scene, retainers approach the palace bringing corn, wine, and sheep as contributions for a banquet (*Odyssey* 4: 621–3). Could this be a memory of the produce levies documented in the Pylos tablets? Again, when Telemachos arrives his horses are unyoked and led to the manger, and the chariot is tilted up against the 'shining wall-face', presumably the opposite wall of the stable building. This formulaic phrase, which occurs also in the *Iliad,* might be a reminiscence of the fine white stucco so often applied to the interior walls of Mycenaean buildings.

Homer emphasizes the great wealth of Menelaos, much of it acquired on expeditions to Cyprus, the Levant, and Egypt (*Odyssey* 4:81 ff.). Particular stress is laid on the Egyptian connections of the royal house. Polybos, who lived in Egyptian Thebes (the wealthiest of all cities), had given Menelaos 'two silver bath-tubs, two tripods, and ten talents of gold', while his wife had given Helen 'a wheeled work-basket of silver with gold inlay on the rim' (*Odyssey* 4:119 ff.).* These traditions accord well with what we know of Bronze Age trade connections between the Peloponnese and the Levant. A recently discovered Egyptian inscription dated *c.* 1400 BC mentions Knossos and Cythera and (possibly) Mycenae and Nauplia in what appears to be a call-over of Aegean place names with Egyptian contacts. Thanks to a recent excavation, we now know that a Minoan trading colony had been established on Cythera as early as *c.* 2300 BC.* Cythera is well placed to control the shipping routes into the Laconian gulf. The colony was destroyed about 1450 BC, and presumably Mycenaean traders then took over the route leading from Laconia via Crete to Phoenicia and Egypt. The gold cups from the Vapheio tomb are usually regarded as being Minoan workmanship, and the treasure also included two alabaster jars and a silver spoon of Egyptian provenance.

THE PALACES OF ALKINOÖS AND ULYSSES

Alkinoös' palace has the standard features of courtyard and great hall, but poetic imagination has enhanced its splendours, and there is a fairytale atmosphere about its bronze walls, silver pillars, and golden

Ill. 96. A gold and niello head, portion of the inlay of a silver cup, found in the propylon of the palace of Nestor. It is possibly a portrait of a member of the Neleid dynasty (see *Ill. 57*).

*A silver cup with gold and niello inlay was found in a fragmentary condition near the outer porch of Nestor's Palace (*Ill. 96*).

*A Fifth Dynasty Egyptian cup was found on Cythera.

doors (*Odyssey* 7:78 ff.). The ageless hounds of gold and silver wrought by Hephaistos to guard the entrance are evidently of supernatural stock. But there is one distinctive and realistic touch in the description which has been thought to embody a memory of Mycenaean architectural decoration. Round the walls of the main hall runs a 'frieze of blue enamel (*kyanos*)' (*Odyssey* 7:87). Tiles of this colour were found at Mycenae, and at Tiryns the palace was decorated with an alabaster frieze in which the spirals were picked out in blue glass paste. The Egyptians had developed such a paste as a substitute for lapis lazuli, and the Mycenaeans seem to have picked up the technique of its manufacture, possibly from the Minoans. *Kyanos* craftsmen are mentioned on a tablet from Mycenae, and in later Greek *kyanos* was the word for lapis lazuli and the Egyptian imitation of it.

The site of Ulysses' palace has not been certainly identified (see above, p. 95), but there can be little doubt that he ruled his island kingdom from a dwelling answering to the Homeric description. His home is pictured as a building of some complexity with upper rooms reached by staircases and one quarter opening out from another. While lacking the great wealth and luxury of the Peloponnesian palaces, it contained a strong-room for precious objects, and special mention is made of a chair and footstool inlaid with ivory and silver (*Odyssey* 21:8–10 and 19:55–6). The existence of palace furniture of this type is confirmed by the Pylos tablets. Other traits in the description seem more in keeping with a 'provincial' establishment: the dung-heap, for instance, in the courtyard near the doors of the main hall, and the feeding trough for geese nearby (*Odyssey* 17:297 and 19:552–3).

The most distinctive feature of the plan was a small side-door towards the rear of the main hall which gave access to a narrow passage leading round to the courtyard. From the passage one could apparently also reach some of the smaller rooms adjoining the hall (*Odyssey* 22:126 ff.). Nothing exactly comparable to this feature has been found in the Mycenaean palaces so far excavated.

The above discussion has tended to confirm the reliability of the descriptions of palaces in the *Odyssey*. They were, as Homer indicates, complex buildings with courts and porticoes, large pillared halls and numerous smaller rooms. They had corridors, bathrooms, staircases and upper stories. Their lavish decoration and opulent furnishings left a lasting impression on the Greek mind. In poorer days the poets recalled their splendours with pride and a touch of nostalgia. Homer has idealized the wealth and graciousness of their appointments, and oversimplified the routine of life in them. There must have been more courtly ceremonial than he allows, and he shows little or no knowledge of the scribal bureaucracy. Nevertheless in essentials his picture is well-founded, and many detailed correspondences with the findings of archaeology serve to authenticate it as a valid, though incomplete, record of regal magnificence in the Mycenaean world.

The wanderings of Ulysses   6

J. V. Luce

IN the ancient world there were, broadly speaking, three main schools of thought on the problem of Ulysses' wanderings. There were those who, like Strabo, accepted an old and widespread tradition that the wanderings took place in the western basin of the Mediterranean, and who set the adventures in various parts of southern Italy and Sicily. Secondly, there were those who, like Crates, supposed the scene to be set in the outer Ocean beyond the Straits of Gibraltar. Thirdly, there were those who held that the wanderings were entirely fictitious. They emphasized the elements of marvel and magic that permeate the story, and insisted that it was a waste of time to try to locate fairyland on the map. Typical of their attitude was the sarcasm of Eratosthenes: 'You will find the course of Odysseus' wanderings when you find the cobbler who sewed up the bag of the winds.'

Similar attitudes can be traced in the widely ramifying discussions of the problem in modern times. The detailed work of Victor Bérard is based on the assumption that Aiaia, Aiolia and the rest are real places and that Homer describes them in sufficient detail for us to recognize and locate them. Ernle Bradford, in his book *Ulysses Found*, has used his wide experience of sailing in the Mediterranean to illuminate the Homeric narrative and claims that the sailing directions and other clues in the *Odyssey* indicate quite precisely the course Ulysses followed. More speculative inquirers have greatly extended the limits of the wanderings. For example, Krichenbauer (in 1877) interpreted the story as a circumnavigation of Africa. More recently Pillot (1969) has located Aiolos in Madeira, the Laistrygonians in Ireland and Calypso in Iceland. It is hardly surprising that, partly in reaction against such extravagances, more cautious scholars explain the 'deep sea yarns' as folktale and fiction owing little or nothing to actual voyaging.

My aim will be to steer a middle course between the Skylla of scepticism and the Charybdis of credulity. When we consider the many miraculous features—one-eyed giants, floating islands, magic potions, six-headed monsters—it must seem almost axiomatic that the wanderings are taking place in Wonderland. But yet, as Strabo well says, 'it is not Homer's way to present a mere recital of marvels in no

Ill. 99

Ill. 97. Opposite: the island of ▶ Stromboli. The mountain (3,136 ft.) is an active volcano constantly emitting gas and lava. Its fires make it a striking sea-mark, particularly at night. Experts believe that it, together with the rest of the Lipari islands, showed even more vulcanism in antiquity. It has probably left its mark on those portions of the *Odyssey* where Ulysses is warned to steer clear of the surf, smoke, fire and noise of the Planktae (*Odyssey* 12:69 and 202). Some ancient writers identified Stromboli with Homeric Aiolia, but this is not plausible.

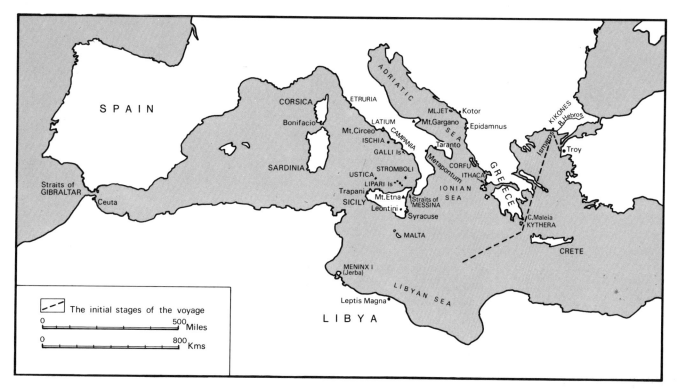

Ills. 98, 99. Opposite: view of the isthmus site at Palaiokastritsa, Corfu. Bérard located the capital of the Phaeacians here, but this is only a conjecture confirmed by no ancient remains. Above: map of the Mediterranean showing the geographical setting for the wanderings of Ulysses.

way related to reality.' Even the sceptical Eratosthenes allowed that 'Homer *intended* to put the wanderings of Ulysses in the western regions.' In my opinion Eratosthenes correctly diagnosed Homer's intention, if by 'western regions' he meant the coasts and islands of the Ionian, Libyan, Sicilian, and Tyrrhenian Seas. Part of Homer's tradition derived ultimately, I believe, from Mycenaean seafaring in these waters. Part of the material is saga and legend formed initially in the troubled period of migrations at the end of the Bronze Age. The narrative also takes some colouring from the initial stages of the Greek colonial movement in the eighth century BC. In support of these contentions I shall review the adventures *seriatim*, picking out such geographical indications as they afford.

Ill. 100

The Cicones were allies of the Trojans (*Iliad* 2:846), and so it was natural for Ulysses to sack one of their cities when his squadron fetched up in their part of Thrace. Herodotus (7:59) located them to the west of the River Hebros, a region of coastal plains varied by the foothills of Mt. Ismaros. In classical times the city of Maroneia was famous for its wine which Pliny described as 'dark in colour, with a strong bouquet, becoming full-bodied with age'. Ulysses mentions the 'plain of the Cicones', the place name Ismaros, and makes much of the very strong and sweet-scented wine that Maron the priest of Apollo at Ismaros gave him in return for his protection (*Odyssey* 9:40, 66, 196–211). We may safely place the first adventure on the coast of Thrace between the rivers Hebros and Nestos. After their defeat Ulysses and his men fled away south before a strong north wind, lying up for two days on an unnamed island or promontory, then sailing on when the gale moderated. They planned to round the Peloponnese and sail north to Ithaca, but the swell, current, and wind off the dreaded Cape Maleia combined to deflect them into the Libyan Sea, and there they were swept along for 'nine days' by 'cruel winds'.

'Nine days' is a time interval that recurs quite frequently in the wanderings, and is not to be taken too literally. However, if we are to suppose that the north-easterly gale continued for all or most of this period, they may well have drifted right across the Libyan Sea to the African coast somewhere in the region of Leptis Magna, a distance of approximately six hundred miles. Ancient tradition located the land of the Lotos-eaters here or hereabouts. Strabo put it in the island of Meninx (Jerba), also known as Lotophagitis. Ancient authorities had much to say about the lotos as a real fruit. According to Polybius it grew on a small spiny tree with yellow foliage, and when ripe was a purplish berry about the size of an olive. Some have identified it with the fruit of the jujube-tree (*zizyphus lotus*). Herodotus compared it to dates for sweetness. It seems to have been a very palatable fruit, and there is evidence that it flourished abundantly on the north African coast between Cyrene and Carthage. But Homer improved on reality by representing it as addictive and as inducing apathy.

So far Ulysses' course can be charted with some precision, but from now on all becomes increasingly vague. He sails on to the land of the Cyclopes, no time or direction being indicated for this stage of the voyage. The Cyclopes lived in caves in rugged mountainous country, with each male Cyclops master of his own small group of wives and children and paying no heed to anyone else. They did not meet in deliberative assemblies and did not recognize the binding force of any laws or customs. Nor did they go in for systematic cultivation of the soil. Their economy was predominantly pastoral, and in this respect quite well developed, to judge from the description of Polyphemos' cave:

> There were baskets laden with cheeses, and the folds were thronged with lambs and kids, each class, the firstlings, the summer lambs, and the little ones, being separately penned. All his well-made vessels, the pails and bowls he used for milking, were swimming with whey.
>
> (*Odyssey* 9:219–23; E. V. Rieu's translation)

Polyphemos himself first appears as a quiet shepherd methodically attending to his flocks and dairy produce. His sudden transformation into a man-eating ogre is dramatically effective, but on reflection we see that his character, like his actions, is composed of inconsistent elements. Thus, at one moment he professes utter contempt for Zeus and all the gods, at another he prays devoutly to his father Poseidon and recalls the predictions of a venerated prophet who used to dwell with his people (*Odyssey* 9:275–8 and 506 ff.).

Ill. 100. Silver stater of Maroneia in Thrace, early fourth century BC. The obverse, pictured here, shows a vine with heavy clusters of grapes. The wine of Maroneia won praise from many ancient writers from Homer on. The inscription reads: *ΕΠΙΠΟΛΥΑΡΗΤΟΥ*, i.e., In [the magistracy] of Polyaretos.

Ill. 101

These inconsistencies probably arise from a conflation of sources in which we may distinguish at least two major elements: saga traditions of contact with primitive tribes in Italy or Sicily, and the folklore motif of a gruesome ogre outwitted by a wily lad. The Cyclopes as a group seem to be very much part of the world of men—they are called 'men' in one passage (*Odyssey* 6:5)—and there is nothing supernatural about their way of life. Homer casts an almost Herodotean eye upon them as he notes their rudimentary social organization, their inability to till the ground or build ships, and their expertise as pastoralists. The picture carries conviction as a sketch of a primitive way of life.

It is interesting to compare it with the picture of the 'Apennine culture' drawn by David Trump in a recent book (*Central and Southern Italy before Rome*, 1966). This distinctive culture seems to have been widespread through the upland regions of central and southern Italy from about 1500 to 1200 BC. Many of the sites are located in remote and rugged terrain not suitable for agriculture, and habitation was frequently in caves. The economy was centred on stockbreeding. An analysis of animal bones from a typical site at Ariano showed that sheep or goats accounted for 42 per cent of the stock, followed by cattle (31 per cent) and pigs (19 per cent). Though Italy had moved into the Bronze Age several centuries earlier, the sites show an almost complete absence of metal tools, and the material equipment generally

Ill. 101. Ulysses and Polyphemos, from an Attic oinochoë, 500–475 BC. The blinded giant reaches out his right hand to feel his favourite ram. Ulysses is making his escape from the cave by clasping his arms round the ram's belly. The composition is adventurous, but anatomically awkward.

seems to have been very limited, except in pottery. Here, by contrast, considerable sophistication is apparent, notably in vessels designed for the slow boiling of milk in cheesemaking and in perforated strainers and dipper sieves for separating curds and whey.

The Apennine culture has been defined mainly as the result of excavations since the Second World War and much still remains to be discovered about it, but it may be worth considering the possibility that some elements in the Cyclops episode derive from saga material based on contacts between Mycenaean merchant adventurers and cave-dwelling Italian pastoralists. Some recent archaeological discoveries show that such contacts occurred. Apennine and Mycenaean pottery has been found in association at Luni in Etruria and also at three sites in the vicinity of Taranto. Mycenaean sherds from Ischia point to a trade route up the Campanian coast close to regions where the Apennine culture was well established.

Such contacts may not always have been peaceful. The impressive cave known as the Grotta Manacorra opens on a sandy beach at the eastern tip of the rugged Gargano peninsula. The cave, together with a settlement on the headland above, showed what Trump calls 'an impoverished version of the later Apennine culture'. Yet, surprisingly, a cleft in the cave yielded a rich hoard of bronze objects including twenty-one swords. Trump remarks that 'this wealth of bronze has never been satisfactorily explained on a site otherwise so poor'. Could it have been loot from an Achaean ship that put in at the beach and was overwhelmed by the natives? Such incidents must have happened often enough in the long centuries of Mycenaean trade and exploration in Italian waters, giving rise to a saga tradition of cave-dwellers of great strength and ferocity. Such a tradition would readily coalesce with the folktale motif of a one-eyed ogre to generate the Polyphemos story.

After escaping from Polyphemos, Ulysses and his men sail on until they reach the island of Aiolos. Again there is no indication of the distance or direction of the voyage. The folktale element is conspicuous in this adventure, with its floating island ringed with a wall of bronze, and its ruler who can tie up the winds in a bag. Homer humanizes Aiolos by endowing him with a patronymic, a family, a palace, and a city, and with a characteristic touch of realism makes him anxious to hear all about the Trojan War. Otherwise there is nothing to identify Aiolia except the datum that on leaving it Ulysses sails for nine days and nights on end, running always before the wind Zephyros, before sighting Ithaca on the tenth day. The time, and the mention of Zephyros, indicate that Homer conceived of Aiolia as lying a long way over the open sea in the quarter to the west or north-west of Ithaca. One should resist the temptation to convert the nine days into a measure of distance. In the economy of the poem they simply serve to cancel out the initial deflection caused by the storm off Cape Maleia. In the ancient world it was commonly thought that Aiolia

Ills. 102, 103. Above: the characteristic Apennine bowl of southern Italy, carinated, and with a tongue handle, but undecorated. Opposite: the Grotta Manacorra on the north coast of Gargano. The great cave opens directly on the beach. This view is taken from the rocky headland which had an open village site of Late Bronze Age to Iron Age date. Inland can be seen the wild country of the Foresta d'Umbria, which makes access by land from Foggia harder than it is by sea from Dalmatia.

was one of the Lipari islands, Stromboli being a popular choice. We now know that these islands were the seat of an ancient and advanced culture whose roots go far back into the Bronze Age. They exported obsidian and were an important link in the chain of communications between the two halves of the Mediterranean. Contact between them and the Aegean can be traced back at least as far as 1600 BC. But these facts do not serve to confirm the identification with Homer's Aiolia, an identification clearly incompatible with the picture of a direct voyage over the open sea from Aiolia to Ithaca. If one is to take the sailing indications seriously, it would be more plausible to look for Aiolia in the Adriatic, and recently A. Rousseau-Leissens* has in fact attempted to locate all the wanderings in this sea, finding Laistrygonia in Kotor and Aiaia in Mljet.

*In *La Géographie de l'Odyssée*, 1963.

Blown back to Aiolos' island, and refused further hospitality, Ulysses and his Companions *row* on for six days before reaching 'Telepylos, the lofty stronghold of Lamos in the Laistrygonian land'. No indication of direction is given, but some interesting details occur in the account of this landfall. The description of the Laistrygonian harbour is particularly graphic:

ll. 104

> There as we entered the glorious harbour, which a sky-towering
> cliff encloses on either side, with no break anywhere,
> and two projecting promontories facing each other
> run out towards the mouth, and there is a narrow entrance,
> there all the rest of them had their oar-swept ships in the inward
> part, they were tied up close together inside the hollow
> harbour, for there was never a swell of surf inside it,
> neither great nor small, but there was a pale calm on it.
>
> (*Odyssey* 10:87–94; Richmond Lattimore's translation)

Echoes of a Norwegian fiord have been detected in this description, with the 'pale calm' a periphrasis for ice. But since ruffled water is normally described as 'dark' in Greek, it is safer to understand 'pale calm' as meaning no more than a still surface reflecting the light.

However, another phrase in the description of Laistrygonia may well contain a hint of high northern latitudes. The poet pictures herdsmen calling to each other as they drive their flocks in and out of the town, and remarks that a sleepless man could earn double wages there 'for the paths of day and night are close together'. Crates took this as a reference to the short summer nights of northern Europe and has been followed by many modern commentators. The phrase is a striking one, and hard to explain in Mediterranean terms. It seems to suggest the long afterglows and early dawns of midsummer in latitudes north of 50°. Some notion of these conditions could have entered the epic tradition at a very early stage, brought perhaps by the earliest Greek immigrants from their Balkan or Danubian homelands, or fostered in the Mycenaean period by trade contacts with the Baltic, along the amber route from the head of the Adriatic.

126

Ill. 104. Opposite: warship on a pyxis from the Tragana tholos tomb, Messenia, twelfth century BC. Bow with ram to right, steering oar to left. Note the sail with sheet running to stern platform, the mast stays, and the prominent fish emblem at the bow.

Ill. 105. A phlyax-scene in the life of Ulysses from an Apulian bell krater, fourth century BC. It depicts *either* the Trojan priestess Theano threatened by Ulysses and Diomedes, *or* Circe threatened by Ulysses and Elpenor.

Disregarding any hint of the far north, Greek tradition located the Laistrygonians at Leontini in eastern Sicily. The Romans put them at Formiae in southern Latium. In neither area, however, is there any harbour answering to Homer's description. In modern times the harbour has been 'recognized' at places as distant as Balaklava and Bonifacio (Corsica). But once again there is not enough distinctive detail in Homer to warrant such precise identifications. On the whole it seems more likely that to him the name Laistrygonians was no more than a convenient label for a savage tribe beyond the confines of his world and out of touch with its culture. Even the Cyclopes know of Zeus, and the Sirens can tell the tale of Troy, but here there is no hint of religion, no contact with history. In the name of the Laistrygonian citadel Telepylos, 'Distant Gate', there may be an echo of the mythical portal of Hesiod's *Theogony* (748–50) 'where Night and Day coming close together hail each other as they pass over the great bronze threshold'. This passage is so reminiscent of Homer's herdsmen hailing one another where 'the paths of night and day are close together' that there must be a close relationship between them. We should perhaps think, not so much in terms of one poet echoing the other, as of both drawing their imagery from a traditional picture of the 'ends of the earth'—a picture which recurs in Parmenides' great image of the 'gates of the paths of Night and Day'. If this is a correct analysis, Homer will in effect be saying that the Laistrygonians are close to the outermost limits of the inhabited world, located far to the west or north-west, where the Sun-god was imagined as passing through some cosmic portal before returning to the east. Such a conception, whatever its ultimate roots, will not imply that Homer himself had any geographical awareness of Spain or north-west Europe or any well-founded knowledge of short nights in high latitudes.

With his fleet reduced to a single ship Ulysses sails on to the island of Aiaia, home of the goddess Circe. Apart from the Cimmerians, who receive incidental mention in the Visit to Hades, human beings now disappear altogether from the scene in the remaining adventures. Ulysses now remarks to his comrades: 'We do not know where is west and where is east', that is to say, they are completely lost with no idea what countries lie to east or west of them. We should take the hint, and not try to locate Aiaia on the map.

The ancients were not so cautious. In the name of Cape Circeo we have a memorial of a widespread belief connecting Circe with Latium. Bérard accepted the ancient tradition about the Circean promontory, but one can only follow him if one is prepared to disregard the plain evidence of the Homeric text. Homer says that Aiaia was 'an island surrounded by the boundless sea' (*Odyssey* 10:195), which can never have been true of Cape Circeo. He also says that in the island are 'the halls and dancing places of Dawn and the rising places of Helios' (*Odyssey* 12:3–4). If anything, this implies a location in the Far East. It could hardly be more inappropriate for the west coast of Italy. But the fact is that Ulysses is now in mythical regions, and we should not try to impose a coherent geographical framework on this stage of the wanderings. We should rather think in terms of the ancient myth of the hero who, with the help and guidance of a goddess, visits the realms of the dead and comes back alive.

For his trip to the House of Hades, Ulysses takes a southerly course from Circe's island, and after a full day's sail reaches the 'confines of deep-flowing Okeanos'. Many passages in the *Iliad* and *Odyssey* combine to show that for Homer, Okeanos was a great river encircling the earth and flowing gently back upon itself in a never-ending course. Okeanos is described as the source of all rivers and the whole sea, but its precise spatial relationship to the seas on which Ulysses sails is never made clear. There is no warrant in the Homeric text for the supposition that he passes through a strait to reach what we would call the ocean. Ingenious theories of a trip to the Straits of Gibraltar are purely speculative. All we are told is that 'sea' merges into 'river', and beyond the river is a bank where a ship can be beached. There, in the words of Circe, as she briefs Ulysses before he sets out:

> You will come to a wild coast and Persephone's Grove, where the tall poplars grow and the willows that so quickly shed their seeds. Beach your boat there by Ocean's swirling stream and march on into Hades' Kingdom of Decay. There the River of Flaming and the River of Lamentation, which is a branch of the Waters of Styx, unite round a pinnacle of rock to pour their thundering streams into Acheron.   (*Odyssey* 10:511–15; E. V. Rieu's translation)

We are now in the Land of the Dead, a land which has no map references, but the description is so graphic that it may owe something to the scenery of an actual locality. K. E. von Baer thought he had found Persephone's Grove, poplars, willows and all, on the Sea of

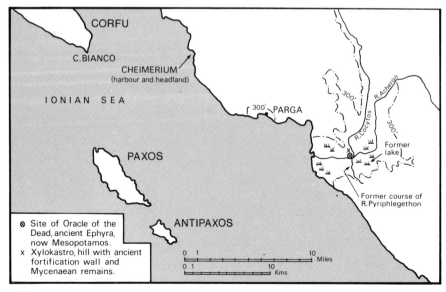

Ill. 106. Map of the district of the lower Acheron in Thesprotia.

Ill. 107. The site of the Oracle of the Dead overlooking the River Acheron in Thesprotia. This view shows the lustral area at the entrance to the Hellenistic shrine, with the hill of Xylokastro, a Mycenaean site, in the background.

*For details of the topography, see N. G. L. Hammond's *Epirus*, 63–9.

Ill. 107

Azov near the mouth of the Protoka. It is obviously far more likely that some part of Greece served as a model, and Pausanias suggested that Homer found the prototypes of his infernal rivers in the district of the lower Acheron in Thesprotia.

Recent archaeological discoveries have lent considerable support to this suggestion. We now know of Mycenaean settlements in the area. A *tholos* tomb has been found near Parga, and Mycenaean sherds have been recovered from the fortified hill of Xylokastro. But even greater significance must be attached to the discovery of an Oracle of the Dead on a rocky spur beside the confluence of the Acheron and Cocytus. Another stream used to flow in from the south at the same point, but has disappeared as a result of drainage work in this century. The locals preserve a tradition that it was highly phosphorescent, and that 'between March and June there used to be a noise of subterranean waters rumbling and echoing'. 'No doubt', as Hammond remarks, 'this stream was the Pyriphlegethon, "the fire-blazer".'* Above the confluence of the three rivers stretched the Acherusian Lake (now drained) which pilgrims coming from the south would cross by boat on their way to consult the Oracle.

The Oracle building as excavated does not antedate the third century BC, but sixth-century votives have been found on the site, and the discovery of Mycenaean sherds and a Mycenaean tomb within the sanctuary area makes it probable that the Oracle had a continuous history stretching back into the Bronze Age. If so, this site (Mesopotamos) must be added to other venerated places, like the Styx waterfall in Arcadia and the cave of Cape Taenaron, that may have influenced epic descriptions of the scenery of Hades. The excavator, S. I. Dakaris, describes the finding of the bones of sheep, cattle and pigs, in small pits, and also grain, libation-dishes and urns that had once held honey.* All this suggests a ritual surprisingly like that used by Ulysses for calling up the ghosts of the dead (*Odyssey* 11:23 ff.). The sceptic will say that the Hellenistic priests obviously modelled their ritual on Homer. But it is equally open to us to suppose that Homer has given us a description of an ancient ritual which continued unaltered down to the Hellenistic period, and that his tradition derived ultimately from necromantic ritual in Bronze Age Thesprotia. Ulysses was closely connected with Thesprotia in ancient tradition— the Thesprotian royal house claimed descent from him—and Homer elsewhere shows an awareness of his Thesprotian background (see pp. 80, 81).

*See his account in *Archaeology*, 15 (1962) 85–93.

One other feature of the adventure in Hades calls for comment. Ulysses locates the 'country and city of the Cimmerians' beside the river Okeanos and apparently on the far side of it near the Grove of Persephone. Described as 'wretched mortals' the Cimmerians must be distinct from the ghosts, but they are shrouded in mist and cloud and never see the light of the sun. Their name created difficulties in antiquity, as can be seen from the variants 'Cerberians' (Keepers of Cerberus?) and 'Cheimerians' (the Wintry Folk, like the Hibernians!). However much we may sympathize with the miseries of their climate we should not accept proposals to identify them with the Cymri of Wales or the Cimbri of Jutland. Greeks of the classical period knew of Cimmerians near the Sea of Azov, and in the seventh century BC Scythian nomads of that name ravaged much of Asia Minor. A possible explanation of their presence in or near the Land of the Dead is that Homer had received a vague report of them as a result of Greek penetration into the Black Sea, and thought them suitable denizens of his sunless Limbo at the world's end. But there are other possibilities. The variant 'Cheimerians' recalls the name Cheimerion, applied to a harbour and headland in Thesprotia north of the Acheron (*Thuc.* 1:46). If this promontory took its name from a local tribe, we may have yet another parallel between the Homeric Hades and the district of the lower Acheron.

After the visit to Hades Ulysses returns to Aiaia where more instructions from Circe form the prelude to the remaining adventures (*Odyssey* 12:37 ff.). This is the only place where alternative routes are described, and it has often been suggested that the passage embodies some vestiges of an ancient pilot or sailing manual. If so, the routes should bear some resemblance to courses known to have been sailed by Greeks in the Bronze Age. It is now accepted that ships from the Greek mainland were visiting the Lipari islands as early as the sixteenth century BC. Such a voyage would imply a passage of the Straits of Messina with all the dangers arising from the complicated tides and currents in this narrow channel between two seas. The Lipari islands have an active volcano in Stromboli, and are known to have been more generally volcanic in ancient times. Further north lie the pleasant islands off the Campanian coast, including Ischia, where Mycenaean pottery has been found. It would not be surprising if these distinctive regions had left some imprint on the records of early Greek voyaging.

With this possibility in mind we may consider what Circe says in more detail. First she tells Ulysses to run past the flowery island of the Sirens. Then she offers him a choice of routes, either past the Wandering (or Clashing) Rocks (Planktae), a place marked by surf and smoke and noise, or else through a narrow strait between Charybdis the 'Sucker-Down' and Skylla the 'Render'. It was the general belief of antiquity that Charybdis was Homer's name for the dangerous currents of the Messina Straits. The *Admiralty Pilot* today remarks that 'the currents and whirlpools, famous from antiquity, are such as to necessitate some caution in the navigation of the strait'. The tidal flow changes direction four times in twenty-four hours and attains a speed of up to four knots. A sailor coming in a small boat from the tideless waters further east must have found these conditions very strange and disturbing. Something of this feeling appears to be reflected in the Homeric description of Charybdis who 'three times each day sucks down the dark water, and three times releases it, a terrible sight' (*Odyssey* 12:105–6). The *Pilot* explains how the whirlpools are related to the tides, and speaks of 'areas where the denser water is sinking', and of 'smooth oily patches . . . where water is welling up from below'.

What of Skylla? Her rock is still pointed out on the Italian side of the strait near the village of Scilla, and experts assure us that it is safer for a small boat to hug this shore, avoiding the shoals and eddies off Cape Peloro. Much ingenuity has been shown in rationalizing her six heads and twelve tentacles (octopus or giant squid) and her yelp (wind or wave moaning in the fissures of the rock). She may still claim us as victims if we stop to scrutinize her too closely, but one point made by the ancient critics is perhaps worth recalling. The northern entrance to the Messina Straits was then, as it still is, a noted place for the capture of sword-fish (*galeotae*) that come there to spawn. And Skylla, as Homer tells us, was in the habit of fishing from her crag for 'dolphins, dog-fish, and larger monsters of the deep' (*Odyssey* 12:95–7).

As for the Planktae, the unusual and distinctive combination of surf, smoke, fire and noise in the Homeric description (*Odyssey* 12:68 and 202) encourages us to make an identification with the volcanic Lipari islands. When Ulysses' ship comes in sight of them he issues the only direct order to his helmsman recorded in all the wanderings: 'Keep the ship well clear of this smoke and surf, and make for the crag' [i.e., of Skylla]. It has been argued, with some plausibility, that this might be an echo of an ancient sailing instruction for the passage from Campania to Sicily.

Bradford points out that the Galli islands at the entrance to the Gulf of Salerno (which he identifies with the Sirens' island) are the last group of islands off the west coast of Italy. Southwards the coast is rugged and dangerously short of anchorages. 'If I were instructing a sailor with neither chart nor compass', he writes, 'how to get down to Sicily from Cape Circeo, I would be inclined to say: "Keep coasting past the islands . . . until you come to a small group at the head of a Gulf. There are three of them close together. At this point, take your departure from the coast and sail south".' This would be a shorter and safer route than following the coast, and would be signposted by Stromboli whose lofty summit (3,136 ft.) would catch the sailor's eye from many miles away. Stromboli's smoking flaring peak has always formed an important, not to say awesome, seamark. From there the voyager had a choice of routes. Keeping well to the east of the volcano—for so we may interpret Ulysses' orders—he could hold on south for the Messina Strait, or he could turn west to sail round Sicily. The latter course would take him through the Lipari archipelago, a route not without its dangers. In short, there is a good case for identifying the two routes sketched by Circe with the alternative passages to east and west of Sicily open to a ship coming south from Campania.

To admit this is not to credit Homer with an accurate notion of the extent of Sicily and its relationship to the Italian peninsula. He may be echoing traditional sailing instructions, but this is not to say that he is visualizing Charybdis in the Messina Strait as we with our map knowledge can so easily do. To him Charybdis was just a strait in the wide western seas. Not far south of it he located the island of Thrinakia. Inevitably Thrinakia was identified with Sicily when the Greeks became familiar with the area, but this attribution is not probable. Homer's description of Thrinakia strongly suggests a small un-inhabited island not rich in natural resources, and therefore in every way unlike Sicily (*Odyssey* 12:260 ff.). In a later passage Homer shows himself to be aware of the existence of Sicily, for which he uses an old name Sikanie (*Odyssey* 24:307). It is therefore safer to regard Thrinakia as a mythical island.

Ulysses and his crew are detained on Thrinakia for a whole month by unfavourable winds blowing from the south and east. This is yet another indication that the poet conceived the adventures as taking place in regions somewhere to the west and north of Ithaca. The crew then lose patience and kill some of the cattle of the Sun-god. After a week of feasting they set sail. Once out of sight of land they are overwhelmed by a sudden storm, and all except Ulysses are drowned. *Ill. 108* Clinging to a piece of wreckage he is swept back to the Charybdis strait where the whirlpool engulfs the timbers of his makeshift raft. He manages to escape by clinging to an ancient fig tree. Eventually the turbulence eases, the timbers float to the surface, and he paddles off out of danger. After drifting for the usual nine days he reaches Ogygia.

Ill. 108. A shipwreck scene from an Attic Geometric oinochoë, late eighth century BC. A man is seated astride the keel of an upturned warship (note the ram). Beside him a helmeted figure is making an attempt to swim for his life. The rest of the crew appear to be floundering helplessly in the water, watched by a shoal of fish. This may be a general theme—there is a quite similar scene of shipwreck on an eighth-century vase from Ischia. But it may well be a specific illustration of the shipwreck of Ulysses off Thrinakia in which Ulysses alone survived (Homer describes Ulysses 'seated on the keel and blown by the winds'). If so, it will be the earliest extant illustration of the *Odyssey*.

So ends the great close-knit tale of adventures with which Ulysses regales his Phaeacian hosts in Scheria. In previous books Homer has described his seven-year stay on Ogygia, and how he came to be wrecked on Scheria and so it remains to discuss the identification of these two places.

Ogygia is described as lying 'at the navel of the sea', that is, the centre of the sea, a lonely and remote place. There Calypso lives in a cavern:

> where a great fire burnt on its appointed hearth, perfuming the island far across with the fragrance of flaming cedar-wood logs and straight-grained incense trees. . . . All round the cave-mouth there flourished a luxuriant copse of alder trees and black poplars and rich scented cypresses: therein roosted birds of long wing, owls and hawks and chattering hook-billed crows—birds of the sea whose livelihood was from the water. A young strong vine loaded with bunches of grapes wreathed the opening of the cave. Four springs quite near together jetted out translucent water in separate rills ingeniously contrived, each to water its own garden-plot. The soft lawns were starred with parsley and violets. Even an immortal coming upon the nook would pause before its beauty and feel his heart made glad.
>
> (*Odyssey* 5:59 ff.; T. E. Shaw's translation)

This charming picture of a terrestrial paradise is as idealized as Marvell's garden, as unplaced as Prospero's island. The experts deal with it after their predilections. For Reiss it was pregnant with chthonic symbolism, with trees, flowers, birds and springs all suggesting the nether world, and Calypso, the 'concealer', a demon of death. Bérard claimed to have located the cave and the four springs near Ceuta by the Straits of Gibraltar. Others have sought this Hesperidean garden in Malta or Madeira.

The most we can say is that Homer conceived of Ogygia as lying far to the west of Ithaca. On leaving it to cross the sea in his makeshift boat Ulysses is directed to sail with the Great Bear always on his left. This instruction, the only Homeric allusion to the practice of steering by the stars, implies a general course from west to east. After sailing for 'seventeen days' he comes in sight of the shadowy mountains of Scheria, and then his boat is smashed in a storm.

Homer nowhere calls Scheria an island, but neither does he call Crete an island, and *insularity* is certainly implied by what Nausikaä says about her people:

> Remote in this sea-beaten home of ours, we are the outposts of mankind and come in contact with no other people.
>
> (*Odyssey* 6:204–5; E. V. Rieu's translation)

Alkinoös conveys a rather different impression when he describes Ulysses as an unknown wanderer who has come 'either from eastern or western peoples' (*Odyssey* 8:29). The *intermediate* position of Scheria implied by his words is consistent with the traditional location in Corfu (ancient Corcyra), an island strategically placed athwart the sea-route between Greece and the West. Thucydides records (1:25) that the Corcyreans prided themselves on their seamanship, and compared themselves in this respect with the Phaeacians, also noted seamen, whom they considered as previous inhabitants of their city and island. This tradition was widely credited in the ancient world. Sceptics (and there were some even in antiquity) stress the mythical and magical aspects of the Homeric account. For example, Alkinoös claims that the gods dine at his feasts, and asserts that his people need no steersmen for 'the ships themselves know the thoughts and intentions of men . . . and very quickly pass across the open sea, shrouded in mist and cloud' (*Odyssey* 7:203 and 8:557–62). Many critics have analysed the fairytale and folklore motifs in the Phaeacian episode, seeing in Scheria an Elysian island where a beautiful princess falls in love with a handsome stranger. Others have detected Minoan features in the culture of the Phaeacians.

A. Shewan, in a series of papers later collected in his book *Homeric Essays*, argued vigorously for the Phaeacians as a 'community of mortals', and discounted the supernatural qualities attributed to them and their ships. He pointed out that Alkinoös is characterized as vain, vinous, and inordinately proud of the accomplishments of his people. The allegedly strong evidence for the supernatural in Phaeacia is mostly found to come from after-dinner speeches by this impulsive

Ill. 109. A Late Geometric Attic spouted bowl, *c.* 735–710 BC. A warship is about to put to sea. The ship is not a bireme—by Geometric convention the rowers on the starboard side are shown above rather than alongside their fellows. The large male figure on the left is about to step aboard, and holds a woman by the wrist. If this is a gesture of farewell, the scene may be interpreted as the departure of the Argo from Lemnos with Jason bidding adieu to Hypsipyle. Alternatively, we may have the abduction of Helen by Paris.

monarch. To take these passages out of context, says Shewan, and to build theories on them is to show a certain insensitivity to the 'gentle raillery' in Homer's portrait of the king. All sailors tend to indulge in exaggeration about their boats. The 'magic ship' passages must be balanced against other places in the narrative where the Phaeacian ships are serviced, launched, and rowed, in the normal way (e.g. *Odyssey* 6:264–9; 8:50–5; 13:22, 78, 113–5).

Thesprotia is brought into connection with Scheria by what Ulysses (in disguise) tells Penelope in a later book (*Odyssey* 19:270 ff.). He says that while in Thesprotia he heard of Ulysses being shipwrecked *nearby* on the land of the Phaeacians. This supports the Corfu–Scheria equation, for Corfu lies close to the northern part of Thesprotia. The equation, if accepted, gives a fixed point near the end of the wanderings, just as the Cicones provide one at the start. We can picture Ulysses' boat breaking up in the open sea some distance to the north-west, with the island in sight on the horizon 'like a shield on the misty sea' (*Odyssey* 5:281). As Bradford has written: 'A "shield" suggests a gradual curve, rising to a main central boss, and sloping away all around. This is exactly what Corfu does look like when approached from the west or north-west, with Mount Pandokrator (nearly 3,000 feet high) forming the boss of the shield.' Bradford goes on to state from personal experience that 'anywhere north of Corfu is a most treacherous place, for it is right in the mouth of the Adriatic, and when the Bora blows, a violent sea and a huge swell roll down to hurl themselves against the island.' Such were the conditions that Homer describes with Ulysses drifting before a northerly gale against the sort of jagged rock-bound coast that Corfu shows to the north and north- *Ill. 98* west.

The last lap in his journey will have been the hundred-mile passage from Corfu to Ithaca, a little long perhaps for the single night allotted to it in the narrative, but Homer does emphasize that the Phaeacian galley travelled extremely fast, with our hero sunk in a sleep 'very like death' (*Odyssey* 13:70–92). Those who take Phaeacia to be in fairyland emphasize the magical overtones of this trance-like sleep in which, as they see it, Ulysses returns from the realms of fancy to the confines of reality. The more practically minded point out that he must have been very tired after his exertions in Scheria. If one can accept that it was Homer's intention to 'give to airy nothing a local habitation and a name', then it would be fairer to say that both views are partly right rather than to dismiss either as wholly mistaken.

Such indications of direction as Homer gives combine to locate the wanderings somewhere in the seas to the west of Ithaca. But the sources of the narrative are complex, and it should not be taken as the record of a single voyage. I have argued that some of the local colour derives from Bronze Age voyages. The extent of these voyages is now well attested by archaeological data, at least for the period after 1600 BC. The Mycenaeans seem to have inherited a route pioneered by the Minoans, a route which went from the Peloponnese up past Ithaca to Corfu, and then across to the 'heel' of Italy. At Scoglio del Tonno (at the entrance to the great harbour of Taranto) there was a Mycenaean emporium whose history can be traced from *c.* 1400 BC onwards. From there the route followed the Italian coast to the Straits of Messina, then turned up past the Lipari islands at least as far as Ischia. A branch route took in the south-east and south-west coasts of Sicily, with a probable extension as far as Malta. Copper ingots of standard Aegean type found in Sardinia, dated *c.* 1200 BC, may indicate another branch route towards the south of France, but there is no evidence of Mycenaean landings here or in the south of Spain. There is, however, some slight evidence for Mycenaean penetration up the Adriatic. At the head of the Adriatic they would have made contact with trade routes up through central Europe to the Baltic. In the Lipari islands they appear to have had a rendezvous with shipping from the western Mediterranean. The Mycenaeans traded jewellery, weapons, and possibly wine, in exchange for copper, tin, gold and amber.

For the period after the Trojan War there is a good deal of scattered evidence in various Greek legends for migrations to Italy and Sicily. For example, Pylian comrades of Nestor were credited with the founding of Metapontum. Thucydides mentions a detachment of Phocians on their way back from Troy who were swept by a storm to Libya, and then made their way to western Sicily to settle near the

Elymians, themselves emigré Trojans. The story of the Phocians is curiously like the initial stages of Ulysses' wanderings, and it seems probable that his saga embodies material derived from this heroic period of Greek migration.

This westward displacement of Greeks in scattered detachments under heroic leaders did not, it seems, last long. Nor did it lead to any important settlements. It was not comparable in weight or purposiveness with the great colonizing movement of the eighth and seventh centuries BC. This latter movement was spearheaded by Euboeans who established themselves on Ischia at least as early as 750 BC. The movement followed the old Mycenaean trade routes, and the new western colonies were planted in areas previously penetrated by Mycenaean influence. In this fact we have the probable explanation of the early and detailed localization of Ulysses' adventures in western waters. The earliest Euboean colonists sailing west past Ithaca would see themselves as following in the track of Ulysses. They would recognize Charybdis in the Messina Strait and the Planktae in the Lipari islands. Once established on Ischia they would be in close touch with the Campanian coast where they were soon to found a settlement at Cumae. It is a reasonable assumption that Cumae then, as later, was the site of an underground oracle. The vulcanism of the region, and the proximity of the gloomy Lake Avernus, later famed as an entrance to the Underworld, would encourage an identification with the scene of Ulysses' visit to the Oracle of the Dead. Noting that Ulysses had sailed a day's journey south from Circe's island to reach the House of Hades, the colonists, we may suppose, would then look for, and find, Aiaia in the Latian promontory that still bears Circe's name. We have noted above how inconsistent this attribution is with the Homeric text (see p. 127), but local pride would discount such difficulties. By similar reasonings, we may suppose, the early colonists in Sicily would come to identify their island with Thrinakia, and would locate the Laistrygonians at Leontini, again regardless of counter-indications in the tradition represented by the *Odyssey*.

Three distinct periods of history underlie the Homeric account of Ulysses' wanderings: the Minoan–Mycenaean pioneering of trade routes to Sicily and western Italy; the folk migrations after the Trojan War; and the early stages of the Greek colonial movement. Each of these periods has coloured the epic tradition in a distinctive way. From the first derives the hazy outline of dangerous sea-routes to coasts and islands of mystery and enchantment. The second is *par excellence* the period of saga formation when the legends of Achaean chieftains raiding and exploring and settling overseas began to take shape. Here, if anywhere, we shall find the Ulysses of history, the 'sacker of cities' and the resourceful wanderer who 'saw the cities of many men and suffered much misery on the sea'. With the third period we reach the age of Homer himself. It was a period when Greek horizons were expanding and when the traditional sagas, particularly those describing overseas adventures, were being retold in the light of new experiences. We can detect something of Homer's own interests and background in the way he handles the tradition. He has no atlas image of the western world, and we should not use his sporadic mentions of sailing times and directions to bring Ulysses from point to point on the map as we know it. But he is aware of distant coasts and peoples distinct from, yet not altogether unrelated to, his own world. He retains the marvels to delight his hearers' fancy, but at the same time he gives the Cyclopes a credible economy, infuses Phaeacia with the spirit of an Ionian *polis*, and even humanizes the confines of Hades with a community of Cimmerians. As Strabo sagely remarked in his discussion of the wanderings: 'These traditions must not be pressed to yield accurate information, but neither are they to be dismissed as baseless and ungrounded.'

Ill. 111. Drawing of a ship from a Late Bronze Age Cypriot vase. Possibly a merchant ship with a deep hold is being used as a troop transport. The three large figures are armed with swords and helmets and look like officers.

7 Ulysses in later Greek literature and art

W. B. Stanford

HOMER and the other early Greek epic poets set the legend of Ulysses in a mould which lasted until the end of the pagan world of Greece and Rome. Not that the writers who succeeded those epic poets felt bound to follow the established legend in every detail. On the contrary they freely added episodes or interpretations of their own. But whenever they wrote about Ulysses they had the epic story in mind. Their opinions divide not so much on what Ulysses did or did not do as on his moral character. Especially in drama Ulysses appears sometimes as a good man, sometimes as a knave. Authors begin to have strong personal feelings about him, in contrast with Homer's objectivity. On the whole Ulysses loses favour from the fifth century onwards, and we can see the gradual growth of that hostility which has dogged his reputation ever since, so that if one consults the Oxford English Dictionary, for example, at the word *Ulyssean* one finds 'characteristic of, or resembling, Ulysses in craft or deceit', not in courage, or endurance, or practical wisdom, or love of home, or piety, as Homer's portrait suggests.

The first major attack on Ulysses' character in extant literature came from a poet who cherished the sterner heroic creed by which a man should die rather than adapt himself ignobly to external influences. Pindar, in two of his *Nemean Odes*, refers to the defeat of Ajax by Ulysses in the contest for the arms of Achilles. Pindar patently admired Ajax and despised Ulysses as 'a deviser of craftiness, an insinuator of mischievous calumnies, always attacking the illustrious and exalting the ignominious'. 'May I never have a character like that!' he exclaims. Pindar had himself been the victim of slander and deceit; hence perhaps his sympathy for the blunt Ajax and his loathing for the plausible Ithacan.

The dramatic poets of the fifth century, both tragic and comic, found an inexhaustible source of interest in the complexities of Ulysses' character. Many of the tragedies about him are now lost. But Ulysses plays notable roles in two of the seven surviving dramas of Sophocles and in five of the nineteen plays attributed to Euripides. The seven surviving plays of Aeschylus are on themes that preclude his appearance. But several of Aeschylus' lost works featured Ulysses

prominently. From fragments of these it looks as if Aeschylus shared
—or at any rate made some of his dramatic characters share—Pindar's
dislike of Ulysses. The slander that Ulysses' father was really Sisyphos,
the sinister ruler of Corinth, and not the blameless Laërtes, first
appears in a play by Aeschylus about the contest for the arms of
Achilles. In another work, *The Bone-gatherers*, a satyric drama, where
one may expect some rude horseplay, Ulysses experienced the foulest
humiliation of his career when a full chamber-pot was emptied over
his head. However he seems to have endured it characteristically
without losing his temper. In Aeschylus' *The Ghost-raisers*, Ulysses was
portrayed as meeting a disgusting and degrading death: a heron flying
overhead scattered ordure on his bald pate, causing his death by
sepsis—a grotesque interpretation of Teiresias' prophecy in the
Odyssey that Ulysses' death would come 'from the sea'. Though
satyric drama normally contained anti-heroic incidents, one may doubt
whether Aeschylus would have devised such repulsive sufferings for
Ulysses if he had admired him.

When one compares the two portraits of Ulysses that emerge in
Sophocles' early play *Ajax* and his later *Philoctetes*, one finds a
surprising contrast. In *Ajax* Ulysses is a model of humane and
civilized conduct. In *Philoctetes* he is a contemptible deceiver. In the
earlier play, Sophocles describes how in consequence of Ulysses'
victory in the contest for the arms of Achilles, Ajax tries to kill or
capture the Greek commanders who insulted him by not awarding
him the prize. To prevent this, the goddess Athena has deceived him
with hallucinations, so that he slaughtered cattle instead of his
enemies. In the opening scene Ulysses appears in the typically
Ulyssean role of an investigator trying to find out what Ajax's
intentions are. Then Athena—a strangely vindictive divinity here—
attempts to make Ulysses gloat over Ajax's insane folly. Ulysses
refuses. Instead he compassionately reflects on the frailty of all human
strength:

> I pity him in his misfortune now—
> Though he's my enemy—yoked as he is, disastrously,
> To utter doom. In this I view my own
> Frail destiny as much as his. For mortal men
> Are little more in life than spectres or dim shades.

On the other hand Ajax and his followers have nothing good to say
about Ulysses. To them Ulysses is a 'knavish fox', 'the dirtiest
offscourings of the host', a villain *capable de tout*. But obviously
Sophocles himself thinks differently. In the final scenes of the play,
when Agamemnon and Menelaos brutally refuse the rites of burial to
Ajax's corpse, Ulysses intervenes and with superb tact persuades
Agamemnon to relent. Further, he magnanimously praises Ajax in the
teeth of Agamemnon's angry resentment, describing him as being
the best man of all the Greeks at Troy now that Achilles is dead.

Ill. 112. This red jasper intaglio of
the Roman period (but the inscription ARISTONOS is in Greek)
presents Ulysses in a pose frequently
found later in classical art. He sits,
wearing his pilos as usual, in a
pensive attitude on a rock covered
by his mantle, holding a sword.
Possibly the location is in Calypso's
island of Ogygia as described in
Odyssey 5:151–3, where Ulysses sits
alone on a promontory yearning for
his home.

In *Philoctetes*, written some forty years after *Ajax*, Ulysses is entirely changed. Now he is a machiavellian emissary of Agamemnon sent to trick the formidable Philoctetes into supporting the Greek cause at Troy. Methodically Ulysses sets about corrupting his young companion, Neoptolemos, Achilles' son, into telling lies. He talks to the young man in terms of cynical disillusionment. When Neoptolemos asks whether Ulysses does not consider lies ugly and shameful, Ulysses replies, 'Not if they save the situation or win some advantage'. Later in the play he shows himself to be a coward as well as a knave, and Neoptolemos despises him for it. In the end Ulysses' detestable villainies are not even successful. The god Herakles has to intervene to win over Philoctetes.

Euripides, Sophocles' younger contemporary, presents Ulysses in an almost entirely evil light. In *Hecuba*, Ulysses plays a leading role, without a single redeeming feature. Before he appears in the play he is described as 'that shifty-minded, popularity-seeking, smooth-spoken traitor'. When he enters he addresses the Trojan women with laconic harshness: Polyxena must die. Hecuba reminds him that he owes his life to her: when he entered Troy disguised as a beggar she recognized him but out of kindness did not betray him. (This is not Homer's version of the incident.) Ulysses, Hecuba says, promised to repay her as soon as he could: now is his chance to keep his promise. Ulysses cynically disregards his promise as being merely a device to avoid death. Hecuba, in furious indignation, denounces all demagogues who will promise anything to win political advantages. Ulysses, with cold logic, replies in terms of political expediency and chauvinism: the request of Achilles for Polyxena's death must be honoured, he says, in order to maintain loyalty and public confidence. Many Greek women have lost their relatives in the war: why shouldn't barbarian women lose some now? When the young princess Polyxena throws herself in supplication at his feet, he remains obdurate. Finally he leads her away for sacrifice.

This is in many ways the most detestable portrait of Ulysses in the whole classical tradition. Euripides presents him as if he were one of the unscrupulous politicians of the last quarter of the fifth century BC in Athens—chauvinistic, callous, ungrateful, pitiless, argumentative, casuistical—all the qualities Euripides detested in the political scene around him. Euripides' blackening of Ulysses' character in this and other plays had a lasting influence on classical drama until the eighteenth century. The serviceable diplomat and statesman of the *Iliad* is transformed into a detestable *politique* whom no humane writer could admire. It was not until well into the nineteenth century that the Ulysses of drama fully escaped from this burden of infamy.

Ulysses with his knock-about adventures and lusty appetite made a congenial figure for the Greek comic writers. No complete comedy about him has survived, but we know from fragments and references that Epicharmos of Syracuse, and Cratinos, Theopompos and

Aristophanes of fifth-century Athens (and several others of the fourth century) made fun of incidents like his spying expedition to Troy and his encounters with the Cyclops, the Sirens and Nausikaä. Nothing of much significance emerges from these glimpses of a comic or satirical Ulysses, except the fact that he seems to have competed closely with that other favourite figure of comedy, Herakles, for popularity among the comic dramatists and their audiences.

In the second half of the fifth century Ulysses became a highly controversial figure. The eminent Sophists Gorgias and Hippias denounced him as treacherous and false. Others, like Alkidamas and Antisthenes praised him highly. To Antisthenes, Ulysses was a kind of proto-Cynic in his disregard of indignities and humiliations and in his fortitude in face of life's dangers and sufferings. Later, the Stoic philosophers and their followers (such as Plutarch and Marcus Aurelius) also admired him.

Plato did not often refer to him. But he commended his self-control under severe provocation, and he introduced him into a brief but memorable scene at the end of the *Republic*. It comes in the famous Vision of Er, when the souls of Homeric heroes are seen assembling to choose bodies for their next reincarnation. Ajax, still angry at his defeat in the contest for the arms of Achilles, chooses to become a lion,

Ills. 113, 114. Two versions of Ulysses' unsuccessful effort to persuade the wrathful Achilles to rejoin the fight against the Trojans as described in *Iliad* 9. On the right: the inside of an Attic red-figure cup by the master-painter Douris; opposite: one side of an Attic red-figure pelike. *c.* 500 BC. The figures of Ulysses leaning intently on his staff are similar, but those of Achilles are markedly different, the Douris figure resembling that in *Ill.* 11. As often, the second hero sent on this embassy, Ajax, a much less frequent subject in classical art than Ulysses, is omitted.

the symbol of unbounded strength and courage. Agamemnon, always eager to assert his overlordship, takes the body of an eagle, the soaring monarch of the skies. Thersites, ambitious to excel in buffoonery, becomes an ape. Last of all comes the soul of Ulysses. After his varied experience of men and monsters he has come to realize the futility of all ambition. What he seeks now is the life of some quiet, humble citizen unburdened with public affairs. He searches for it purposefully among the bodies that the other heroes have tossed aside like unwanted bargains at a sale. When he finds an incarnation for this quiet humble life he seizes it gladly. Even if he had been given first choice, he says, he would have chosen this 'unofficial' life.

Here Plato shows genuine sympathy for Ulysses. During the era of literature previous to the publication of the *Republic*, Ulysses had certainly been stigmatized by writers like Sophocles and Euripides for his political activities. If he had been all that they had said—ambitious, unscrupulous, hated for his successes, disliked by the good, denounced by the honourable—Ulysses might well have chosen the life of an obscure, non-political citizen for his next reincarnation. In a sense, too, Plato's vision was uncannily prophetic. Late in the European literary tradition Ulysses did in fact become reincarnated in the body of such a socially and politically undistinguished person, when James Joyce re-created him in Leopold Bloom, that mild and inoffensive citizen of twentieth-century Dublin.

After Plato, a new feature can be discerned in Greek writings on Ulysses. First, under the influence of the Cynic and Stoic philosophers, Ulysses became an allegorical figure, especially in his Odyssean aspects. He was seen partly as the Pilgrim Man, the *homo viator* making his way with fortitude and resourcefulness through the trials and temptations of human life. He also became an exemplar of another Stoic ideal, the Cosmopolitan Man, the Citizen of the World, who has travelled widely and who regards all mankind as his fellows. The earliest surviving work on the allegorical approach to Homer in general and to Ulysses in particular—though as a method of interpretation allegorization can be traced back to the sixth century—is by a certain Herakleitos in the first century AD. He claims that Homer, regarding Ulysses as 'an instrument of all manly virtue', used him to expound his philosophy of life. The Lotos-eaters represent the temptation of gluttony; the Cyclops, the menace of savage anger; Circe, the allurements of strange vice; Charybdis, voracious extravagance; Skylla, multifarious shamelessness; the Cattle of the Sun, the pangs of hunger; the Sirens, the desire for historical knowledge; Ulysses' journey to the Land of Shades, the indomitable search for secret lore. In the light of such doctrines as these, Homer (Herakleitos enthusiastically asserts) is 'the great hierophant of Heaven and of the gods, who opened to men's souls the closed and untrodden paths to Heaven'.

This energetic and arresting work—fanciful though much of it was—became the foundation of an immense body of speculative literature about Ulysses, as will be exemplified later. It helped to justify pagan philosophers, Christian apologists and modern school-teachers in presenting Ulysses, despite the execrations poured on him in the plays of Euripides and Sophocles (and in second-rate works like the *Cassandra* of the Hellenistic writer Lycophron), as a commendable hero for adults and schoolchildren alike.

From the first decade of the fifth century onwards the visual arts in Greece also produced some remarkable variations in the characterization of Ulysses. He begins now to appear in Greek vase-paintings as a distinct and arresting personality. Whether this development was linked with the growing interest in drama cannot now be determined. But at any rate the artistic effects were admirable, as may be seen in the work of several brilliant artists—notably the 'Eucharides painter', *Ill. 11* presenting a superbly relaxed, but very alert Ulysses in the embassy to Achilles, and also Douris, Makron, and the 'Tyskiewicz painter' in *Ill. 114* other versions of the same episode. (This embassy was a favourite *Ill. 113* theme in Greek art round the beginning of the fifth century. Over a dozen pictures of it survive on vases from this period, beginning with

Ill. 115. The capture of Dolon by Ulysses (left) and Diomedes (right) on an imperfectly preserved oinochoë. A fine archaic representation (cf. *Ill. 13*) which keeps close to the description in *Iliad* 10: Dolon in the centre carries a quiver for his arrows and wears a wolfskin over his clothes. Ulysses and Diomedes wear their traveller's hats (*petasoi*) and animal-skins to keep them warm on their night-raid.

Ill. 10

Ill. 14

Ill. 15

Ill. 18

Ills. 13, 115

a Caeretan hydria of 520–10 BC.) An equally memorable picture of Ulysses appears on an Attic skyphos by the 'Brygos painter' *c.* 490 BC. Here the subject is Ulysses in conversation with Nestor. Ulysses' expression is quizzical and humorous as he sits at ease looking up at Nestor, as if, perhaps, he was expecting to have to listen to another of the old man's long-winded stories.

Two paintings by Douris, both on one cup of about 490 BC, also deserve particular praise. The first presents two scenes from the conflict between Ulysses and Ajax for the arms of Achilles. On one side Athena watches the Greek commanders as they cast their votes. She turns with favour to the left where the votes for Ulysses are mounting up much faster than those for Ajax on the right. The other side shows Ulysses and Ajax being restrained by Greeks as they try to attack each other with drawn swords on either side of Agamemnon, who stands over the controversial arms. (There are other versions of this scene.) The second of these masterpieces by Douris illustrates a generous action by Ulysses after the suicide of his rival Ajax. We see Ulysses, with a grave, heavily-bearded face, giving the arms of Achilles to Achilles' young son Neoptolemos. These are brilliantly executed scenes, one of a violent action, the other of a peaceful gesture. But it can hardly be said that they present Ulysses as subtly as the scenes from the embassy already mentioned.

One not very important incident in Ulysses' career at Troy, the killing of Dolon (*Iliad* 10), occurs on no fewer than four vases before 475 BC (some other identifications are uncertain), notably on a black-figure fragment and on a red-figure cup attributed to the 'Dokimasia painter'. Small fragments of a version of the same scene by Euphronios also survive. After 475 BC other Ulyssean episodes from the *Iliad* and

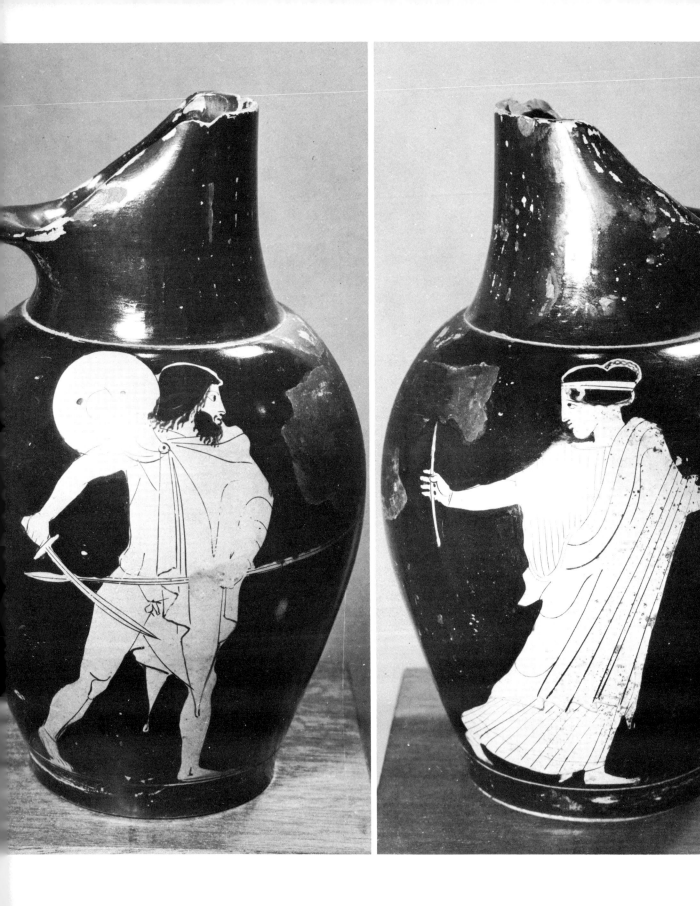

Ill. 116. Opposite: two sides of an Attic oinochoë (*c.* 460 BC) showing Ulysses advancing on Circe with sword and spear (a non-Homeric addition—cf. *Ill. 26*).

Ill. 117. This cover of a fine red-figure pyxis by Aison (late fifth century BC) gives a lively kind of strip-cartoon of the encounter of Ulysses and Nausikaä (see *Ill. 32*). Ulysses, with the traditional branch to cover his nakedness, follows Athena who directs him towards the Phaeacian princess past a fleeing handmaid. Beyond Nausikaä, another handmaid washes clothes (as in the previous incident in *Odyssey* 6:85 ff.), while behind Ulysses another girl runs very fast away from the disreputable-looking intruder.

the other epics became popular, especially his encounters with Chryseïs, Helen, Patroklos and Telephos, his stealing of the Palladium, and his exploits during the Sack of Troy.

Scenes from Ulysses' Odyssean adventures were even more frequent during the fifth and fourth centuries. Over a hundred of them have been listed in a recent monograph. As might have been expected, the Circe incident with its opportunities for depicting animals as well as men and a demi-goddess attracted many artists. A black-figure Attic lekythos (*c.* 500–475 BC) from Eretria shows Circe offering her potion to a seated Ulysses whose relaxed pose, with the right-leg crossed over the left, recalls the paintings with Achilles and with Nestor already noticed. An oinochoë dating from about 460 BC realistically illustrates Ulysses threatening Circe with his sword, while she retreats holding her wand in one hand and her magical cup in the other. Comic versions will be considered later.

Ill. 116

Ulysses' visit to Hades produced at least one masterpiece. An Attic red-figure pelike (about 440 BC) attributed to the 'Lykaon painter' shows Ulysses seated on a rock with the bodies of sacrificed animals in front of him. Beyond them Elpenor's ghost rises out of the ground, while the god Hermes, wearing his winged hat and boots and carrying his herald's staff, moves forward from behind Ulysses. Similar in some

Ill. 27

respects, but not quite so effective, is a Lucanian calyx krater of
uncertain date (from perhaps the earlier part of the fourth century)
showing Ulysses seated in Hades, sword in hand, between two
Companions, while the head of Teiresias emerges macabrely from the
ground in front of them.

Another favourite theme, the temptation by the Sirens, is pictured
on a well known red-figure Attic stamnos from the second quarter of   *Ill. 33*
the fifth century. Ulysses' ship, his Companions, and his own figure
tied to the mast, are impressively, though rather statically delineated.
But the vertically descending dumpy Siren is almost ludicrous. One
may well prefer the more formalized versions on an earlier black-
figure oinochoë (about 520 BC) and a slightly later lekythos, or even
the crude, but forceful, scene on a Corinthian aryballos (about 570 BC).   *Ill. 28*

Ulysses' meeting with Nausikaä and her handmaidens in Phaeacia
appears in several varied interpretations, notably on a red-figure
pyxis (end of the fifth century) by Aison. On it a naked Ulysses,   *Ill. 117*
modestly bending down, with the scarf of Leukothea still round his
shoulders, encouraged by a majestic Athena, moves towards a calmly
waiting Nausikaä while two handmaidens retreat in alarm (and
another obliviously goes on washing clothes)—a charming, though
rather disjointed composition. A red-figure Attic amphora (450–40   *Ill. 32*

148

Ills. 118, 119. Two sides of an Attic red-figure skyphos from Chiusi by the 'Penelope painter', *c.* 440 BC. Opposite: Telemachos stands before Penelope in her traditional pose of sadness. In the background is the loom on which Penelope wove (and unwove) the shroud for Ulysses' father—her ruse for delaying the Suitors' demands. Above: Ulysses disguised as a beggar, with various accoutrements, has his foot washed in the presence of Eumaios, the swineherd, by a servant named Antiphata (not in the literary tradition).

Ills. 39, 40

BC) is better organized, but here it seems that Nausikaä is about to run away in fright at the unprepossessing appearance of the shipwrecked Ulysses. In Homer's account she bravely stood her ground.

Various episodes in Ulysses' return to Ithaca were also favoured. One side of a superb red-figure Attic skyphos from the second half of the fifth century shows Telemachos contemplating a grieving Penelope seated on a stool in front of her ornately decorated loom. On the other Ulysses, wearing the pilos over dark curling hair and carrying various objects on a pole over his shoulder, is having his left foot held above a basin by a happy-looking woman. Despite the fact that she is named Antiphata on the vase (perhaps a slip of memory on the artist's part) this most likely represents Eurykleia recognizing the scar on Ulysses' leg as described in *Odyssey* 19. Behind the woman, Eumaios offers a present to Ulysses (not according to Homer, either). Some identifications of Eumaios on other vases are questionable. The slaying of the Suitors is represented on two notable vases. On a red-figure Attic skyphos (about 450 BC) by the 'Penelope painter' Ulysses with two women behind him (probably servants) draws an arrow on his bowstring against three Suitors dramatically posed on and around a dining couch. Influence by Polygnotos has been suggested here.

One painting—on a Lucanian red-figure hydria of the late fifth century, from Paestum—has baffled all attempts at identification. A figure captioned 'Ulysses' sits with bowed head on a heap of stones. He holds a sword, while a woman offers him a round box tied with a ribbon. In the background is a youth captioned 'Telemachos' and some other women. No convincing explanation has been offered. Possibly the scene was taken from a lost drama about Ulysses.

Comic treatments of events in Ulysses' career also occur in vase-paintings. We have already noticed something of the kind in an early version of the blinding of Polyphemos, but a comic intention is not certain there. Deliberately comic treatment is apparent on skyphoi from the Kabeirion at Thebes (about 400 BC and later) presenting burlesque versions of the Circe incident. A Paestan crater (about 340–20 BC) also seems to be intended as a burlesque of Ulysses' encounter with the Sirens. Ulysses has a Silenos-like head, like a comic mask, and the Companions who, contrary to Homer's version, obviously can hear the Sirens' song, seem to be in a state of carefree intoxication. Ulysses is equally ugly on a red-figure fourth-century Apulian oinochoë which depicts him stealing the Palladium, while Diomedes, looking like an African slave, stands by. A Lucanian

Ills. 120, 121

Ill. 122

Ills. 120–122. Three burlesque versions of Ulysses' adventures. On the first Boeotian skyphos, *c.* 400 BC, (above left) a pot-bellied and noticeably phallic Ulysses strides over two amphorae (parodying his raft in *Odyssey* 5) while a comic head of the North Wind blows him on. On the second Boeotian skyphos, *c.* 400 BC, (left) a grotesquely emaciated and scraggy-bearded Ulysses receives the magic potion from a negroid Circe. On the red-figure Apulian oinochoë, fourth century BC, (opposite) a comic Ulysses carries off the Palladium with Diomedes (contrast *Ill. 17*).

third-century calyx crater shows a scene from a 'phlyax' comedy: a virago-like Queen Arete accompanied by a passive Alkinoös harangues a dazed-looking Ulysses in a pilos (with a ribbon attached) and a short cloak. This is in fact the latest extant representation of Ulysses on a painted vase. But scenes from his adventures continued to appear on moulded Megarian bowls and Samian ware.

Ulysses also appeared in large-scale paintings from the fifth century onwards. Unfortunately no early originals of these have survived, but a good deal can be learnt about their subject-matter and treatment from descriptions in later writers, especially the elder Pliny in his *Natural history* and Pausanias in his *Description of Greece*.

Polygnotos, the earliest of the Greek masters of mural painting, who was active in Athens during the first half of the fifth century, composed several works on Iliadic and Odyssean themes. His two paintings of the Sack of Troy contained representations of the Wooden Horse, of Ulysses in armour and of Ulysses sparing a son of his Trojan friend, Antenor, and killing another Trojan boy. His picture of Hades for the Club House of the Cnidians in Delphi was particularly famous. In it (according to Pausanias) one could see two Companions of Ulysses carrying black rams for Ulysses' sacrifice to the Underworld powers (as described in *Odyssey* 11), Elpenor in sailor's dress with Ulysses (who squatted down, holding a drawn sword, over the trench for the blood, while the prophet Teiresias advanced towards him), and the ghost of Ulysses' mother, Antikleia. Other elements in the composition were not taken from Homer's description of Hades: for example, the ghosts of the four chief enemies of Ulysses among the Greeks at Troy —the two Ajaxes, Palamedes and Thersites—were shown in a group together. One painting by Polygnotos seems to have been specially

Ill. 6

influential—his composition showing Achilles among the daughters of Lykomedes in Skyros. Whether it included Ulysses in his role of detective (as in the celebrated Pompeian painting) cannot be determined on the present evidence. It is not certain, either, that Ulysses appeared in Polygnotos' painting of Nausikaä and her handmaidens washing clothes at the river. These last two works were in the art gallery of the Acropolis in Athens. The same collection contained *Ulysses stealing the bow of Philoctetes*, *Diomedes stealing the Palladium* (probably with Ulysses), and *The Sacrifice of Polyxena*. (Pausanias does not record who painted these.) Another famous work by Polygnotos was in Plataea. It showed Ulysses at the climactic moment just after he had killed the Suitors. (There was another painting on this theme in Corinth, by an unknown artist.) Obviously Polygnotos found Ulysses a congenial subject. Since, according to Aristotle, his style of painting was idealistic in the sense that it aimed at ennobling his subjects, we may take it that he presented the more heroic aspects of Ulysses' character. Polygnotos probably influenced contemporary vase-painting strongly. His brother, Aristophon, painted Ulysses' entry into Troy as a spy. Aristophon also introduced an allegorical element into paintings on the Ulysses theme, presenting a group

Ill. 124. Another Greek terracotta relief from Melos, *c.* 460 BC. This shows Eurykleia washing the feet of Ulysses in the presence of a wondering Penelope and a rather abstracted Telemachos (cf. *Ill. 37*).

consisting of Ulysses, Priam and Helen, with figures representing Credulity and Craftiness in attendance.

Polygnotos' celebrated successor, Zeuxis, painted a Penelope, but it is unknown whether it also included Ulysses. Another renowned artist of the fifth century, Parrhasios, was especially interested in scenes of psychological interest, and he excelled in subtleties of facial expression. These he could have exploited effectively in his celebrated painting of Ulysses feigning madness to avoid conscription for the Trojan War. Parrhasios also included Ulysses in a picture illustrating the healing of Telephos, and possibly also in his picture of Philoctetes. Yet despite his acknowledged mastery, this artist met defeat at the hands of a rival in a competition for paintings on the theme of Ulysses' victory over Ajax in the contest for the arms of Achilles. The successful artist, Timanthes, also produced one of the most celebrated paintings of antiquity, *The Sacrifice of Iphigeneia*. Cicero and others specially praised its subtle gradations of grief as expressed in the faces and postures of the protagonists, Calchas, the prophet, Ulysses, Menelaos and Agamemnon (whose head was veiled to show that his agony as a father who had to sacrifice his own daughter was inexpressible).

Several other Greek painters found a congenial subject in Ulysses. Some attempted to rival earlier works. Athenion of Megara produced a new version of *The Detection of Achilles in Skyros*, while Euphranor

Ill. 7

Ill. 127. Opposite: a Roman statuette of Ulysses, wearing his customary pilos, holding up a wine-bowl. This probably formed part of a group in which Ulysses offered wine to the Cyclops.

tried to surpass Parrhasios' *Madness of Ulysses*. The elder Nikias (and possibly the younger Nikias) painted new versions of scenes in Hades. Others chose less celebrated themes. Pamphilos, the teacher of Apelles, portrayed Ulysses on his raft; and a painting (of uncertain origin) on wood in Cyzicus depicted him with his mother Antikleia.

In relying on literary sources, as we must, for information about these lost works we cannot be sure that the information is always entirely trustworthy. For example Pliny, our chief authority for Greek painting, says that the conical felt cap (*pilos* in Greek, *pileus* in Latin), which Ulysses often wears in ancient art, was first given to him in a painting by the fourth-century painter Nikomachos: another source attributes it to the fifth-century painter Apollodoros. Both are wrong. The pilos is clearly to be seen on Ulysses in earlier vase-paintings. Nor can it be taken as proving that the figure wearing it is Ulysses: it was also worn by seamen, shepherds, and craftsmen, and helmets of this shape were in use in the fifth century BC.

When one turns to Greek sculpture, bronze-work, and terracottas, one finds fewer representations of Ulysses. The earliest of them (if the identification with Ulysses is correct) is the figure on a turtle on one of the metopes (*c.* 560 BC) from the mouth of the river Sele at Paestum, as already mentioned. Next—and about a hundred years later—comes the series of terracotta reliefs from Melos. Though not masterpieces, they show marked tenderness and subtlety of feeling in their presentations of scenes from the home-coming of Ulysses. We see him meeting with a group consisting of Penelope, Telemachos, Laërtes (or perhaps Philoitios) and Eumaios, conversing with Penelope, and having his feet washed by Eurykleia in the presence of Telemachos and a pensive-looking Penelope (who seems to be wondering more about the stranger's identity than she does in the *Odyssey*).

Very fortunately, what seems to be an excellent example of a major artist's conception of Ulysses in the style of the Parthenon frieze has been recently discovered. It is a clay impression of a metal belt-buckle. A finely proportioned and nobly posed Ulysses, holding his spear, sits grieving deeply, his shield (with its traditional Gorgon-head on it), and a pilos beside him. It probably dates from the middle of the fifth century, and perhaps, as has been suggested in the article reporting the discovery, it illustrates the grief of Ulysses at the suicide of Ajax as described in Sophocles' *Ajax*. Similar representations of a mourning Ulysses appear later on gems, on a small bronze from Minorca, and most notably on a bronze cheek-piece of a helmet from Megara in the late fifth or early fourth century BC, which shows a noble and handsome figure wearing a pilos, leaning against a rock, and gazing sadly ahead, with two spears and a sword nearby. It used to be thought that these represented Ulysses yearning for Ithaca on Calypso's island as described in *Odyssey* 5. But the presence of arms and armour suggests a more warlike setting than Ogygia and the connexion with the *Ajax* may be valid for all.

Ill. 123
Ill. 38
Ill. 124

Ill. 125

Ill. 126

Nothing else survives in these genres from the fifth century in Greece. It is known, however, from literary sources that the sculptor Onatas of Aigina included Ulysses in a group portraying the nine Greek heroes who cast lots for the honour of fighting a duel with Hector (as described in *Iliad* 7); and that Lykios, the son of the celebrated Myron, included Ulysses and the Trojan prophet Helenos when illustrating a scene from the *Aithiopis*, because (as Pausanias records) these two had the highest reputation for wisdom in the two armies.

A forceful, though rather crude, group of reliefs from the limestone frieze at Gjölbaschi-Trysa in Lycia, dating from the first decade of the fourth century, presents scenes from the Trojan War and from Ulysses' Odyssean adventures. The slaying of the Suitors is robustly modelled, *Ill. 41* and includes the older motif of a Suitor trying to use a table as a shield.

The most heroic of all the surviving statues of Ulysses is the handsome and dynamic figure in the Doge's Palace in Venice, probably *Ill. 2* a copy of a fourth-century work. Here we have a full acceptance that Ulysses was the equal in courage and nobility of bearing to any of the other Homeric champions, as he stands ready to meet some formidable foe. There is a heroic quality, too, in the statue in Rome of Ulysses *Ill. 127* holding up a bowl of wine (presumably to the Cyclops). In a well-preserved bronze statuette of the Roman period he looks more like a *Ill. 3* rather worried philosopher. In complete contrast to these is the curious *Creeping Ulysses*, a much later work (*c.* 50 BC). This is Ulysses in *Ill. 128* one of his less conventionally heroic exploits—perhaps creeping into Troy on his spying mission (see p. 30). He appears in an even less dignified pose in an absurd but not unpleasing marble figure of his escape under the ram from the Cyclops' cave.

Ill. 128. This marble statue from Rome, *c.* AD 50, is quite unique. The curious figure of Ulysses is creeping cautiously somewhere (perhaps into or out of Troy on his spying expedition described in *Odyssey* 4: 242–58). The head, which looks naturalistic in profile as here, has a distinctly classical appearance in full face.

Ill. 130. Opposite: on this oval bezel ▶ of a gold ring (fourth century BC) Ulysses walks with a dog (presumably Argos) in a variation on the scene described in *Odyssey* 17: 292 ff.

Ill. 129. Another version of the non-Homeric exploit of Ulysses on a turtle (from a gem, now lost). Here (unlike *Ill. 46*) the hero is clearly recognizable by his pilos.

Ill. 31

Finally there is the starkly unforgettable head of Ulysses from the recently discovered group of Odyssean figures in the Cave of Tiberius at Sperlonga. Its wide, staring eyes, its mouth wide open in grief or horror, and its general expression of immeasurable agony, imply that it comes from an excruciating moment in Ulysses' experience. Probably (since fragments of a formidable Skylla were also found on the site) it records the moment when he saw six of his Companions being dragged by Skylla's long tentacles into her cave to be devoured there. 'That', Homer says in *Odyssey* 12: 258–9, 'was the most piteous sight that I ever saw in all my sufferings and searchings over the paths of the sea.' A masterpiece of sensational sculpture, the head has stylistically much in common with the Laocoön group by Rhodian sculptors in the second half of the second century BC (*frontispiece*).

Terracotta figurines and plaques also featured incidents from the adventures of Ulysses, especially when he was passing the Sirens or having his feet washed by Eurykleia (with some variations from the description in *Odyssey* 19), or conversing with the grieving Penelope. Most of them are run-of-the-mill work. But one unusually effective piece of late Tanagra work shows a matronly Calypso sitting on an ornate chair at the entrance to her cave, facing a rather apologetic-looking Ulysses beside a ship's prow, while a small cupid flutters inanely between them—an entertainingly sentimental rendering of the scene described with so much restraint in *Odyssey* 5.

Coins, too, and engraved gems attest the popularity of the Ulysses legend. He appears on mintings from Cyzicus in the fifth century, from Ithaca in the fourth and third centuries, and possibly from Mantineia in the early fourth century BC. If the identification of the latter is valid, the picture shows Ulysses planting his oar among 'men who do not know the sea' as prescribed by Teiresias in *Odyssey* 11: 123.

Greek (as well as Etruscan and Roman) gems displayed a wide range of Ulyssean exploits, most commonly the killing of Dolon, the negotiations with Philoctetes, the stealing of the Palladium, the Wooden Horse, and the encounters with Polyphemos, Circe, the Sirens, Calypso, the dog Argos, and Penelope. Some themes rarely seen elsewhere are also found, notably the bag of the winds, the building of the raft, the planting of the oar, and Ulysses' ride on the turtle's back. Specially memorable as a work of art is a sard intaglio of the Roman period (but probably from a Hellenistic model) signed (in Greek) with the name 'Felix' showing Ulysses and Diomedes stealing the Palladium (see p. 30).

In general, it can be said that the Greek artists of the classical period and later portrayed Ulysses as vividly and as variously as the Greek writers. But one notable feature of the literary tradition is absent from Greek art—the presentation of Ulysses as a corrupt villain. He appears in comic and undignified scenes, yes. But the iniquitous monster of Euripides is not to be found in any Greek work of art, except in a late Graeco-Roman piece to be noticed in Chapter 8.

8 Ulysses in Etruscan and Latin traditions

W. B. Stanford

THERE is evidence for knowledge of Ulysses' adventures as early as the seventh century in Italy. How did it arrive there? Were his adventures part of a common prehistoric European stock of stories about brave and clever heroes? Or were they first told in Italy by migrants from Troy, or Greece, or the Greek lands in Asia Minor? Greek writers claimed that several cities in Italy had been founded by the sons of Ulysses, and even that Ulysses was a co-founder of Rome with Aeneas the Trojan. Similarly they asserted that 'Latinus' and 'Romanus' were originally the names of children or grandchildren of Ulysses (see p. 59). Naturally such pro-Greek genealogies were not universally approved of by orthodox Romans. On the other hand Roman writers generally accepted the tradition that several of Ulysses' Odyssean exploits occurred in Italy and Sicily. Further, the powerful Roman *gens Mamilia* claimed descent from Ulysses' son Telegonos, and minted several coins with an effigy of their ancestor. (An early one, about 170 BC, shows Ulysses on the prow of a ship. On another, about 83 BC, he is seen meeting his dog Argos. On the obverse of the second coin is Mercury, Ulysses' ancestor on his mother's side. The Argos theme was repeated on Roman 'restored coins', *contorniates*, of the Roman imperial period.)

The earliest references to Ulysses in Italy are on Etruscan inscriptions. They call him *Utuse* (with several variants). This has been taken as an adaptation of *Odysseus* (though a derivation from the pseudonym *Outis*, used by Ulysses to deceive the Cyclops, has also been conjectured). No Etruscan literature survives to record the local beliefs about Ulysses. But late Greek writers say that he went to Etruria after the fall of Troy, and was named *Nanos* by the Etruscans, and died there. Plutarch mentions a curious tradition among the Etruscans that Ulysses got a reputation for unusual sleepiness among them.

Etruscan art often uses scenes from his adventures. As early as the seventh century BC, ivory buckets from Etruria show the Companions escaping from the Cyclops. (But Ulysses himself is not clearly identifiable on them.) More uncommon is the representation of Ulysses as a forceful charioteer on a sixth-century bronze plate from

Ills. 131, 132. Opposite: Etruscan mirror-case from Cervetri. The relief on the medallion represents the meeting of Ulysses and Penelope. Ulysses, wearing his customary pilos, stands on the left and gesticulates to Penelope, who looks towards him in a thoughtful attitude. In the centre is perhaps Athena (or Eurykleia) and the dog Argos. Below them are heads of (presumably) slain Suitors. Below: Argos is also shown with Ulysses on a Roman coin of C. Mamilius Limetanus (82–79 BC), whose family claimed descent from Ulysses.

Chiusi. Etruscan burial urns, *stelai* and sarcophagi portray many scenes from Ulysses' Trojan and Odyssean adventures—the sacrifice of Iphigeneia, the negotiations with Telephos and with Philoctetes, his encounters with Circe, Polyphemos, Skylla, the Sirens (a favourite theme in Etruria), and the Suitors, and his return to Penelope. To notice only a few out of a rich diversity: a burial urn (about 300 BC) from Torre San Severo shows a powerful representation of Ulysses threatening Circe in the presence of two Companions with animals' heads. The massively built Ulysses with a stern, heavy-featured face grasps Circe by the hair with his left hand and with the other points his sword up towards her heart, while the Companions watch rather nonchalantly. On another urn (now in Leyden) Ulysses, wearing an ornate pilos, is escaping with five Companions on a fine ship while from the shore a humanized Polyphemos, with two eyes in his handsome head, hurls a rock after them, and a small winged goddess brandishing a sword encourages the Greeks. In the background are a cave, sheep and rocks. It is a curiously tranquil rendering of an essentially violent scene. Also from Torre San Severo is a fourth-century wooden sarcophagus showing Ulysses sacrificing a ram (presumably as in *Odyssey* 11). An alabaster urn of the third or second century BC from Volterra presents two scenes: Ulysses at the Suitors' banquet, and then slaying them with a formidable spear.

Ill. 135

Ill. 131

Etruscan bronze mirrors from the fifth century BC onwards depict several Ulyssean incidents—with Circe, with Teiresias in Hades, and with Penelope. The theme of Ulysses on the turtle appears on a third-century BC specimen: here Ulysses seems to be wearing a long, narrow scarf, which suggests that the riding of the turtle in this case (as on an Etruscan scarab) is connected with Leukothea's intervention to save Ulysses after his raft had been shipwrecked on his voyage from Ogygia, rather than with the Skylla and Charybdis incident (see p. 48).

Among Etruscan wall-paintings the most striking presentation of an Odyssean theme is the horrific picture of the blinding of Polyphemos from the 'Tomb of the Underworld' at Tarquinia (fourth or third century BC). The huge, round eye of a fat, pot-bellied giant is being pierced by a long pointed stake held by a figure (presumably Ulysses) of which only a few fragments remain. A touch of compassion for the suffering monster is perhaps intended in the mild eyes of the watching sheep. Pictures like this make one all the more regretful that there are no literary records of the Etruscan attitudes to Ulysses and his exploits (see p. 164).

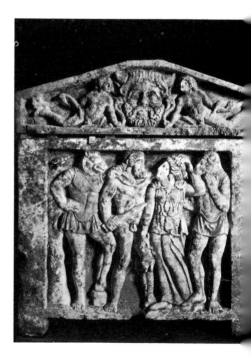

The Romans called Ulysses *Ulixes*, a transliteration apparently of his second Greek name (see p. 13). The difference from the Etruscan *Utuse* suggests that they derived their earliest knowledge of Ulysses from different sources, the Etruscans being influenced more by the Ionian and epic traditions, the Latins by the western Greek and the folklore traditions. Ulysses begins to take a prominent place in Latin literature in the third century BC when Livius Andronicus translated

162

Ills. 133–136. A selection from the many varied and imaginative presentations of Ulysses in Etruscan art. On the small sixth-century bronze plate from the foot of an Etruscan cist from Chiusi (opposite, top), a sturdy Ulysses vigorously drives a four-horse chariot (perhaps as on the François vase, *Ill. 45*). Opposite, bottom: a sarcophagus relief (*c.* 300 BC) from Torre San Severo forcefully depicts a formidable Ulysses threatening a rather impassive Circe with his sword, watched by two bewitched Companions. The panel showing a banquet scene, probably of the Suitors as in *Odyssey* 21, from Volterra on an alabaster funeral urn (right). From there, too, on another Etruscan burial urn, comes the highly decorative version of Ulysses passing three Sirens (below). These are shown as conventional-looking females playing musical instruments —very different from the sinister bird-creatures of early art.

the *Odyssey* into Latin. Two early Roman dramatists, Accius and Pacuvius, wrote plays on the competition between Ulysses and Ajax for the arms of Achilles. Only fragments of their works survive, and one cannot be sure what their attitudes to the two contrasting heroes were.

In the second half of the second century BC, after the Roman annexation of Greece, educated Romans began to be able to read the descriptions of Ulysses in Greek literature for themselves. A century later we find frequent references to Ulysses among the Augustan writers and their successors. Horace for the most part followed the Greek Stoic philosophers in admiring Ulysses. Writing as a philosophic man of the world, he describes Homer's hero as a

> Choice pattern of the manly and the wise.

Horace goes on to point out a contrast between his own slack semi-Epicurean life, spent in feasting and pleasure (like that of the Suitors of Penelope or the Phaeacians) and the life of such a virtuous hero. However Horace elsewhere described Ulysses as 'two-faced' and 'avaricious'.

Cicero praised Ulysses for his stoicism and for his affability—a quality which he himself, as an aspiring politician of unpatrician family, would wish to emulate. Cicero discussed the question of whether Ulysses was morally justified in feigning madness to avoid conscription for the Trojan War, and quoted from an earlier Roman writer (probably Accius or Pacuvius) who presented Ulysses as being denounced for cowardice, but concludes: 'It was better for him to

164

Ills. 137, 138. Opposite: a drawing of the horrifying version of the blinding of Polyphemos on an Etruscan mural-painting from the 'Tomb of the Underworld' at Tarquinia. Two notable features are the olive leaves on the stake (showing that the artist knew about Homer's description in *Odyssey* 9:320) and the mild-eyed sheep on the right of Polyphemos. Right: Ulysses and Circe on a Roman lamp from Pozzuoli. Circe holds her magic wand alertly while Ulysses talks to her.

battle with both the enemy and the waves, as he did, than to desert Greece when it was united for waging war against the barbarians.' Elsewhere Cicero meditates on the meaning of Ulysses' encounter with the Sirens. Their lure, he believes, was not sensual but intellectual. They offered men of philosophical mind the pleasure of contemplating the loftier truths of life, not merely factual knowledge. The desire for contemplation of these loftier truths is the sign, he thinks, of superior men.

Similarly Seneca in his philosophical writings praised Ulysses as a man 'unconquered by labours', 'scorning pleasures' and 'victorious in all lands', and admired him as a model of patriotism, family loyalty and prudence. But in his tragedies he views Ulysses much less favourably. In the *Trojan Women* he followed the example of Euripides in vilifying the versatile Greek hero as 'an artist in crime', full of deceitfulness and cunning. Yet, being a Roman used to the stern exigencies of power-politics under the Emperors, Seneca shows rather more sympathy than Euripides for Ulysses. Seneca's Ulysses pleads that in arranging for the death of Astyanax he is merely 'the minister of a harsh decree': his demands are not his own; they express the general will of the Greek commanders who fear that, if this son of Hector were to survive, a war of revenge might follow in the next generation. Ulysses is spared the abominable act of hurling Astyanax from the walls with his own hand. The child throws himself down, and even Ulysses is moved by his courage.

The Augustan poet Ovid was particularly well endowed to appreciate Ulysses' personality. Ovid was a man of superb intelligence and brilliant rhetorical ability; in his public life he suffered much from envy and malice; he found the company of women congenial and sympathetic; and he had to endure the sorrows of exile. Ovid's main presentation of Ulysses comes in the thirteenth book of his *Metamorphoses*, where he re-tells the story of the contest between Ulysses and Ajax for the arms of Achilles. The poet's rhetorical purpose is clear: he intends to illustrate the recurrent conflict for man's highest praise between men of action and men of counsel—in other words, between brawn and brain—and he does not disguise his own preference for intelligence as personified in Ulysses. In a later poem, the *Tristia*, written after Ovid had been banished by Augustus to the Black Sea, Ovid wrote of Ulysses as a fellow-exile. In his erotic poems he admires Ulysses' amorous successes. Here one can see fore- *Ill. 138* shadowings of a role that the Homeric hero will play much more fully in modern literature—Ulysses the Amorist.

Another highly influential Latin author who described Ulysses was Statius, writing in the first century AD. In his unfinished epic about Achilles, he tells us how Ulysses came to Skyros to enlist Achilles for the Trojan War. Statius' attitude to Ulysses is ambiguous: on the one hand he describes him as 'crafty', 'giving a sidelong glance', 'smiling secretly'; on the other hand he is 'keen', 'sagacious', 'provident'. His

Ill. 139. A striking action-picture of the bringing of the Wooden Horse into Troy on a Roman wall-painting from Pompeii, late first century AD. The dark massed figures in the background suggest the impending disaster.

conduct on the whole is dignified. But on one occasion Statius allows Roman bias against Greek cleverness to colour his narrative. When King Lykomedes gives Ulysses permission to display his fateful gifts (Ulysses is not disguised as a merchant in this version), the poet exclaims:

> Alas, the simple one, too innocent! Those crafty gifts, and all Ulysses' variousness, he little knew!

Virgil has been left to the end of this survey, though chronologically he precedes Horace, Ovid and Statius, because in his *Aeneid* he affected the attitude of medieval Western Europeans towards the Troy Tale more strongly than any other author. Virgil accepted the belief, propagated by Roman writers of the third century BC, that the Romans originated in Troy. Aeneas, the hero of Virgil's great epic, is a Trojan prince from whose son, Iulus, descended the Julian family to which Virgil's patron, Augustus, was attached. By marriage with Lavinia, daughter of King Latinus of Latium (Virgil does not refer to the legend that Latinus was a son of Ulysses), Aeneas became a prince of the Latin people by whom Rome was ultimately founded. So the Romans considered themselves the new Trojans. As such, they regarded the Greeks, the destroyers of Troy, as their hereditary enemies. Naturally, too, Ulysses, the Greek whose Wooden Horse had finally breached the walls, was held to be the arch-enemy of them all.

Ill. 139

Ulysses does not appear personally in Virgil's account of the Sack of Troy in *Aeneid* 2, but he is referred to as 'harsh', 'dreadful', 'the instigator of crimes', 'the descendant of Aeolus' (a reference to the suggestion that the crafty Sisyphos was his father), 'a coiner of smooth talk', and 'a deviser of crimes'. These censures, however, are voiced by enemies of Ulysses and not by the poet himself, who in fact refers sympathetically elsewhere to the sufferings of Ulysses. But the general impression given by the *Aeneid* is that Ulysses was a lying scoundrel.

The opinions of other eminent Romans varied widely. Augustus in a lost tragedy seems to have preferred Ajax as an example for good Romans. The Emperor Caligula, to judge from his description of his great-grandmother as 'a Ulysses in petticoats', did not admire him either. On the other hand, Nero took only Ulysses' statue from a group of Greek heroic figures at Olympia, and Marcus Aurelius and Julian respected Ulysses for his stoicism. The Emperor Hadrian, an enthusiastic philhellene, asked the oracle at Delphi about the birth-place and parentage of Homer, and was told:

> Homer belongs to Ithaca, Telemachos was his father,
> Epicaste, the daughter of Nestor, his mother.

The chief new factor in the Latin phase of the legend of Ulysses is the pro-Trojan feeling fostered by propagandists for the Julian Emperors. This affected the reputation of Ulysses unfavourably all through the medieval period. A second Roman attitude increased this hostility. To the average Roman the ideal hero was a man of grave, stable and inflexible character, like Cato or Regulus. Greek versatility, dexterity, adaptability and ingenuity were regarded as signs of weakness and inferiority. Rome's greatest satirist, Juvenal, in a famous diatribe pilloried the hungry Greeklings who infested the imperial capital. 'A nation of playboys', he scornfully called them. 'Romans, I can't bear a Graecized Rome.' To Juvenal, Greece seemed the homeland of liars— *Graecia mendax*—and he mocked Ulysses' stories in Phaeacia.

A third cause of antipathy towards Ulysses became prevalent in the second century AD, especially in the Latin-speaking regions of Europe. In the post-classical period some enterprising, but second-rate, writers decided that it would be profitable to produce new versions of the Troy Tale in competition with the Homeric poems and the other early Greek epics. In these concoctions (the most celebrated were those of 'Dictys the Cretan' and 'Dares the Phrygian'), the authors depreciated the heroes whom Homer admired and gave prominence to minor figures like the Trojan Troilos, famous after Homer's time for his tragic love for Cressida. As a result of wide belief in their forgeries, the Homeric portrait of Ulysses as a prominent and honoured hero among the Greeks at Troy came to be discredited.

Ills. 140, 141. Opposite: here we have two sections of one of the finest and most comprehensive artistic representations in antiquity of Ulysses' Odyssean adventures, the mural paintings of the Esquiline Villa in Rome, first century BC. In one of them (top), Ulysses and his Companions are being attacked by the Laistrygonians as in *Odyssey* 10:118–23. In the other (bottom), the Laistrygonians attack the ships of Ulysses while he and his Companions try to escape. Only one of Ulysses' twelve ships survived this onslaught.

In general, then, in Western Europe at the end of the pagan Graeco-Roman period, Ulysses' reputation had sunk low. He now bears a triple load of infamy—as the arch-enemy of the Trojan ancestors of the Roman Emperors, as the kind of tricky 'Greekling' that solid Romans despised and as the anti-hero of the latest popular accounts of the fall of Troy.

This villainization of Ulysses is not apparent in the art of the Roman period, except perhaps in a silver bowl to be described later. Indeed most of the artistic presentations of Ulysses in the Roman area, apart from copies of earlier Greek works, are sadly undistinguished. But one superb set of masterpieces deserves particular attention—the magnificent murals from the Esquiline Villa in Rome, painted in the second half of the first century BC. The panels depict dreamlike
Ill. 142
Ills. 140, 141
landscapes from Hades and from the countries of the Cyclopes, of the Laistrygonians, and of Circe. Figures of the various protagonists appear. But in a strange way it is the landscape that dominates each incident—landscapes in which the contours of the hills, promontories, rocks, and trees, have been subtly formalized to suggest the mood of the incident, while scattered figures—a group of nymphs sunning themselves in Circe's island or a giant pursuing a Greek in Laistrygonia—add human footnotes, as it were. The colourings, too, create an atmosphere of mythological timelessness, emblematic of an age when Odyssean adventures were no longer calls to personal emulation and action. Strangely, their nearest equivalent in the whole Ulysses tradition is Pascoli's *Ultimo Viaggio*, to be noticed later.

Masterpieces, too, but quite different in mood and technique, are the well-known figure-paintings from the walls of houses in Pompeii,
Ill. 7
Ill. 6, 144
showing the Sacrifice of Iphigeneia, several versions of the Detection of Achilles, of Ulysses with Circe, and of Ulysses with Penelope. To what extent these are directly copied or adapted from the Greek classical versions of the same themes one cannot tell. (The gravely pensive Penelope in the scene with Ulysses distinctly resembles the
Ill. 124
figure on the Melian relief as already noticed.) But despite their dramatic force they do not add anything significantly new to the characterization of Ulysses.

Following this fashion, Petronius Arbiter in his *Satyricon* makes his *parvenu* Trimalchio have paintings of Ulysses on his walls. A writer who flourished in the third century AD, Philostratos the Younger, has described two paintings of Ulysses. One is on a popular theme, *The Detection of Achilles*. In it, we are told, Ulysses 'being a clever fellow and competent in hunting out secret affairs' keeps his eyes fixed on the ground while, disguised as a merchant, he waits for Achilles to reveal himself. The other painting is described as showing Greeks in grief over a dead comrade. Philostratos says that Ulysses is easily recognizable among them from 'his watchful and rigid expression'.

◀ *Ill. 142.* Opposite: another section of the magnificent Esquiline murals: Ulysses in Hades. The cavernous approach is typical of the superbly atmospheric scenic effects which these masterpieces achieve. The figures matter little: the landscape is hauntingly evocative.

Ill. 143

Ill. 143. A large and remarkable mosaic from the House of Dionysos at Dougga in Tunisia, third century AD. Ulysses and his ship are similar to that in *Ill. 29* and elsewhere, but the Sirens have become partly bird-figures again. A remarkable and perhaps intentionally satirical feature is the interest shown by the Companions in the sea-food displayed by the figure on the left, not in the Sirens.

As Romans grew fonder of Greek-style art another form of interior decoration also became fashionable—floor-mosaics, which were first widely used by Greeks in the Hellenistic period. The adventures of Ulysses begin to occur on these in the early imperial period and are fairly frequent from the third century onwards. Examples have been found in Italy, Sicily, Portugal, North Africa and Israel. Ulysses and his Companions passing the Sirens was a popular subject, perhaps for its allegorical implications. Nine versions of it have been found, including a massive composition of the third century AD from Dougga in Tunisia. Here the temptation offered by the Sirens is not (as in *Odyssey* 12) boundless knowledge, but music, played by the bird-footed trio. But while Ulysses, towering erect over his Companions in the rather puny boat gazes longingly towards them, the Companions are turned in the other direction towards a fisherman who displays a particularly large lobster—perhaps a touch of humour or satire, suitable for a Roman dining-room. Scenes from Ulysses' encounter with the Cyclops also recur. In Nero's Golden House (first century AD) and at Piazza Armerina (third or fourth century) he was to be seen giving wine to the giant, and a later composition now in the National Museum in Rome showed his escape under the ram. A rarer theme— Ulysses being helped by Leukothea—has probably been correctly identified on a second-century mosaic now in the Vatican. The central scene in a mosaic at Hadrumetum (Sousse) shows a variation of the detection of Achilles in Skyros: a companion of Ulysses sounds a trumpet suddenly, and Achilles snatches up the arms which Ulysses has brought. Possibly one of the Antioch mosaics in the House of the Red Pavement at Antioch depicts Ulysses (the face is destroyed) taking Astyanax from Andromache.

A new medium of illustration began in Rome under the early Emperors. This consisted of small marble reliefs portraying scenes from the Homeric poems, sometimes accompanied by quotations from the text (*tabulae Iliacae* and *tabulae Odysseacae*). Ulysses appears here in some scenes from the *Iliad* and on a plaque illustrating all twenty-four books of the *Odyssey*. There is also a fragment called the *tabula Rondanini* depicting the Circe incident. These are rather like modern

Ill. 144. Opposite: a sombrely ▶ impressive Roman wall-painting of Ulysses with Penelope, from Pompeii, first century AD. Penelope seems to be wondering who this stranger is: can it be Ulysses, or is it some trick the gods are playing on her (*Odyssey* 23 : 62–68)? Eurykleia stands expectantly in the shadow on the left.

strip cartoons. The emphasis is on action, not on character, and the artistry is minimal. Their influence was widely felt, even as far as India where the striking Gandhara relief of the Trojan Horse (with Sinon, Laocoön, and a Cassandra in Indian dress), dating from the second half of the second century AD, shows features resembling a *tabula Iliaca*.

These Homeric tablets may have been derived to some extent from Hellenistic illustrated editions of the *Iliad* and *Odyssey*. No fragments of such editions have appeared as yet among the Egyptian papyri, but there is a parchment codex of the *Iliad*, dating probably from the fifth century AD, in the Ambrosian Library in Milan, which has illustrations of Ulysses with Chryseïs, and with Nestor and Diomedes. The most famous and most valuable manuscript of the *Iliad*, the tenth-century Codex Venetus A, is also illustrated, but Ulysses is not portrayed in it. Unfortunately no early illustrated edition of the *Odyssey* has survived.

Also in the early Imperial period, Roman sarcophagi frequently present Ulyssean scenes. Recurrent themes were the detection of Achilles and the encounters with Philoctetes, Polyphemos, Circe and the Sirens, together with the recognition by the dog Argos (now a Roman favourite) and the slaying of the Suitors. As will be noticed

Ill. 146. A drawing of a section from the illustrations to the *Odyssey* on the Roman marble relief acquired by the Marquis Rondanini (now lost). On the lower left (according to the inscription), Hermes gives Ulysses the magic *Moly*-plant; centre right, Ulysses threatens Circe with his sword; top, Circe releases the bewitched Companions.

174

Ills. 145, 147. Opposite: this silver cup from Hoby (a Roman copy of a Greek fifth-century BC work) shows Ulysses (with Neoptolemos behind him) trying to persuade Philoctetes to join the Greeks at Troy (cf. *Ill. 16*). Right: the eccentric version, uncomplimentary to Ulysses, of the Judgement of the Arms of Achilles on the 'Stroganoff bowl' (sixth century AD, from an earlier model). A prim-looking Athena obviously favours the noble-looking Ajax on the left (in contradiction to her usual preference for Ulysses) while an ignoble Ulysses vainly tries to turn her attention to him.

later, Ulysses continued to appear even on Christian sarcophagi for a while.

Graeco-Roman silverware followed the same fashion. Pliny, writing in the first century AD, refers to an embossed base of a silver bowl by the eminent silversmith Pytheas, which portrayed Ulysses and Diomedes stealing the Palladium. It has not survived. Among extant pieces two are specially noteworthy. The fine pair of silver-gilt cups found at Hoby in Denmark (signed Cheirosophos and probably dating from the first century BC) portray Ulysses addressing Philoctetes on Lemnos and asleep among other Greek warriors. The other piece, the 'Stroganoff bowl' (dating from the sixth century AD) presents the judgement between Ulysses and Ajax for the arms of Achilles. A Britannia-like Athena stands in the centre between Ajax and Ulysses. Ajax is a stately, noble figure. Ulysses in contrast is ugly and dressed like a slave. In the heat of his argument he contorts himself upwards in an undignified way and points to an emblematical figure of Persuasion in the sky above him. This looks like an expression of the strong anti-Ulyssean feeling which we have already observed in the literature of the Roman period. As such it is exceptional in both Greek and Roman classical art.

Ill. 145

Ill. 147

175

W. B. Stanford

In our quest for Ulysses, we enter an area of enormous complexity when we follow his career out of the classical periods of Greece and Rome into the Middle Ages. Ulysses now begins to speak in many new languages—Italian, Spanish, French, German, English, Irish and others—and he has to adapt himself to new customs and ideals. The classical tradition survived to some extent in the Greek-speaking parts of Eastern Europe, as will be noticed later. But in the West, now overrun by barbarians, knowledge of Greek disappeared almost completely. Even the Latin writers of the high style like Virgil and Ovid became unintelligible except to scholars. Consequently for a thousand years the Ulysses of popular literature was the despicable, or at any rate dubious, figure of the spurious accounts of the Trojan War concocted by 'Dictys of Crete' and 'Dares the Phrygian'. And the fact that some of the rulers of Western Europe claimed descent from Trojan princes helped to increase chauvinistic prejudice against Ulysses as the destroyer of Troy.

In this period, too, another powerful factor came into play, first for, and then against, Ulysses. The earlier Fathers of the Christian Church on the whole accepted Ulysses as a morally commendable person in so far as any pagan could be so. When they wished to appeal to educated Greeks and Romans in terms of pre-Christian Graeco-Roman literature, they found it useful to point to 'Christian' qualities, so to speak, in some of the famous pagan figures. As pagan philosophers had already seen, the Odyssean adventures of Ulysses offered acceptable analogies for human life viewed as a voyage or a pilgrimage. This was especially true of Ulysses' adventure with the Sirens. Again and again early Christian apologists used this incident as a parable for expounding the value of prudence and wisdom in resisting sensual and lustful temptations (for the Sirens were now generally taken as embodiments of erotic enticement). In such allegorizations Ulysses was seen as 'the wise Ithacan', *sapiens Ithacus*. His name *Ulixes* was ingeniously explained as meaning 'stranger to all things' (because 'true wisdom stands equally aloof from all the things of this world'). Basil of Cappadocia quoted with approval the view that the purpose of Homer's poems was to praise virtue, adding:

Ill. 148. Opposite: this richly elaborate Franco-Flemish tapestry, 1472–4, shows the embassy to Troy to demand the return of Helen before the start of the Trojan War. Three scenes are shown: at the bottom right, Ulysses and Diomedes are at the gates of Troy. On the left side, Ulysses and Diomedes are shown addressing Priam, high on his throne and surrounded by his sons, including Hector, Paris, Deiphobus and Troilus. The presence of Diomedes as an ambassador here is a post-Homeric version of the incident, following an account of the war by 'Dares the Phrygian' and other medieval writers. In the *Iliad*, Menelaos accompanies Ulysses (cf. *Ill. 8*). At the top right of the tapestry there is a separate scene showing Achilles killing Teuthras, king of Mysia, one of Troy's allies (despite the fact that the war had not yet begun).

177

Thus by his story of Odysseus among the Phaeacians . . . the poet seeks to say aloud to mankind, 'Ye men must strive after virtue which swims to land alongside the shipwrecked mariner and makes him who has been washed naked ashore more worthy of honour than the frivolous Phaeacians'.

Others, like Clement of Alexandria and Ambrose, offered similar praise. Often these Christian interpreters followed the Stoics and Neoplatonists in suggesting very far-fetched allegorizations of Odyssean features. For example the plant called *Moly*, which Hermes gave to Ulysses to protect him from Circe's enchantments, was interpreted as the gift of faith, 'a holy physic', and became a favourite topic for writers and artists. So for a while Ulysses became a kind of pre-Christian patriarch almost ranking with Job or Jonah, and fourth-century Christians did not consider it incongruous to bury a fellow-Christian in a sarcophagus depicting Ulysses passing the Sirens.

Ill. 149

But from the fifth century onwards Ulysses gradually disappeared from the mainstream of European art. Personages more acceptable to the Christian ethos took his place, though symbolic representations of Circe and the Sirens occasionally recurred in ecclesiastical sculpture (as, for example, the Circe on the twelfth-century tympanum in the cathedral at Vézelay). Ulysses does not return to prominence in the visual arts until much later. This eclipse was partly due to the fact that the bitter theological controversies that arose between the Eastern and Western Christians in the ninth century, culminating in the Great Schism of 1054, drew the much-suffering Ulysses into their Charybdis-like vortices. Western Catholics began to distrust and dislike the Greeks for ecclesiastical and political reasons. The words 'Greek' and 'Byzantine' came to imply deviousness and perfidy. We have seen already how the pagan Romans tended to despise the Greeks for

Ill. 149. This fourth-century Christian sarcophagus portraying Ulysses and his shipmates as they pass the Sirens (here with bird-like feet) perhaps exemplifies the early Christian admiration for Ulysses as a Pilgrim Man, and possibly alludes to the analogy between Ulysses tied to the mast and Christ on the Cross.

Ill. 150. Drawings from a manuscript of Herrade of Landsberg's *Hortus Deliciarum* (thirteenth century). The two upper scenes show the Companions being bewitched and then seized by angelic-looking Sirens. In the other, 'Duke Ulixes', accoutred in the armour of the period, stands loosely tied to the mast accompanied by another knight, while Companions fend off Sirens.

Ill. 157

ethical weaknesses. Now the Roman Church anathematized Greek ecclesiastics on doctrinal grounds, and some of the *odium ecclesiasticum* seeped into the field of secular literature to contaminate the reputations of Homer and Ulysses.

A new era in the literary career of Ulysses began about 1160 when Benoît de Sainte-Maure produced his *Roman de Troie*. This was the first notable presentation of the Troy Tale in a language other than Greek or Latin. Benoît's title itself is significant in contrast with the conventional title of the last major Latin poem on the Troy theme which appeared about the same time—the *De bello Troiano* of Joseph of Exeter. Though Benoît's word *Roman* did not then imply what our term 'romance' does, it marks a new departure in the wanderings of the Ulysses legend. Ulysses now enters the world of chivalry and knightly love, dressed in the rich court costume or the costly armour of a French prince, and speaking French. Within the next century Germany, Italy and the Netherlands produced their own vernacular translations or adaptations of Benoît's poem, and after that England, Scotland and Spain, and eventually almost all the civilized countries of Europe had versions in their own language.

On the whole the portraits of Ulysses offered in these versions are uncomplimentary. The anti-Ulyssean attitude of Dares and the *Aeneid* prevails. In Benoît's *Roman* Ulysses is an unrivalled trickster, never speaking the truth for a whole day, given to mockery and derision (though he also surpasses everyone in his great beauty and is wonderfully skilled in fine speech). Benoît blames Ulysses for wickedness in the Palamedes and Ajax incidents, and pictures him (following Dictys) as slinking away from the detestation of the other Greek princes. When Benoît goes on to describe Ulysses' Odyssean adventures he shows more respect and liking for him than Dictys did. We see Ulysses loved by his wife and people in joy, peace and happiness, and delighted with his grandson, born to 'Telemacus' and 'Nausica' (that *pucele proz et sage*). Ulysses' death later at the hand of Telegonos is more compassionately described than by Dictys, and Circe mourns Ulysses inconsolably. One gets the general impression that Benoît himself warmed to Ulysses despite the hostility of Dares and Dictys.

It is unnecessary to describe the slight variations on Benoît's portrait of Ulysses to be found in subsequent accounts of the Troy Tale such as *The Gest Hystoriale of the Destruction of Troy* (1287), *The Seege or Batayle of Troye* (early fourteenth century), Lydgate's still delightful *Siege of Troy* (1420), and (the first printed English version) Caxton's pedestrian, but enormously influential, prose *Recuyell of Historyes of Troye* (*c.* 1474). To show how complex the tradition had become by that time one may note that this last work was an adaptation of Raoul Lefèvre's French rendering of Guido delle Colonne's Latin paraphrase of Benoît de Sainte-Maure's amplification of Dares' and Dictys' travesties of the Greek epic narratives of the Troy Tale. On the whole Ulysses appears in an unpleasant light in

179

these versions (and in many others not mentioned here). He is 'falsest in his fare and full of deceit'; he is 'full of wiles and slighty in essays'; he is a disgrace even to the Greek army. But there are some exceptions. John Gower, for example, in his *Confessio amantis* (1393) follows Horace and Ovid in praising Ulysses as a 'worthy knight' and a man of universal knowledge. But, sad to say, he turned to black magic in a desire to discover forbidden knowledge and so was destroyed in the end (according to Gower).

As a result of this revival of interest in the Troy Tale Ulysses gradually came back again into the visual arts of Western Europe. This happened first of all in illustrations to books. Copies of Benoît's book in Britain, France, Spain, Switzerland, and Germany contained notable pictures of Ulysses' exploits at Troy and on his return home. (Some particularly fine examples are in the copy of Lydgate's *Siege of Troy* in the Rylands Library in Manchester.) But Ulysses was not confined to these. His encounter with the Sirens appears in the celebrated *Hortus Deliciarum* (*Garden of Delights*) of Herrade of Landsberg in the second half of the thirteenth century. The same incident,

Ills. 151, 152

Ill. 150

Ills. *151, 152*. Two illustrations from John Lydgate's *Siege of Troy* (1420). In the centre of the first (opposite) Ulysses and Diomedes treacherously kill Palamedes (Ulysses' rival) in a well—the worst crime in Ulysses' record (but not mentioned in Homer). The second (right) shows three scenes from the post-Homeric and medieval version of Ulysses' last days, including an energetic representation of his death at the hand of Telegonos, his son by Circe.

P tciuple mne auc fouffur
ilc doit tes cunanus offur
M ne toy ou cfjcual de fuſt

together with the Cyclops episode, also appears on a magnificently designed page in an illustrated manuscript of Aristotle's *Nicomachean Ethics*. Here he is restored to his former status as an eminent exemplar of prudence. A fifteenth-century copy of Jacques Malet's play, *The Destruction of Troy the Great*, emphasizes a different quality of Ulysses, his prowess as a warrior, in scenes of violence and bloodshed. Many other celebrated medieval works offered further versions, for example several fifteenth-century copies of Christine de Pisan's *Letter of Othea to Hector* (mainly based on Ovid), of Orosius' *History*, of Boccaccio's *De claris mulieribus*, of Boethius' *De consolatione philosophiae* and of Seneca's *Tragedies*.

Ills. 153, 154

These were all small-scale pictures seen only by readers. More popular views of Ulysses' exploits could be seen on *cassoni*, majolica ware, and bread-dishes in the fifteenth century. But Ulysses had more space for displaying his exploits on tapestries, as can be seen on several fine fifteenth-century pieces. Specially rich are two which portray him demanding Helen back from the Trojans, and a pair depicting Ulysses and Penelope separately, where Ulysses is posed on board ship in a rich dress, young-looking, with dreamy, but rather sly, eyes, fondling a pet leopard, and labelled in Latin 'the eloquent Ulysses', while Penelope is at her loom, dreamy-eyed and young, too, and rather

Ills. 148, 155, 156

ingénue. Both have regressed a long way from the mature characters described by Homer.

It is important here, before we consider one of the most remarkable and influential characterizations of Ulysses ever conceived, that a distinction should be made between the medieval attitude to scientific investigation and our own. We in modern times resemble the ancient Greeks in regarding scientific inquiry as being a good thing in itself. We generally accept the principle that scientists should pursue their research and experimentation to the furthest limit of feasibility, though products like the atomic bomb and bacteriological warfare may cause us misgivings. To the conventional man of the Middle Ages, on the contrary, it seemed both wicked and dangerous to pry into the inner secrets of nature and to try to unlock her hidden forces. To do so was to commit the sin of *curiositas*, condemned by Augustine and Thomas Aquinas. Experimental science in those days was chiefly in the dubious hands of alchemists, and the borders between scientific research and the practice of the Black Art were often traversed. That was the main reason why Gower and others ultimately shrank back from Ulysses' insatiable desire for knowledge and branded him as a

Ills. 155, 156. An opulent pair of Franco-Flemish tapestries, 1480–3, portraying 'the eloquent Ulysses' (FACUNDUS ULIXES) dreamily stroking a pet leopard (opposite) and a slightly petulant-looking Penelope at her loom (right) with a Latin pentametric inscription asserting 'I shall always be the wife of Ulysses'.

PENELODE COIVNX SEPER VLIXIS ERO

sorcerer. Eventually the revival of Greek learning and Greek ideals at the Renaissance changed this fear of *curiositas* into admiration and emulation.

We can see the contrast between the medieval and the modern attitudes to intellectual curiosity powerfully expressed in Dante's brief but brilliant portrait of Ulysses in his *Inferno*. Dante, composing his *Divine Comedy* early in the fourteenth century, long before Gower and Lydgate, was predominantly medieval in his theology and philosophy. But his vision of Ulysses in the twenty-sixth canto of the *Inferno* seems to escape for a moment from contemporary disapproval of Ulyssean *curiositas* and to catch a prophetic glimpse of the mood of the coming Renaissance.

In the *Inferno*, Dante comes with Virgil, his guide, to the part of the Malebolge reserved for fraudulent counsellors. The flames that devour these deceivers flash like fireflies in the dark gulf. One flame, strangely cloven at the top, arouses Dante's curiosity. He asks who is in it. Virgil answers that the flame contains Diomedes and Ulysses, who are consumed there eternally for their part in overthrowing Troy where Rome's first ancestors lived. If Dante had seen nothing more than this familiar figure of Latin detestation, he would hardly have evoked his spirit in his visit to Hell; but Dante was apparently not satisfied with this conventional verdict. He relates that a sudden desire seized him to hear Ulysses speak for himself. At his earnest request, Virgil consents to ask Ulysses about his death. Then the taller peak of the ancient flame begins to shudder and murmur. A voice—Ulysses is not named—plunges without greeting or preface into a stark narrative. Ulysses tells a tale never heard before of his last voyage: how, after leaving Circe,

> Not fondness for my son, nor reverence
> Of my old father, nor return of love,
> That should have crown'd Penelope with joy,
> Could overcome in me the zeal I had
> T' explore the world, and search the ways of life,
> Man's evil and his virtue. Forth I sail'd
> Into the deep illimitable main,
> With but one bark, and the small faithful band
> That yet cleav'd to me. . . .
>
> *Inferno* 26 (Cary's translation)

In terse, metallic phrases he describes how he sailed on relentlessly. At length he and his Companions, now old and slow, reached the pillars of Hercules, believed by classical writers to mark the limit of legitimate exploration. There he took his fatal decision. In one of the most famous examples of Ulysses' proverbial eloquence he roused his enfeebled Companions to a last effort:

> O brothers! I began, who to the west
> Through perils without number now have reach'd,

Ill. 157. Opposite: in this arresting illustration in a late fifteenth-century manuscript of Raoul Lefèvre's very popular French version of the medieval Troy Tale, we see three Greeks (perhaps Ulysses, Menelaos and Neoptolemos) inside the Wooden Horse, with the hatch open and a ladder ready for their descent. The horse stands at a breach in the wall beside the Dardanian Gate (*la Porte Dardane*) of a splendidly architectured *Ville de Troie* where (in a development of the episode) some Trojans have been killed by the invading Greeks.

Ill. 158. Perhaps the most voluptu-
ously sensual in an innocent kind of
way of all representations of Circe in
her enchanted forest is this detail of
Circe and her Lovers in a Landscape by
Dosso Dossi in the early sixteenth
century (opposite). The semi-human
face of the creature on the left
implies that it is a bewitched lover.
The other animals look like nature's
work. A curious detail is the book of
magic at the feet of this smooth
Madonna-like Circe.

To this the short remaining watch, that yet
Our senses have to wake, refuse not proof
Of the unpeopled world, following the track
Of Phoebus. Call to mind from whence we sprang:
Ye were not form'd to live the life of brutes,
But virtue to pursue and knowledge high
                    Inferno 26 (Cary's translation)

They sailed on southwards. A dim mysterious mountain appeared in the distance. They were filled with gladness. Suddenly a whirlwind struck the ship and it sank. When Ulysses has finished speaking, his flame becomes 'erect and still'. Without groan, boast, or curse, he moves firmly away. His austere and majestic self-restraint contrasts with the abject lamentations of the fraudulent counsellor who comes next to Dante's view.

This brilliant, but puzzling, episode has caused much speculation and controversy, especially about Dante's personal attitude towards Ulysses. Clearly Dante feels admiration for Ulysses. We can sense this in the superb magniloquence of Ulysses' speech to the Companions with its splendid, ringing call to heroic action. Here, for a moment, Dante transcends the medieval Roman-biased antipathy towards Ulysses and sees him as a superbly heroic figure. For a moment, too, Dante admires his defiant search for dangerous knowledge, his *curiositas*. Ulysses' voice, as Dante gives it life here in the early fourteenth century, speaks prophetically for the spirit of the Renaissance soon to begin in Italy. Nevertheless this Ulysses is left to burn for ever in Hell, both for his traditional guilt as the prime enemy of 'the Roman seed' and because his 'false counsel' led himself and his Companions to their doom. The contrast with Homer's Ulysses is clear. Though he, too, was a man of *curiositas* he respects the will of the gods and he constantly strives to return home: he is homeward-bound, centripetal, dutiful, and pious. Dante's doomed hero is outward-bound, centrifugal, impious; and he is romantic, too, in the sense that the romantic hero ever yearns for new experiences in far-away lands, while the classical spirit endeavours to make the best of normal and familiar life. Dante's conception of Ulysses points on to other ever-questing, ill-fated figures in later sea-tales—the Flying Dutchman and Captain Ahab, for example. We shall see that two of the most vivid embodiments of Ulysses in modern times—those of Tennyson and Kazantzakis—were directly inspired by this new conception.

10

Ulysses from the sixteenth to the nineteenth century

W. B. Stanford

THE revival of Greek studies in the fifteenth century ensured that the Greek writers on the Ulysses theme would be studied again in Western Europe. But, as we have seen, the classical Greek authors were far from being unanimously favourable towards Ulysses. The strictures of Euripides in several of his plays, and of Sophocles in his *Philoctetes*, could not be ignored. However, two favourite Greek writers, Homer and Plutarch, now stood out as strong champions of Ulysses' integrity and nobility. Gradually, under their influence, Ulysses was accepted as a model for wise rulers as well as for prudent voyagers on the journey of life. In England, for example, Sir Thomas Elyot commended 'the witty Ulisses' as a model for monarchs in *The Governour* (1531), addressed to Henry VIII, and so, too, Roger Ashcham, tutor of Elizabeth I, in his *Scholemaster* (1570). Most influential of all was George Chapman in his famous translations of the *Iliad* and *Odyssey* (1598–1615). Chapman adored 'divine Homer' and idolized Ulysses as 'the much-sustaining, patient, heavenly man' and '. . . . the wise and God-observing man.'

The Ulysses of Shakespeare's *Troilus and Cressida* is a much disputed figure. Some quotations will illustrate how the critics have disagreed about him. 'The wily Ulysses, delighting in the caricature of his compeers, is the most ridiculous of the Greek heroes.' 'Ulysses is the real hero of the play, the chief, or at least the great, purpose of which is the utterance of the Ulyssean view of life.' 'Ulysses who is intended to represent the wise man of the play is as trivial of mind as the rest.' 'Shakespeare's Ulysses is a medieval knight of the legend of Troy who has been modernized into a *politique*—but who still retains a Greek touch of concern for "the still and mental parts".' 'The combination of psychological insight, cold malice and artistic gusto with which Ulysses sets out to stir up trouble puts him in a totally different, and lower, camp from perpetrators of crimes of passion, reminding us, in retrospect, of Pandulph . . . and, in prospect, of Iago. . . . As a deranger of degree and fomentor of the very anarchy he pretends to hate, he turns out to be an advance agent of his own Universal Wolf.' 'Ulysses . . . is the much-experienced man of the world, possessed of its highest

◀ *Ill. 159.* Ulysses was a favourite theme on domestic vessels and furniture during the Renaissance. This majolica plate (opposite), probably from the Duchy of Urbino in the last quarter of the sixteenth century, shows Ulysses and Ajax contending for the arms of Achilles, watched by other Greek soldiers. They are dressed in what was then thought to be ancient Greek armour.

and broadest wisdom, which yet always remains worldly wisdom and never rises into the spiritual contemplation of a Prospero. He sees all the unworthiness of human life but will use it for high worldly ends.'

The present writer has presented his own views elsewhere. Here it must suffice to suggest that, despite much criticism, in the play Ulysses is essentially an influence for good, if one accepts that 'law and order' are the essentials of civilized life. His famous discourse on 'degree' in society is as superb in its eloquence as his *orazion picciola* in Dante. Equally splendid in style and argument is his appeal to the angry, fame-intoxicated, love-infatuated Achilles, warning him against inaction and ingratitude. In his dealings with the pitiful Troilus, Ulysses is frank but compassionate. He does indeed use 'the blockish Ajax' as a pawn in an Autolycan piece of deceit. Yet the ultimate impression is that of a man who in a chaotic world of self-centred pseudo-heroes tries to hold things together *pro bono publico*, very much in the manner of Homer's Ulysses in the *Iliad*. An element of trickery and deceit is certainly emphasized in Ulysses' conduct in *Troilus and Cressida*, but in that age of machiavellian statesmanship Shakespeare can hardly have meant it to be seen as particularly damnable.

In other countries besides England one can see a similar conflict between pro-Ulyssean and anti-Ulyssean attitudes. Ulysses found a valiant champion in Germany in the middle of the sixteenth century in the person of Hans Sachs, who wrote several stories and comedies about his Odyssean adventures, with appropriate conclusions or epilogues praising his virtues. For example, when Ulysses is saved from Skylla and Charybdis by clinging to a fig tree, it shows that when men have sinned and God has sent punishment on all, the wise man will not despair but will cling to the sweet fig tree of Hope. Similarly, in his encounters with Circe, Calypso, and the Suitors, Ulysses is seen as an exemplar of steadfastness, wisdom, caution, patience and piety. In France there was a period of admiration for him in the sixteenth and early seventeenth centuries. In 1604 Salomon Certon, in the dedication to his translation of the *Odyssey*, thought it complimentary to compare the career of Henry IV with that of Ulysses. Most memorable of all is Joachim du Bellay's brief but deeply sympathetic evocation of Ulysses in the celebrated sonnet in his *Regrets* (1558) beginning *Heureux qui comme Ulysse*, expressing his own poignant yearning to return from the stately palaces of Rome to *la douceur Angevine* of his native Lyré, in phrases derived directly from the *Odyssey* and Ovid's *Tristia*.

Early in the seventeenth century, French admiration and sympathy for Ulysses began to decline. Three forces were working against him. The first was the natural inclination of the French to side with the Latin heritage against the Greek—an inclination which was strongly stimulated by Scaliger's attack on Greek literature and championship of the Latin style in his *Poetic* of 1561. The second was the influence of Euripides on the French dramatists. Later, a third force became strong.

Ill. 160. Many representations of Ulysses appeared in book illustrations after the invention of printing, especially in editions of plays. Here we have a fantastic version of Ulysses viewing the strange fauna of Circe's island, which appeared in a printing of a play entitled *Ulisse et Circé* by 'Monsieur L.A.D.S.M.' (published in Gherardi's *Théâtre italien*, 5th edn., Vol. III, Amsterdam 1721). Ulysses and Circe are conventional figures of the period, but the animals are an extraordinary menagerie, especially the clown-faced donkey which a maidservant is belabouring.

This was the growing formality of court etiquette. René Rapin in his *Comparaison entre Virgile et Homère* (published in Paris in 1668) denounced Ulysses virulently, his accusations at times quite untrue, as when he alleges that Ulysses let the Phaeacians make him drunk, that he forgot his wife and son while he stayed with 'that prostitute Calypso', and that he let all his Companions perish in order to save his own skin. He sees Ulysses as a congenital liar and deceiver, entirely motivated by self-interest.

Intelligent French critics saw the obvious fallacy in such attacks. René Le Bossu wrote effectively in defence of Ulysses in his *Traité du poème épique*, following Horace and the early Christian Fathers in finding high moral edification in Ulysses' career. So, too, Archbishop Fénelon in his famous *Aventures de Télémaque* (1699), where Ulysses is consistently praised for all the good qualities of an exemplary French prince. Minerva tells Telemachos:

Ills. 161, 162. Two renderings of the Ulysses theme by Francesco Primaticcio, the sixteenth-century artist who designed the enormous series of murals at Fontainebleau, now destroyed. Drawings of it survive, including the tender recognition scene between Ulysses and Penelope (opposite, below). But most striking of all is the strange easel-painting (*c.* 1563) of Ulysses fondling the chin of Penelope's statue-like, calmly meditative head after their reunion in Ithaca (right). No picture ancient or modern better recaptures—but with tantalizing emblematical overtones—Ulysses' quiet joy in contemplating his beautiful long-lost wife after he has recounted his adventures to her (*Odyssey* 23 : 296 ff.).

> Ulysses your father is the wisest of men: his heart is like a deep well, no-one could draw out its secrets. He loves the truth, and never says anything that hurts it. He speaks only what is necessary. Wisdom, like a seal, always keeps his lips closed to any useless word.

Even Homer himself might say that this went too far in praising Ulysses, and others have found this conception of Ulysses as a Bourbon prince rather pretentious, priggish, and even a bore.

Meanwhile the many portraits of Ulysses by French dramatists had been much less commendatory. Here the main influences were those of Euripides and Seneca. Robert Garnier's *La Troade* in 1579 is all on the side of Hecuba and Andromache against Ulysses. When Andromache denounces Ulysses as a perjured, untrustworthy, shameless, fraudulent villain, Ulysses is not given an opportunity to reply, though even Seneca had allowed him that amount of fair play. Similarly, in Racine's *Iphigénie*, Ulysses (as in Rotrou's play on the same theme) appears as a smooth, unscrupulous go-between—perhaps a little less repulsive than Rapin's villain, but still unpleasant. Curiously, twelve years earlier Racine in his *Remarques sur l'Odyssée d'Homère* had expressed a lively admiration for Homer, finding him *un beau caractère d'un esprit fort et résolu,* and *un esprit délicat et fort.*

Spain's richest contribution to the Ulysses tradition also appeared in the seventeenth century—Calderón's interpretations of Ulysses' encounter with Circe in two dazzling dramas: *El major encanto amor*, 1635 ('Love the greatest enchantment') and its Christianized version *Los encantos de la culpa* ('The sorceries of sin'). Following the interpretation of the Stoic philosophers and early Christian Fathers, Calderón presents Ulysses as the Pilgrim Man beset by sensual enticements. In an opalescently rich style and with luxuriantly exotic imagery reminiscent of *the Arabian Nights*, Calderón describes (in the second play) how Sin (i.e. Circe) tempts Ulysses in all his five senses. Ultimately, he survives all allurements and sails away in 'the saving vessel of the sovereign Church', voicing a final curse on 'cruel Circe', to the sound of 'Happy voyage' from an angelic choir.

Calderón's masterpiece presents one feature which other less-gifted authors overdid—the use of the Ulysses legend for theological propaganda. We see an absurdly elaborate development of this propagandist function in a work by Jacobus Hugo. In his *Vera historia Romana* (1655) he argued that the *Iliad, Odyssey* and *Aeneid* were allegorical foreshadowings of post-Tridentine Catholic truth. Thus, in the *Odyssey*, Ulysses represented St. Peter, and Penelope was Mother Church threatened by wicked Reformers in the guise of Suitors. Telemachos, who prefigures the Pope, duly protects Mother

Ills. *163–165*. Opposite and above: two lunettes by Annibale Carracci in the Camerino Farnese, Rome, showing a queenly Circe receiving a handsome young Ulysses accompanied by Hermes (not the Homeric version), and the ship of Ulysses passing the rock of the Sirens. Note the skulls and bones of former victims (bottom left) mentioned in *Odyssey* 12:45–6. Below: *The Trojan Horse*, a fresco by Giulio Romano in the Ducal Palace, Mantua.

Church until St. Peter returns and triumphantly slays the heretics. An earlier example of the same kind of extravaganza had previously appeared in the Netherlands. Joost van den Vondel in his *Palamedes*, or *Murdered Innocence* (1625) had portrayed Ulysses as a wicked Calvinist. Protestant writers, on the other hand, tended to be more on Ulysses' side (as we have seen already in Ascham's and Chapman's work).

Ulysses' fortunes went through similar vicissitudes in other national literatures after the Renaissance. Each nation tended to present him as an exemplar of its own heroic ideals. For example, Portuguese writers like Gabriel Pereira de Castro in his *Ulyssea* (1636) portrayed him as a forerunner of their own intrepid explorers Vasco da Gama and Magellan. (There was a tradition in Portugal that Lisbon was founded by Ulysses.) But these nationalistic versions of the tradition produced no major reincarnation of the ever-changing hero.

Ill. 160

By the middle of the sixteenth century Ulysses had become a very common figure in European art. He continued to appear in tapestry-work. For example a Franco-Flemish work (*c.* 1515–25) presents four scenes from Ulysses' life: his feigned madness to avoid enlistment for the Trojan War, his detection of Achilles in Skyros, his embassy to

Ills. 166, 167. Two contrasting portrayals of Ulysses scenes by Pellegrino Tibaldi, both from the former Palazzo Poggi (now the University) in Bologna (see pp. 202, 203 and *Ills. 1, 34*). Opposite, below: the tremendous Polyphemos being blinded by Ulysses (clambering on a rock, not as in *Odyssey* 9). To the left of the Cyclops are the remains of Companions whom he has devoured and on the lower right are his club and pan-pipes (suggesting the later representations of the Cyclops, in Theocritos and other Hellenistic writers, as a pastoral swain in love with the nymph Galatea). The other, much more elegant composition (right) shows a rarely depicted scene: the sea-nymph Leukothea saves Ulysses from drowning when his raft is being shipwrecked (*Odyssey* 5: 333–51) by giving him her unsinkable head-veil.

Ill. 165

Priam, and his theft of the Palladium. Florentine weavers also executed a 'history' of Ulysses, and there are other versions of his adventures in England, Madrid and Stockholm. Rubens designed a set of eight pieces on Achilles and Ulysses for Brussels weavers, and in France, Simon Vouet produced a series of paintings about Ulysses for the Hôtel de Bullion in Paris which were reproduced on tapestries now to be seen in the Château de Cheverny. The sacrifice of Iphigeneia, which generally included Ulysses among the participants, remained a popular theme, as in the Gobelins set designed by Antoine and Charles Coypel and in the Beauvais tapestry designed by Desoria in 1792.

It was in the middle of the sixteenth century that Francis I of France commissioned what was perhaps the most elaborate series of pictures of Ulysses that the world has ever seen. Francis, probably prompted by knowledge of earlier frescoes about Ulysses and the Trojan War in Italian palaces (such as Pordenone's in Ferrara and Giulio Romano's in the Ducal Palace in Mantua) ordered a stupendous Ulysses Gallery for his new palace at Fontainebleau. The gallery extended for almost one hundred and fifty yards and displayed fifty-eight scenes, each measuring eight feet by six, from the life of Ulysses. They began with the embarkation of the Greeks after the fall of Troy and ended with a representation of Ulysses receiving the homage of his subjects in Ithaca after his victory over the Suitors. Unhappily the Gallery was subsequently destroyed. Luckily, however, a pupil of Rubens, Theodoor van Thulden, published a set of engravings of the frescoes,

Ills. 168–170. It was Pintoricchio who produced the first of the more celebrated Renaissance paintings of Ulysses—this picture of Penelope at her loom, first presented as a fresco in 1509 and later transferred to canvas (above). Telemachos, in the centre, has apparently just returned from his journey in search of his father. He comes eagerly towards Penelope (whose expression is rather reserved). The three male figures behind him may be Suitors of Penelope. Ulysses disguised as a beggar, stands in a doorway to the right. Through the window one can see two events in his wanderings: the encounters with the Sirens (the three are in the water) and with Circe (on the promontory). Opposite: two versions of the meeting of Ulysses and Nausikaä. Above is Rubens' conception of the scene (only the figures are his: the landscape is by Lukas van Uden): a queenly Nausikaä on the right greets the naked Ulysses, while her handmaidens crouch away behind her in terror and others on the left re-load the wagon for return. Below: Pieter Lastman's more romantic version (1609) in which a John-the-Baptist-like Ulysses supplicates a more juvenile princess.

which, although inferior work, give a fair idea of the originals. A few other drawings and engravings of individual scenes are also extant. The chief artists were Francesco Primaticcio, who drafted the original designs, and Niccolo dell' Abbate of Modena, who added some original work of his own. (The exact extent of their work is uncertain, and assistants were also employed.) Primaticcio also included a representation of Ulysses in his designs for the four great wardrobes in the King's Closet at Fontainebleau. Here various heroes of antiquity were paired with the four cardinal virtues. Ulysses, as usual, went with Prudence. (A drawing of this survives in the Louvre.)

Ill. 161

Fortunately one masterpiece by Primaticcio on the Ulysses theme has survived—his exquisite easel-painting of Ulysses recounting his adventures to Penelope after their reunion. Superb delicacy, tenderness, and subtlety of gesture, combined with manneristic distinction, make this one of the most memorable compositions in the whole pictorial tradition. Since it is an adaptation from one of the scenes in the Ulysses Gallery, we can sadly estimate from it how great the total effect of all Primaticcio's work there must have been. (A drawing by Rubens of Primaticcio's *Ulysses meeting the shade of Teiresias in Hades* has also been preserved.)

Ill. 162

There were several other impressive mural-paintings of the Ithacan hero and his adventures, such as those by G. B. Castello in Bergamo, Stradano in Florence, and Annibale Carracci in Rome. Tibaldi's series in the University of Bologna are particularly evocative in his highly manneristic style. In his version of the stealing of the Cattle of the Sun, for example, there is an unforgettably eerie and foreboding

Ills. 163, 164
Ills. 1, 34, 166, 167

Ill. 171. One of two versions by Nicolas Poussin of the often-painted detection of Achilles on Skyros, *c.* 1656 (cf. *Ill. 6*). On the left Achilles reveals himself by trying on the helmet and sword instead of the trinkets that attract the genuine princesses. Probably the figure close behind him restraining his companion is Ulysses. The satyr-figure behind Achilles adds a touch of Renaissance irony.

Ill. 172. A tremendous conception of the building of the Trojan Horse, by Tiepolo *c.* 1760. While Greek workmen toil vigorously at the white effigy, the two figures watching on the left are presumably Ulysses, its planner, and Epeios, who supervised the construction (*Odyssey* 8:493) with the help of Athena. If the city in the background is Troy, the Trojan watchmen must have been singularly unobservant.

Ill. 168

look in the wide staring eyes of the Companion in the left foreground and of the cow (or ox) on the right: all the horror of the events to follow is suggested there. His version of *Ulysses and the Cyclops* suggests the enormous size of Polyphemos very effectively and puts a macabre heap of human bones beside him. Tibaldi's series contained one rarely depicted scene—the sea-nymph Leukothea saving Ulysses' life before he reached Phaeacia. Here Ulysses lies prone on his raft gazing up at Leukothea (not Calypso, as sometimes suggested) while she, bending towards him, gives him the head-veil which will save him from the storm. Poseidon looms angrily in the background. In the eighteenth century, the most remarkable Ulysses frescoes are those of Tiepolo in the Villa Valmarana, based on incidents in the *Iliad* and the *Aeneid*.

Ulysses is such a common figure in easel-paintings in the sixteenth, seventeenth, and eighteenth centuries that a full description of them would take many pages. We can mention only a few. The earliest of the more celebrated works is an imaginative composition by Pintoricchio in 1509. But, as it happens, Ulysses is not one of the outstanding figures in it. Pintoricchio, still under the influence of medieval romance, preferred to give prominence to a dashing young Telemachos and a winsome Penelope. Scenes by other painters were mostly taken from Ovid and the Troy Tale, but, exceptionally, Niccolo Giolfino chose the Ulysses of Dante's *Inferno*. Some incidents became positively hackneyed. Over seventy versions of *Achilles in*

Skyros have been listed (e.g. by Domenico Corvi, G. B. Pittoni, Rubens, Tibaldi, Van Dyck, and two versions by Poussin), over forty of the Circe episode (e.g. by de Bray, Dosso Dossi, Bernardino Nocchi and J. Tengnagel), and fifteen with Nausikaä (e.g. by P. Lastman, C. Moeyaert, Guido Reni, Rubens and P. C. van Aalst). Other recurrent themes were Ulysses' pretended madness, the killing of Astyanax, the adventures with Polyphemos, Aiolos, the Sirens, and Calypso, and his return to Penelope. More unusual were Claude's *Ulysses returning Chryseïs to her father*, L. Giordano's *Ulysses ploughing in Ithaca*, and M. Preti's *Ulysses taking Astyanax from Andromache*. Pittoni and Corvi revived a favourite theme of classical antiquity with their renderings of *The sacrifice of Polyxena*. Ulysses is not the dominant figure in all of these, and, as is to be expected in major works of art, the artists are frequently more concerned with formal or scenic aspects of their subjects rather than with portraiture or characterization. But undeniably the artists of the Renaissance and later found frequent stimulus in the subtle and adventurous Ulysses.

Ill. 171
Ill. 158
Ills. 169, 170
Ill. 174

Early in the eighteenth century, in England, Alexander Pope's very popular translations of the *Iliad* and *Odyssey* did much to strengthen Ulysses' reputation as an admirable hero. Despite the strict standards of poetic decorum that prevailed in his time, Pope rejected the censures on Ulysses' unorthodox conduct by critics like Rapin and the Alexandrian scholars. Instead of judging the manners and morals of Ithaca by those of Versailles or Windsor, Pope made a genuine effort to understand them in the perspective of their own era on the principle of *autres temps, autres mœurs*. His footnotes frequently defend Ulysses from charges of immodesty or incivility and they show a sensitive and well-informed appreciation of the nuances of Ulysses' character and conduct.

Another celebrated writer of the early eighteenth century discussed Ulysses philosophically and scientifically. Giambattista Vico in his *Scienza Nuova* (1725) employed the long-established method of interpreting the Homeric poems allegorically. But while the Christian Fathers and the pagan philosophers had concerned themselves chiefly with moral or divine questions, Vico, a rationalist, took the view that these poems were allegories of political and economic developments. For example, when Ulysses 'strings up the Suitors like thrushes in a net' it means that 'Ulysses binds them to cultivate the fields . . . just as Coriolanus sought to reduce the plebeians who were not satisfied with the agrarian law of Servius Tullius.' Similarly he explains the stories of Circe and the Sirens as portraying 'the politics of the heroic cities' and as emblems of the struggle between the plebeians and patricians. His interpretations are full of inaccuracies and absurdities. But he illustrates how varied the uses of the allegorical approach to Ulysses could be, and he helped to stimulate the imagination of James Joyce later.

Ill. 173. Opposite: a detail showing the crowded ship of Ulysses from Turner's tempestuous canvas *Ulysses deriding Polyphemos* (1829), one of the most dramatic pieces in the whole artistic tradition. Ulysses, dressed in scarlet and standing on the poop of his ship, shouts his defiance at the shadowy figure of the Cyclops above the cliff (as in *Odyssey* 9:491 ff.). Some of the Companions try to prevent him from this foolhardy action. Others amidships (addressed by an urgent figure with arms raised) are trying to row away as fast as they can. Others unfurl the sails. Sea-nymphs at the bows help to speed the ship onward.

Vico was typical of eighteenth-century rationalism. Later in that century a writer more famous than either Pope or Vico adopted a different approach. In 1770 Goethe began to study Homer in the Greek. He fell deeply under the influence of Ulysses' personality. Goethe admired Ulysses' freedom of action, his fixity of purpose, his all-pervading alertness and his intelligence. He found it convenient, too, in his infidelities to Christiane, to remember how Ulysses had yielded to the divine charms of Circe and Calypso while remaining ultimately faithful to Penelope. In 1786 Goethe began work on a tragedy to be called *Ulysses in Phaeacia*. In contrast with Homer's story, here Nausikaä would fall passionately in love with the handsome stranger and eventually would kill herself when she discovered that he was married and determined to return home. Ulysses and Nausikaä were to represent the *Urmenschen*, the unspoilt, uninhibited primal humanity that Goethe believed he had found in the Homeric poems. But the world order would be revealed as being inhumane: inhumane in the daemonic power of attraction in Ulysses' character; inhumane in the love that would drive the girl to destruction. Eventually Goethe lost interest in the theme—the outline of his plot and a few fragments have been preserved—and never finished it. (Subsequently several other German writers tried to complete it with small success.) After Goethe, Heine in his North Sea poems saw himself as a storm-tossed wanderer like Ulysses, but he did not create a full portrait of the hero.

To return to England: in 1808 Charles Lamb published an unpretentious little book, *The adventures of Ulysses*. Based on Chapman's translation and notes, it recaptured some of that element of mystical and moralistic allegory which eighteenth-century rationalism had made unfashionable. When his publisher objected to breaches of decorum in Homer's narrative, Lamb stoutly replied*:

> If you want a book which is not occasionally to shock, you should not have thought of a tale so full of anthropophagi and wonders. I cannot alter these things without enervating the book, and I will not alter them, if the penalty should be that you and all the London booksellers should refuse it.

In the outcome, Lamb's book remained a favourite for the best part of a century and directly inspired Joyce's *Ulysses*.

The growing romanticism of the early decades of the nineteenth century found an idol in Byron. As a writer, Byron himself never attempted a full portrait of Ulysses, perhaps because Ulysses' attachment to his wife and homeland were antipathetic to him. But we can see something of the Byronic mood in the next great reincarnation of Ulysses—that by Tennyson. Tennyson, after the death of his friend Arthur Hallam, wrote his magnificent lyrical monologue *Ulysses*. It expressed, as he said himself, 'the need of going forward and braving the struggle of life, perhaps more simply than anything in *In Memoriam*'. Within its seventy lines *Ulysses* is a poem of remarkably

*From *Letters of Charles Lamb,* ed. E. V. Lucas, London 1912, pp. 403–6.

Ill. 174. Opposite: Claude Lorrain exercised his talent for depicting classical scenery in this thoroughly anachronistic but finely composed picture of a rather rare scene in the artistic presentations of Ulysses, namely, his mission to return Chryseïs to her father Chryses, the priest of Apollo. It was Agamemnon's taking of Chryseïs as his concubine that caused the plague sent by Apollo as described in *Iliad* 1: 8 ff.; and it was when Agamemnon seized Achilles' concubine Briseïs in her place that the fateful wrath of Achilles began.

Ills. 175–177. Above: Bouchardon's dramatic conception of the scene in *Odyssey* 11:23 ff., where Ulysses evokes the spirit of the prophet Teiresias in Hades. The artist has followed Homer in many details. On the right are the bodies of animals sacrificed to the Dead, and behind them stand Companions who helped in the sacrifice. In the centre Ulysses wards off a crowd of unnamed ghosts with his bronze sword, to allow the ghost of Teiresias (crouching with his prophet's staff) to drink from the pool of blood that will give him strength to prophesy. The two works by Henry Fuseli are equally powerful. The pen and watercolour drawing (below) illustrates the scene in *Odyssey* 22 when Ulysses slaughters the Suitors mercilessly. His tremendous bow has never been more powerfully represented. Beside him stands Telemachos, spear in hand, while the Suitors sprawl back over the banqueting table. Fuseli's painting (opposite) presents a Goya-like image of a favourite theme in early Greek art, but uncommon in the later tradition, Ulysses' escape from the Cyclops under the ram.

varied moods. Ulysses has now, it seems, been at home in Ithaca for some time after his return. At first he shows a peevish discontent with normal life, a craving for sensational adventures abroad, and an egotistic feeling that people do not truly understand him, which belong to nineteenth-century romanticism rather than to any period in the classical tradition. But gradually the heroic temper reasserts itself. He remembers his exploits at Troy before his wanderings. Then the influence of Dante's great embodiment of the hero asserts itself, and in the end we see this new-world Ulysses setting off on his voyages again,

> To follow knowledge like a sinking star
> Beyond the utmost bound of human thought,

and determined

> To strive, to seek, to fight, and not to yield.

Ill. 178. Ingres' nobly conceived representation of a frequent subject, the embassy to Achilles (cf. *Ills. 11, 113, 114*). On the left is Achilles, holding the lyre that he plays to soothe his wrath as in *Iliad* 9:194, accompanied by young Patroklos (posed with a suitable 'Grecian bend'), faced by Ulysses (in the centre) with the massive-limbed Ajax and the old Phoenix who have come to persuade him to accept honourable amends from Agamemnon.

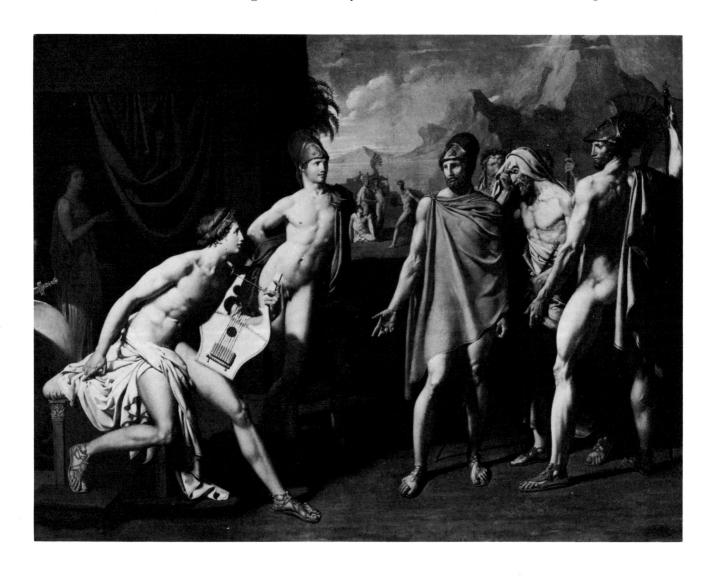

Ill. 179. A Pre-Raphaelite Circe by Edward Burne-Jones. Dark-eyed, she mixes her magic potion watched by two of her animals, while the ships of Ulysses approach on the right.

By this time a drastic change had come over the presentation of figures from antiquity in the visual arts as a consequence of Winckelmann's *Reflections on the painting and sculpture of the Greeks* (1755) and his *History of the art of antiquity* (1764). Artists now tried to present figures from the ancient world—and frequently Ulysses—in what were believed to be the costumes of their time rather than in modern or idealized dress. Much of the resulting neo-classicism was jejune, as Diderot scathingly indicated in his *Salons* of 1759–71. (But Diderot favourably noticed Bouchardon's vivid and imaginative conception of Ulysses among the ghosts in Hades.) We see this tendency clearly in John Flaxman's celebrated illustrations to the *Odyssey* in *Ill. 175* 1793, which now seem too smooth and pallid. One would think that they belonged to a totally different world from Fuseli's powerful and even horrific interpretations of similar scenes, especially his *Escape* *Ills. 176, 177* *from Polyphemos* and *The slaying of the Suitors*. A few other artists also rose above the conventionally classical or neo-classical norms. Ingres *Ill. 178* made memorable compositions from Ulysses' embassy to Achilles, as well as from his encounters with the Phaeacians and with Eurykleia.

Turner's *Ulysses deriding Polyphemos* (1829) is a masterpiece of atmospheric romanticism, but Ulysses himself is a negligible figure. A few other compositions out of very many may be briefly mentioned: a bust of Ulysses by David and a model of *Ulysses receiving the armour of Achilles* by Thorwaldsen; paintings by Angelica Kauffmann, Gustave Moreau, Etienne Garnier, the two Böcklins, William Etty, and Samuel Palmer. Wedgwood pottery made Ulysses familiar to many families in England with a design by Joseph Wright of Derby entitled *Ulysses and the young Telemachos.*

One nineteenth-century painter seems to have been unusually captivated by the idea of Ulysses. This was Friedrich Preller of Germany. A visit to Southern Italy in 1830 inspired him to paint seven Odyssean landscapes. He followed these in 1856–60 with sixteen compositions on the same theme. Besides the more commonly presented scenes with the Cyclops, Circe, Nausikaä and the Phaeacians, these included Ulysses' departure from Troy, his battle with the Cicones, his visit to the Underworld and his meetings with Eumaios and Laërtes. Preller produced a third series of woodcuts on the Ulysses theme in the 1870s. But they failed to win fame.

Ill. 180. William Etty, an adept in female nudes, has moved the three Sirens to the forefront of this arm-wavy painting. Below them is the Homeric heap of bones augmented with the not yet putrescent corpse of a recent victim. Behind, Ulysses quite understandably makes muscular efforts to break his bonds. His Companions are presumably blind as well as deaf.

11   Ulysses in modern times

W. B. Stanford

PERHAPS the least Homeric, but yet one of the most beautiful, of all versions of the Ulysses legend emerged in the *Ultimo Viaggio* or 'Last Voyage' by Giovanni Pascoli in 1904. In the opening scene of this poem, Ulysses—like Tennyson's Ulysses at first—feels the centrifugal longings of Dante's doomed hero. But he has lost his moral strength and energy. We see him sitting drowsily at his fireside in Ithaca waiting for the gentle death prophesied by Teiresias in *Odyssey* 11. But death delays, and Ulysses' feeling of loneliness and futility increases as the years slip by. His halls have no banquets or music now. As he sits brooding, Penelope watches him and, sensing danger in his reveries, tries to revive loving memories of the past. She fails. At last Ulysses decides to leave Ithaca. He seeks out his old Companions—a non-Homeric detail this, since in the *Odyssey* all of them perished before he returned to Ithaca—and addresses them with a mild and gentle eloquence quite unlike his vigorous Odyssean style. He tells them that he is like the sea, varicoloured and changeful, and speaks of his yearning to visit again Calypso's violet-covered island and the other wonderful lands of his Odyssean voyages. Eventually they set sail and first come to Circe's island. They find nothing, none of its past wonders—only the rustling of the leaves in the forest and far away the everlasting music of the sea. Next they come to the land of the Cyclops. There, too, they find nothing to revive their former deeds of heroism. In the same way they visit the Sirens, the Lotos-eaters, the Laistrygonians, the Land of the Dead, the Cattle of the Sun, the Wandering Rocks, Skylla and Charybdis, without danger and without adventure, as if those monsters were no more than the wispy fantasies of an opium dream. The feeling of futility and emptiness increases with each episode in the voyage. In the end Ulysses is drowned. His body floats ashore on Calypso's island. She shrouds it in the cloud of her flowing hair, while a mysterious cry is heard announcing that the best fate for man is total annihilation. The poem's all pervading mood of disillusionment and pessimism—and in the end, nihilism—entirely contradicts the spirit of Dante's and Tennyson's poems about Ulysses.

Pascoli's conception of Ulysses was not unchallenged by other Italian writers. Arturo Graf, prompted by Dante, Tennyson and Pascoli (and also by an Italian treatise comparing Dante's Ulysses with Christopher Columbus), described how a dynamic Ulysses sailed across the Atlantic and discovered the New World. In even stronger contrast, Gabriele d'Annunzio presented a Ulysses who blended the self-assertiveness of a Nietzschean superman with the bombastic arrogance of a proto-Fascist. He defies Fate and the gods and the normal restraints on human conduct alike—all for the sake of self-glorification. Neither Christianity nor humanity must stand in the way of his triumphant progress. All in all d'Annunzio sounds the brassiest and most bombastic note in the Ulysses tradition, ancient and modern. His way of praising Ulysses could be more damaging to Ulysses' reputation than any of Euripides' or Rapin's censures.

So far in this chapter we have been considering only poets. In 1890 two celebrated prose writers, H. Rider Haggard and Andrew Lang, collaborated in a novel about Ulysses called *The World's Desire*. Here, Ulysses has the remarkable experience of meeting Moses and the Children of Israel; and before he dies he becomes involved with the Spirit of Primeval Evil. The 'world's desire' which he seeks is the supreme manifestation of spiritual beauty that only Helen of Troy can provide. A vague pseudo-mysticism and a diluted eighteen-ninetyish eroticism pervade the whole work. Emile Gebhart's *Dernières aventures du divin Ulysse* (1902) was curiously like Pascoli's *Ultimo Viaggio* in its narrative. But its tone is harsh, sardonic, cruel and embittered. In the end Ulysses is killed by Telegonos (who is portrayed as a sinister, sadistic youth) under a mass of tottering masonry. Other prose-writers' versions of Ulyssean themes were sentimental (like J. W. Mackail's *Love's Looking-Glass* in 1891, and L. S. Amery's *Last voyage of Ulysses* in 1934), or cynical (like Leon Feuchtwanger's *Odysseus and the Sirens* in 1949), or sordid (like Jean Giono's *Naissance de l'Odyssée* in 1938), or erotic (like Eyvind Johnson's *Strändernas Svall* in 1946), or science-fictional (like A. C. Clarke's *2001: a space Odyssey* in 1968, also filmed).

During the same period the potentialities of Ulysses for dramatic purposes were not neglected. Robert Bridges faithfully, but rather flatly, portrayed the Iliadic Ulysses in his *Achilles in Skyros* (1890) and the Odyssean in his *Return of Ulysses* (1890). *Ulysses* by Stephen Phillips (1902) gained some reputation for a while. Its Ulysses is more subservient to feminine influence than elsewhere, and the erotic element is strong in several scenes. But these works, and many others which need not to be recalled, failed to make any major contribution to the Ulysses legend. Nor need we delay to examine the various ways in which Ulysses was used as a lay figure for political satire, as in Ugo Foscolo's play, *Ajax* (1811), in which Ulysses represents General Fouché; Ajax, General Moreau; Agamemnon, Napoleon; and Calchas, Pope Pius VII; or André Gide's dramatic dialogue, *Philoctète*,

Ill. 181. Opposite: a scene in the performance of Monteverdi's *Il ritorno d'Ulisse in patria* performed at the Glyndebourne Festival in 1972 and 1973. Ulysses, disguised as a beggar after his return to Ithaca, listens to the melodious address of a cosily armoured Athena. Athena's expression admirably catches that spirit of intimate geniality towards Ulysses—unique between an Olympian divinity and a mortal in the Homeric poems—that Homer subtly conveys in their conversation in *Odyssey* 13:287 ff. (but there Athena is not wearing armour).

in which Ulysses represents the injustice of the French towards Dreyfus; or a squib called *Ulysses-up-to-date* (1923) in which Ulysses carries all the odious stigmata of Lloyd George.

More original were two plays written early in the present century: Stanislaw Wyspianski's *Powrót Odysa* or 'Return of Odysseus' (1907) and Gerhart Hauptmann's *Der Bogen des Odysseus* or 'Bow of Odysseus' (1912). In the first play the effect of Freudian psychology is clearly perceptible. Ulysses is hag-ridden by feelings of guilt and remorse—in fact, a typical Oedipus-figure, which is certainly not justified in the classical legend. In the second, Hauptmann re-enacts the Odyssean episodes in which Ulysses is disguised as a beggar. This Ulysses is a strange mixture of demonic power and grotesque idiocy. At times he raves like a Teutonic *Urmensch*. In the end, after a brilliantly contrived series of encounters, he slaughters the Suitors and regains his kingdom. But Penelope means little or nothing to him.

Ulysses returned to a more conventional atmosphere in a sparklingly witty play by the French dramatist Giraudoux, *La guerre de Troie n'aura pas lieu* (1935). Its subject is the Greek embassy to Troy demanding Helen back before the outbreak of war. He appears first as an ambassador among a group of leading Trojans. His manner is forthright and brusque, but not disagreeable. A salty Homeric humour and an unusual candour of phrase make it clear that this is neither the discreet

Ills. 182, 183. A comic *Odyssey* again in art after over two thousand years (see *Ills. 120–122*): two lithographs by Honoré Daumier in *Charivari*, 1842 (from the *Histoire Ancienne* series). Left: Penelope dreams of her absent husband (not in the way she dreams in *Odyssey* 19:535 ff.). Right: a caricature of the reunion of Ulysses and Penelope (contrast *Ill. 162*).

Ill. 184. Opposite: an illustration by ▶ Henry Moore to Edward Sackville-West's melodrama for broadcasting, *The Rescue*. An unusual picture both stylistically, with its statuesque yet spectral figures, and in theme: Phemios (the bard of Ithaca) conversing with Telemachos, who holds a spear (and a distinctly non-Homeric temple in the background).

216

negotiator nor the callous power-politician. In the next scene Ulysses remains alone with Hector. Each with an intuitive confidence in the other speaks frankly of himself and his motives. Hector describes himself as a figure of young manhood, devoted to his young wife and to the child that is to be born. His is *la joie de vivre, la confiance de vivre, l'élan vers ce qui est juste et naturel*. Ulysses in reply characterizes himself as *l'homme adulte*, devoted to a thirty-year-old wife and a growing son, valuing *la volupté de vivre et la méfiance de la vie*. They continue in a kind of confessional litany: Hector stands for *la chasse, le courage, la fidélité, l'amour*; Ulysses for *la circonspection devant les dieux*—a notable, though possibly ironical, reference to his long-forgotten Homeric piety—*les hommes et les choses*. Hector compares himself to a Phrygian oak and a falcon who stares into the sun; Ulysses chooses the symbolism of the olive tree and the owl. In the end Hector admits that he feels unequal to Ulysses.

Out of many subsequent dramatizations of the Ulysses theme—at present almost every year produces a new variation—one may pick out the recent opera *Ulysses* by Luigi Dallapiccola (first performed in 1968). Here Ulysses' main motivation in his Odyssean adventures is a search for his own identity and for the key to the mystery of life. His name in the Cyclops incident, 'No-man', becomes a symbol of his doubts about who he really is. He searches for the answers in his encounters with Calypso, Nausikaä, Circe, Antikleia and Penelope. In the end he sails away again from Ithaca. Alone in a small boat he is granted a prophetic vision of the Christian God which satisfies his questionings and makes him feel lonely no longer. Dallapiccola was familiar, when he was writing this opera, with the Ulysses of Dante, Tennyson and Joyce, and had strong memories of a film entitled *The Odyssey of Homer* produced in Italy by Giuseppe de Liguoro. Dallapiccola's Ulysses is notable as a re-creation of the god-befriended hero of the Homeric poems. But the Homeric hero was pious by nature: Dallapiccola's hero only reaches his knowledge of God after agonizing doubts and uncertainties—a symbol of modern man's quest for faith.

The fact that Dallapiccola had previously studied Monteverdi's opera *Il ritorno d'Ulisse in patria* (1641) is a reminder that Ulysses has made several other appearances in the musical world. An opera about his adventures with Circe was composed by G. Zamponi in 1650. He appeared in Handel's *Deidamia* in 1739 and in the Iphigeneia operas by Scarlatti and Gluck. Other muscians have composed works about his encounters with Nausikaä and Circe, his return to Ithaca and his death at the hands of his son, Telegonos.

In contrast with the extraordinary activity of writers on the Ulysses theme in these last hundred years, artists seem to have become rather less attracted by it. Perhaps Honoré Daumier's comic lithographs of

218

Ill. 185. Picasso's image of the Sirens. A central round-faced being (is she Parthenope, Ligeia, or Leukosia: who can tell?) has her equally round mouth wide open, presumably in full song. Her body merges, in mermaid fashion, into a fish's tail. (Mermaids and Sirens are often interchanged in the later tradition.) Below her on the right is the dark mask-like face of one of her sisters. The older, bird-nature of the Sirens is suggested by the creature on the left. In the background are hints of Ulysses and the mast of his ship.

Ill. 181

Ills. 182, 183

Penelope and Ulysses for *Charivari* in 1842 indicated a feeling among artists that the classical heroic themes had become too hackneyed for serious treatment. At any rate twentieth-century artists on the whole preferred to interpret themes more adaptable to symbolical and

Ill. 185
Ill. 186

Ill. 188

psycho-analytical interpretation, though Picasso's triptych *Ulysses and the Sirens*, Dali's *Return of Ulysses* and Braque's highly formalized *Ulysses and Circe* are notable exceptions, together with Chagall's brilliant large-scale mosaic for the Faculty of Law and Economics of the University of Nice in 1968. This last-mentioned work presents Ulysses as 'the Mediterranean hero of intelligence' in nine scenes based on the *Odyssey*, including his reunion with Penelope in their nuptial bed and his death in Ithaca (as prophesied by Teiresias). Here Chagall rejects the Dantesque and Tennysonian conception of Ulysses as dying far from his home, and follows the Homeric tradition with one significant innovation: among the visions of the past that come to Ulysses as he dies is a figure, which could be an angel or a siren, with arms extended as on a crucifix. Among more conventional twentieth-century presentations are a pale *Ulysses and Nausikaä* by the Russian painter V. A. Serov the Elder, Russell Flint's *Ulysses in Hades* and *Ulysses slaying the Suitors*, and Bryson Burrough's *Calypso's island*.

Ill. 186. Salavador Dali's brush and pen drawing (with ink-blots) of the *Return of Ulysses* suggests something of the quality of the Esquiline murals with its emphasis on mysterious scenery (cf. *Ills. 140–142*).

Book-illustrations have evoked some noteworthy portraits of Ulysses by eminent artists—Henry Moore, for example, in Edward Sackville-West's *The Rescue* (a melodrama based on the *Odyssey*) and the Greek artist Ghika in the English version of Kazantzakis' *Odyssey*. Among recent illustrators of Homer's *Odyssey* four deserve special mention: Rudolf Kock (1931), André François (1947), Buckland Wright (1948) and Henri Laurens (1952).

Ills. 190, 191
Ill. 184

Ills. 192–194

Ulysses has also appeared as the leading character in films. The most ambitious screening of the *Odyssey* as yet was the Italian production by Dino de Laurentis in 1954, with Kirk Douglas as a rather less than princely Ulysses and Silvana Mangano doubling the parts of a voluptuous Circe and a modest Penelope (which was intended to be psychologically significant). Joseph Strick directed a film version of Joyce's *Ulysses* in 1966, with Milo O'Shea and Barbara Jefford in the leading roles. But despite talented acting it was hardly equal to Joyce's masterpiece.

Joyce's *Ulysses* and its only modern rival in scope and scale, Kazantzakis' *Odyssey*, now remain to be considered. These offer by far the fullest and most detailed presentations of Ulysses in existence, much fuller even than Homer's. (The account of Ulysses in the *Iliad* and *Odyssey* amounts to about 100,000 words, Joyce's to over 250,000, Kazantzakis' to over 330,000 in its English translation by Kimon Friar.) They are remarkable, too, in the candour and fairness of their portraits of Ulysses. As we have seen, most of the post-Homeric writers generally presented a partisan view of Ulysses, either as an out-and-out villain or as an admirably prudent hero. In Joyce and Kazantzakis we find both his virtues and his faults fully displayed and explored to a depth quite unparalleled in any of the earlier tradition. Perhaps no other ancient hero has been so fully and elaborately reincarnated in modern times as in these books by an Irish and a Greek author.

James Joyce was introduced to the story of Ulysses through an edition of Lamb's *Adventures of Ulysses*, which was set as a textbook for an examination in 1894. Joyce himself wrote:*

> I was twelve years old when I studied the Trojan War, but the story of Ulysses alone remained in my recollection. It was the mysticism that pleased me.

What he meant here by 'mysticism', apparently, was the allegorical implication of the *Odyssey* which Lamb had derived from Chapman's translation. His *Ulysses*, published in 1922, was the portentous sequel to his juvenile studies. In the meantime Joyce had read the presentations of Ulysses by Virgil, Ovid, Dante, Shakespeare, Racine, Fénelon, Tennyson, Phillips, d'Annunzio and Hauptmann, besides works by Bérard and Samuel Butler on the authorship and geography of the *Odyssey*.

*Quoted in Herbert Gorman, *James Joyce*, London 1941.

Ill. 187. Opposite: Bryson Burrough's *Calypso's Island* makes Calypso appear bored with life and with Ulysses in a way that Homer certainly does not imply in *Odyssey* 5. Perhaps the mood is more a comment on the world of 1928 (when the picture was painted) than an attempt to re-create the heroic age. The figure of Ulysses resembles several in the earlier artistic tradition (cf. *Ills. 112, 126*), but he seems even more dejected now than formerly.

Both in form and content *Ulysses* is intended to be understood as something much more than a naturalistic (and at times expressionistic) novel of modern city life. As its chief characters, Dedalus and Bloom, make their ultimately converging ways through the streets of Dublin, they re-enact the experiences of Telemachos and Odysseus among modern equivalents of Odyssean places and characters. Lotosland now centres on a Turkish bath, Hades on a suburban cemetery; Nestor has become a tedious schoolmaster, Circe a brothel-keeper. Sometimes the Odyssean order is dislocated or telescoped, and sometimes the analogies are rather far-fetched. But Joyce kept the parellelism constantly in mind, both as a structural model and as a symbolic undertone.

In presenting the Homeric aspects of his hero Joyce concentrates attention mainly on Bloom's Odyssean adventures and characteristics. But some Iliadic qualities are also noticed. Bloom, though thwarted by his social condition from any prominence in politics, is not without secret ambitions to excel as a *politique*. In his delirium in Nighttown, he sees himself as 'Alderman Sir Leo Bloom', later to be the popular Lord Mayor of Dublin. In the final catechism before his return to his wife it is revealed that if he were given a chance he would try to be a genuine political and social reformer:

> because at the turning-point of human existence he desired to amend many social conditions, the product of inequality and avarice and international animosity.

He had thought deeply on justice and on what Shakespeare's Ulysses calls 'degree'. He had loved rectitude from his earliest youth. Schemes for increasing Ireland's wealth and prosperity abound in his fertile brain. But in his more realistic moments he knows he will never be a national leader. The best use he can, and does, make of his sagacity and tact is to pacify and moderate the passions and follies of his bourgeois associates.

Similarly, though an ordinary citizen of Dublin had little opportunity to show the martial valour of an Iliadic hero, Bloom, given an opportunity, can be as brave in conflict and as loyal to a Companion as Homer's Ulysses. In the incident at Barney Kiernan's public house (a modern Cyclops' cave where an uncouth nationalist represents Polyphemos), Bloom defends the Jews with firm courage, standing alone in a circle of wrathful enemies as staunchly as Odysseus in the *Iliad*. Later, protecting Dedalus as he lies helpless on the street, Bloom shows himself to be a worthy successor to the hero who fought so stubborn a rearguard action over the body of Achilles in the *Aithiopis*. Other qualities of Homer's hero are to be found in Bloom—prudence ('Gob, he's a prudent member and no mistake'), caution ('Mr Cautious Calmer'), wiliness, resourcefulness, tactfulness, self-control, skill in negotiation, intellectual and manual versatility, endurance, emotional resilience. Bloom also has a strong element of eroticism in his

Ill. 188. Opposite: part of a brilliant ▶ mosaic by Chagall in the Faculty of Law of the University of Nice. Above we see Ulysses and his Companions sailing past the Sirens. (The Siren plunging downwards on the left is doubtless taken from *Ill. 33.*) They are half-angelic, half-birdlike figures. Ulysses strangely holds a winged creature in his arms. Below is the death of Ulysses in the presence of (perhaps) Penelope, Telemachos, Athena and the dog Argos. The most remarkable feature is the winged being on the left whose outstretched arms, as on a cross, suggest an archangelic or even a Christian welcome for Ulysses' soul. Contrast *Ill. 143.*

character. Far from romanticizing this as some of his immediate predecessors had done, Joyce makes it sordid for the most part. He reduces the Nausikaä incident, so delicately and charmingly presented in *Odyssey* 6, to a parody of novelettish sentimentality and furtive autoeroticism. His treatment of Calypso is only a little less repulsive. His adaptation of the Circe episode reaches a degree of phantasmagorical hideousness unrivalled in the whole tradition. Yet one feels that Joyce is not savagely and rancorously satirizing Bloom's unheroic love-affairs in the manner of a Juvenal or a Swift. Joyce has compassion for his unheroic hero, and neither condemns nor mocks him. Nor does he moralize about him. Bloom feels no guilt or remorse for his amorous infidelities towards his equally unfaithful Penelope. His only restraint is prudence, that primordial quality of Ulysses.

Joyce found one element in Homer's *Odyssey* thoroughly distasteful. He hated all kinds of physical violence. So he sought a less sanguinary climax to his novel than Ulysses' ruthless slaughter of the Suitors in *Odyssey* 22 (though Homer, as we have seen, modified the savagery of that incident by making Ulysses refuse to exult over the carnage). Joyce's problem, then, was how to make Bloom triumph over his wife's paramour without resorting to violence. He solved it ingeniously by substituting a psychological victory for the physical one. Bloom overcomes the suspicions, jealousies and fears in his own heart by—to use Joyce's own terms—'abnegation' and 'equanimity' (Stoic virtues, these), and by recognizing

> the futility of triumph or protest or vindication: the inanity of extolled virtue: the lethargy of nescient matter: the apathy of the stars.

In this way Bloom, when he returns to his humble Ithaca in 7 Eccles Street, Dublin, achieves peace of mind and even a vestigial happiness as he unrancorously kisses his faithless Penelope and falls asleep.

It should be remembered that Joyce's Ulysses has none of the traditional piety of Homer's Ulysses to sustain him in his trials and sufferings. He is no longer the god-fearing, god-beloved hero of the *Odyssey*. Bloom, originally a Jew, then vaguely Protestant and Catholic in turn, is now an agnostic atheist. He is not interested in God, nor—so far as Joyce's indications go—is God interested in him. Without a patron goddess like Athena to protect and encourage him, he (like Joyce estranged from the Church of his ancestors) has to battle his way through all the difficulties of a long summer day in a hostile city entirely on his own resources.

This is the chief difference between the character of Joyce's hero and Homer's. Otherwise they have much in common—notably intellectual curiosity ('Mister Knowall') and exilic yearnings for a faraway home (in Bloom's case the New Jerusalem of the Zionist), besides the characteristics already noted. One quality, hinted at but not emphasized in Homer, becomes especially prominent at the end of

Ill. 191

Ill. 189. Opposite: the right-hand side of a not very imaginative version of *Ulysses and Circe* by the French artist André Bauchant in 1942. The Circe episode has probably been the most widely popular of all the Odyssean themes, combining as it does mystery, magic and sexuality, and offering a rich field for allegorical interpretation.

Ulysses—the loneliness of the hero. When Dedalus finally leaves him, Bloom feels a 'lonechill' like

> the cold of interstellar space, thousands of degrees below freezing point, or the absolute zero of Fahrenheit, Centigrade or Réaumur.

Here Joyce no doubt expresses some of the loneliness that he himself felt in exile from Ireland and perhaps, too, something of the *De profundis* of Everyman in face of the dehumanization of life in the scientific age.

All-in-all, Joyce's Leopold Bloom stands out as one of the supreme reincarnations of Ulysses. Here in *Ulysses*, for the first time since Homer, we have a full and balanced presentation of the many-sided hero, portrayed not as a villain or an ideal hero but as a sympathetic Everyman, and an enterprising Citizen of the World, who meets the

Ills. 190, 191. Two masterly drawings by Matisse to illustrate a limited edition of Joyce's *Ulysses* in 1935. Above: a virile Cyclops, seated (as in *Ills. 22, 44*), receives the stake of a faceless Ulysses into his wide, hair-embowered eye. His distorted right thigh skilfully suggests his huge dimensions. Opposite: Nausikaä, here presented with two handmaidens (much braver than in *Odyssey 6*) on each side (linked in the conventional pattern for the Three Graces), is supplicated by Ulysses. The economy of line is fully matched by the economy of clothing.

226

trials of life with courage and resourcefulness. The externals of Bloom's Odyssey are un-epic and anti-heroic. But his mind and spirit have not lost their ancient fire.

The second of the two vast modern portraits of Ulysses is *The Odyssey* published by Nikos Kazantzakis in 1938. (He had previously produced a play about the return of Ulysses in 1928.) Other modern Greek poets, notably Seferis and Cavafy, have written subtle and nostalgic lyrics about the Greekest of the Greek heroes. But they are minuscule compared with Kazantzakis' enormous poem. Here, Ulysses sets off again on the most extensive travels of his whole career, ever outward-bound, from Ithaca through Crete, Egypt, Africa and the Far East to the South Pole. In the opening scenes Ulysses, having killed the Suitors and regained his kingdom, begins to feel discontented (like Tennyson's Ulysses) with his quiet life in his island home. He chooses new Companions, gets drunk with them and sacks his own palace. Soon he sails off, leaving Telemachos (now married to Nausikaä) to rule Ithaca. He goes to Sparta where he finds Helen still beautiful and restless, but Menelaos flabby and complacent. He tries to rekindle the heroic flame in Menelaos. He fails. In disgust Ulysses takes Helen away from him. They sail off together to Crete. *Ill. 192*

At this point one might think that Kazantzakis was about to write a romantic or erotic narrative like Rider Haggard's *World's Desire*. But it is not so. Kazantzakis himself has explained that Ulysses had no erotic motive when he took Helen away with him from Sparta: he intended to use her as a new Wooden Horse for the destruction of the decadent Cretan civilization. In fact she was only one of the many stages in his outward-bound journey.

After a storm at sea Ulysses and Helen come to Crete (the native *Ill. 193* island of Kazantzakis himself). They meet King Minos and witness a bull-spectacle. When a host of invading Dorians approaches, Ulysses helps them (as he had done at Sparta) to unite with the local proletariat and set up a new dynasty in Crete. Leaving Helen there, Ulysses sails on to Egypt, where he finds a third example of a decaying civilization. (Kazantzakis emphasizes this motif in the earlier part of his work, influenced presumably by Marxism as elsewhere in his writings.) He joins the revolutionaries, is imprisoned, escapes, and, like another Moses, leads a band of freedom-loving spirits across the desert. As he presses southwards, his Companions follow wearily like the toiling shipmates of Dante's questing hero.

Meanwhile Ulysses has grown conscious of increasing loneliness (like Joyce's Bloom). Now he leaves his comrades and climbs a mountain alone. At the summit he adopts the posture of an oriental mystic, immerses himself in austere meditation, ascends the scale of mystical enlightenment, rising above all mundane concepts—the Ego, Race, Mankind, and the Earth itself—and experiences a dazzling vision of the universe. Three earlier hero-strivers appear—Tantalos, Herakles and Prometheus. Finally God comes in the form of an old tramp, bent down, chewing a lump of bread, exhausted and out of breath from climbing the mountain. God is tired, lonely and frightened. Ulysses decides to help him by founding an ideal city in the desert.

In these episodes one can see two traditional characteristics of Ulysses—his political ability and his piety. But they are changed. In politics this Ulysses—so far—is a revolutionary idealist in the Marxian mode, hoping to create a Utopia on earth, and not a pragmatic opportunist as in the earlier tradition. His piety, too, is no longer conventional and easy-going as in Homer, but questioning and ascetic. (Kazantzakis himself spent some time in the practice of mystical asceticism among the Orthodox communities on Mount Athos.) Eventually his conception of God becomes so rarefied that he is virtually a pantheist.

After his paradoxical vision of the Deity, Ulysses formulates his own creed. It emphasizes God's dependence on man and man's duty to love not only mankind, but animals and plants and the whole of creation. Its last maxim is:

The greatest virtue on earth is, not to become free,
but to seek freedom in a ruthless, sleepless strife.

This devotion to freedom, so characteristic of the Greeks ancient and modern, remains the dominant motive of the whole poem. Ultimately, as Kazantzakis saw, total freedom means total solitude and total separation from God and man. At this time, however, Ulysses is still concerned with the welfare of his fellow man. He founds his New *Ill. 194* Jerusalem. It is a totally communistic Utopia. Shortly after the elaborate ceremony of inauguration a volcano erupts and destroys it. A few inhabitants survive to seek another ideal city elsewhere. Ulysses is left alone, his hair now snow-white as a result of the catastrophe. After this he ceases to concern himself with others, seeking, instead, self-knowledge and self-conquest in the manner of an Indian Yogi.

A richly imaginative series of adventures follows, each a step forward on the ascent to mystical enlightenment. Ulysses encounters sages, princes, priests, courtesans, artists and symbolical figures (like 'Lord One', a lonely, pathetic warrior reminiscent of Don Quixote), and learns in various ways from them. He turns southwards towards the frozen wastes of the Antarctic. He reaches the last limit of mankind, the terrible twin rocks of Yes and No. He sails resolutely between them and finds that they are ordinary cliffs inhabited by seabirds. Now the sun—a dominant symbol of life and joy all through the poem—grows weak. Intense cold begins. Death appears, looking like a mirror-image of Ulysses himself, now old and weak. Ulysses welcomes him as a long-expected friend.

Ulysses prepares to die. He has a vision of his past life. Symbolical figures offer him conventional salvation. This he refuses. He says

Ills. 192–194. Three fine drawings by the Greek artist Ghika, to illustrate Kimon Friar's translation of *The Odyssey* by Nikos Kazantzakis, a sequel to Homer's *Odyssey*. Opposite: **the beautiful Helen of Sparta (and Troy) is observed by one of** Ulysses' sailors while Ulysses himself, uninterested, steers the ship away from Greece. Above left: Ulysses (bottom left) glumly watches Helen's coquetries with the Minotaur. Above right: Ulysses contemplates the building of his Utopian city in Egypt.

farewell to his spiritual ancestors, his personal friends and Companions, to all animals, to the elements, to his senses and mind, and last of all—ironically perhaps—to his dog Argos who welcomed him so poignantly on his return to Ithaca. A man's best friend, it seems, is his dog. Temptations come to him in various forms. He resists. Enigmatically a little negro boy appears, perhaps embodying the temptation of life itself (with a suggestion of the primeval African element in Kazantzakis' heritage). Ulysses laughs and talks playfully with him for a while. ('Be cheerful', *chairete*, has always been the traditional Greek form of farewell.) The last words of the poem are:

> Then flesh dissolved, glances congealed, the heart's pulse stopped,
> and the great mind leapt to the peak of its holy freedom,
> fluttered with empty wings, then upright through the air
> soared high and freed itself from its last cage, its freedom.
> All things like frail mist scattered till but one brave cry
> for a brief moment hung in the calm benighted waters:
> "Forward, my lads, sail on, for Death's breeze blows in
> a fair wind."

Joyce's *Ulysses* and Kazantzakis' *Odyssey* portrayed more fully and elaborately than ever before the two main contrasting conceptions of

Ulysses in the post-Homeric tradition—the home-seeker and the home-deserter. Since then many other writers have offered new interpretations of this ever-challenging theme in poems, plays, novels and critical studies. We end our quest for Ulysses in the literary world here, not because the story is over, but because in the writings of this Irish novelist and this Greek poet, two major phases in Ulysses' unending odyssey have reached a fitting conclusion. The Irish homeward-bound wanderer, Leopold Bloom, is now at rest beside his Penelope in a quiet terrace house, and the neo-Greek Ulysses, valuing freedom above all things, has died with a cheerful word on his lips in the desolate icefields of Antarctica. Where his next major reincarnation will lead him, who can say?

Conclusion

W. B. Stanford

OUR quest for Ulysses has led us through some three thousand years and from Ithaca to the North and South Poles. Historically, it would appear that an Achaean prince of Western Greece, born and bred in the island now called Itháki, and named something like *Oulixes* or *Odysseus*, won renown among the commanders in the Trojan War for his exceptional intelligence and resourcefulness. After his death folklore added to his exploits, and traditional stories about Wily Lads and Jack-the-giant-killers were attached to his name. He was also credited with wanderings comparable to those of the Argonauts, which in turn were embellished with material drawn from memories of the period of migrations after the Trojan War and from the experiences of early merchant-seamen and colonists. Probably towards the end of the eighth century BC—five hundred years or so after the Sack of Troy—a great poet, Homer, composed one of his two major poems about Odysseus and portrayed him as an eminent figure in the other. Out of the traditional material, the genius of Homer created a complex and subtle character in which fact and fiction, history and legend, were fused with elements from the poet's own creative imagination to make a vivid new personality destined to be remembered in every subsequent era of European literature.

We have seen too, that recent archaeological discoveries have helped us to recognize authentic features of Bronze Age Greek civilization in Homer's descriptions of the world of Ulysses. Now that so much of the long lost Mycenaean period has been rediscovered, many features of the *Odyssey*, which were once regarded as poetic fictions, can be better understood in their historical and geographical perspectives. We will indeed never, as one sceptical Greek commentator on Homeric geography remarked, find the cobbler who stitched the bag of the winds for Aiolos, but we can now in all probability see some of the palaces that Ulysses could have visited in his day, and we can trace the trade-routes which may have provided material for Homer's account of Ulysses' wanderings.

Perhaps most fascinating of all is the personality who emerges first in the *Iliad* and the *Odyssey* and is still a living figure in contemporary thought. Homer clearly admired Ulysses, though he did not disguise what we have called his Autolycan heredity—his trickiness and at times deceitfulness. Subsequent writers for the most part found it impossible to maintain the ethical equilibrium of Homer's attitude. With a few exceptions they presented Ulysses either as a villain or a public benefactor, a rogue or a noble hero, a liar or a lofty philosopher. This was the nemesis of his supreme quality, cleverness, that neutral quality which can be used with equal facility for good or evil purposes. To some extent Ulysses is like a chameleon in his literary career, taking his colour from the mind and mood of each writer who re-creates him; yet despite all his changes he continues to be distinctively himself.

In art the tradition has been less full of sharp contrasts. Artists are usually more concerned with aesthetic effects than with ethical interpretations. They revelled in Ulysses' variegated adventures as subjects for pictorial representations, but they rarely added significantly to his characterization, though sometimes they emphasized the comic or tragic or sinister aspects of his exploits. In other words, the artistic tradition is almost entirely illustrative of Ulysses' literary career rather than creative in extending it. They took some traditional episode, explored its dramatic and ethical implications, constructed a satisfying art-form out of it—and that was artistically all they desired. From time to time memorable portraits of Ulysses have been produced, but no major artist seems to have felt such strong personal empathy towards Ulysses as, for example, writers like Euripides or Dante or Tennyson or Joyce, all of whom drastically altered and adapted the traditional legend to express their own feelings.

On the other hand, as the illustrations in this book will, it is hoped, demonstrate, the visual arts have deepened our understanding of Ulysses' personality and adventures. As in so much of the Ulysses tradition, while the manners and costume vary drastically, the essence of 'the man of many devices' and of his associates remains unchanged. It may be noted, too, that on the whole the practitioners of the visual arts have rarely presented Ulysses as so villainous a type as many writers from the fifth century BC downwards portrayed him. Artists have generally been content to depict his skilful stratagems and his tempestuous adventures without moralistic prejudice or political bias. In this way the artists are closer to the open-minded spirit of Homer in the *Iliad* and the *Odyssey* than were most of his literary successors.

So in a very remarkable way the word used by Homer in the first line of the *Odyssey* has been true in almost every one of the twenty-seven centuries since that poem was composed—*polytropos*, 'the man of many turns'. Turn by turn in every epoch he has been adapted to the currently fashionable type of wise or clever man—a Sophist in fifth-century Athens and a power-politician during the Peloponnesian War; a polished orator in Rome; an emblem of a prudent Everyman among pagan philosophers and early Christians; a magician in the Middle Ages; an example of statesmanship in the sixteenth century; a

Catholic in Spain and a Protestant in England; and so on to James Joyce's alert and sensitive canvasser for advertisements in twentieth-century Dublin. Among romanticists he becomes a romantic, among Stoics a Stoic, among amorists an amorist, among wanderers a wanderer. Always the adaptable man, he has sometimes been presented as a mere opportunist. But at his best—in Homer and Sophocles as in Dante and Kazantzakis—he shows a courage and firmness of purpose that are wholly admirable. That is why several writers in times of personal despondency have found an emblem of hope and encouragement in him.

Finally there is the sheer vitality of his personality as a constant source of inspiration for writers and artists alike—and even for imaginative scientists, too, as when the command module of the lunar exploration spacecraft, Apollo 13, in 1970 was named *Odyssey* (and there is an *Odysseus* among the minor planets). Every year Ulysses is re-created in some book, or play, or film, or painting, or statue, not as a mere figure of antiquity but as a contemporary personality. In fact the quest for Ulysses is essentially a quest for a deeper understanding of man's ever-voyaging indomitable spirit. It will never be concluded as long as there are writers and artists and scientists and thinkers who share in the aim of Tennyson's Ulysses:

> To strive, to seek, to find, and not to yield.

The final paradox, then, is that though Ulysses goes back so far into the earliest epoch of European civilization, he remains an emblem of things to come, more so than any other hero of antiquity. As the Greek Kazantzakis has expressed it—and who better qualified in our time to understand 'the Greekest of the Greeks'?—Ulysses always looks forward, not back; he 'goes on ceaselessly, his neck stretched forward like the leader of birds migrating'.

Bibliography

Abbreviations

AJA = *American Journal of Archaeology*

AJP = *American Journal of Philology*

BCH = *Bullétin de Corréspondence Hellenique*

BICS = *Bulletin of the Institute of Classical Studies* (London University)

BSA = *Annual of the British School at Athens*

CP = *Classical Philology*

CQ = *Classical Quarterly*

CR = *Classical Review*

HSCP = *Harvard Studies in Classical Philology*

JHS = *Journal of Hellenic Studies*

Chapters *1, 2, 7–11*

HISTORY AND LITERATURE

Altenburg, F. W. *Ulixes qualis ab Homero in Odyssea descriptus sit,* Schleusingen 1837.

Antin, P. 'Les Sirènes et Ulysse dans l'œuvre de Saint Jérôme', *Revue des Études Latines* XXXIX (1961): 232–41.

Audisio, G. *Ulysse ou l'intelligence,* Paris 1954.

Bartlett, P. B. 'The heroes of Chapman's Homer', *Review of English Studies* XVII (1941): 257–80.

Bertoni, G. 'Ulisse nella "Divina Commedia" e nei poeti moderni', *Arcadia* XIV, Vols. V–VI n.s. (1931): 19–31.

Bonet, J. P. *Homero en España,* Barcelona 1953.

Bradley, E. A. 'The hybris of Odysseus', *Soundings* LI (1968): 33–44.

Broche, G. E. *Examen des remarques de Racine sur l'Odyssée d'Homère,* Paris 1946.

Budgen, F. *James Joyce and the making of Ulysses,* London 1934.

Buffière, F. *Les mythes d'Homère et la pensée grecque,* Paris 1956.

Cesareo, P. 'L'evoluzione storica del carattere d'Ulisse', *Rivista di Storia Antica* III (1898): 75–102; IV (1899): 17–38, 383–412.

Clarke, H. 'Homer and Mikiewicz: *Pan Tadeusz* and the Odyssean heritage,' *Indiana Slavic Studies* III (1959): 7–25.

Croiset, M. 'Observations sur la légende primitive d'Ulysse', *Mémoires de l'Institut National de France, Académie des inscriptions et belles lettres* XXXVIII 2 (1911): 171–214.

Daremberg-Saglio. *See* Séchan.

Davaux, Jean. 'Etudes sur le personnage d'Ulysse dans la littérature grecque d'Homère à Sophocle', unpublished thesis, Louvain 1946.

Dimock, G. B. 'The name of Odysseus', *The Hudson Review* IX (1956): 52–76.

Dunger, H. *Die Sage von trojanischen Kriege in den Bearbeitungen des Mittelalters und ihren antiken Quellen,* Leipzig 1869.

Finley, M. I. *The world of Odysseus,* London 1956.

Finsler, G. *Homer in der Neuzeit von Dante bis Goethe,* Berlin 1912.

Friedrich, H. 'Dante und die Antike Odysseus in der Hölle', *Gymnasium* LXXIII (1966): 9–26.

Fries, C. *Studien zur Odyssee,* Vol. I, 'Das Zagmukfest auf Siberia', Vol. II, 'Odysseus der Bhikshu', Leipzig 1910, 1911.

Garassino, A. 'Ulisse nel teatro greco', *Athene et Roma* X (1930): 219–51.

Gaude, P. *Das Odysseusthema in der neuen deutschen Literatur, besonders bei Hauptmann und Lienhard,* Halle 1916.

Gemser, B. 'Odysseus-Utnapistim', *Archiv f. Orientforschung* III (1926): fasc. 5–6, 134–6.

Germain, G. *Genèse de l'Odyssée,* Paris 1954.

Gilbert, S. *James Joyce's Ulysses,* London 1952.

Glaser, E. 'The Odyssean adventures in Gabriel Pereira de Castro's *Ulyssea*', *Bullétin des Études Portugaises* n.s. XXIV (1963): 25–75.

Grégoire, H. 'Euripide, Ulysse et Alcibiade', *Bullétin de la classe des lettres, Acad. Roy. Belgique* XIX (1933): 83–106.

Guthrie, W. K. C. 'Odysseus in the *Ajax*', *Greece and Rome* XLVII (1947): 115–119.

Hackmann, O. *Die Polyphemesage in der Volksüberliefung,* Helsingfors 1904.

Harsh, P. W. 'Penelope and Odysseus in *Odyssey* XIX', *AJP* LXXI (1950): 1–21.

Hart, W. M. 'High comedy in the *Odyssey*', *University of California Publications in Classical Philology* XII (1943): 263–8.

Hartlaube, G. F. 'Der gotische Odysseus', *Antaios* III (1962): 412–60.

Hartmann, A. *Untersuchungen über die Sage vom Tod des Odysseus,* Munich 1917.

Havelock, E. A. 'Parmenides and Odysseus', *Harvard Studies in Classical Philology* LXIII (1958): 133–43.

Houben, J. A. *Qualem Homerus in Odyssea finxerit Ulixem,* Trier 1856, 1860; *Qualem Homerus in Iliade finxerit Ulixem,* Trier 1869.

Hugo, J. *Origo Italiae ac Romae ad hanc diem ignota,* Rome 1655.

Hunger, G. 'Die Odysseusgestalt in Odyssee und Ilias', dissertation, Kiel 1962.

Hunger, H. *Lexikon der griechischen und römischen Mythologie,* Vienna 1953.

Joyce, James. *Ulysses,* 2nd ed., London 1960.

Kazantzakis, Nikos. *The Odyssey: a modern sequel,* translated by Kimon Friar, London and New York 1958.

Kettner, G. *Goethes Nausikäa,* Berlin 1912.

Knight, D. *Pope and the heroic tradition,* New Haven 1951.

Kretschmar, O. *Beiträge zur Characteristik des homerischen Odysseus,* Trier 1963.

Lessing, E. *The voyages of Ulysses,* London 1966.

Loiseau, A. 'La légende d'Ulysse dans la littérature portugaise', *Revue de la Société des Études Historiques* LI (1885): 469–74.

Lord, G. de F. *Homeric renaissance: The Odyssey of George Chapman,* London 1956.

Mahaffy, J. P. 'The degradation of Ulysses in Greek literature', *Hermathena* I (1874): 265–75.

Marcowitz, G. *Ulixis ingenium quale et Homerus finxerit et tragici,* Dusseldorf 1854.

Martorana, M. *Ulisse nella letteratura Latina,* Palermo and Rome 1926.

Masqueray, P. 'Agamemnon, Ménélas, Ulysse, dans Euripide', *Revue des Études Anciennes* VI (1904): 171–204.

Matzig, R. B. *Odysseus. Studie zu antiken Stoffen in der modernen Literatur, besonders im Drama,* St Gall 1949.

Menrad, J. *Der Urmythus der Odyssee und seine dichterische Erneuerung,* London 1910.

Meyer, E. 'Der Ursprung des Odysseus Mythus', *Hermes* XXX (1895): 241–73.

Müller, H. *Odysseus, Mann, Seele, und Schicksal,* 2nd ed., Chemnitz 1932.

Osterwald, K. W. *Hermes–Odysseus,* Halle 1853.

Paetz, B. *Kirke und Odysseus. Uberlieferung und Deutung von Homer bis Calderon,* Berlin 1970.

Page, D. L. *The Homeric Odyssey,* Oxford 1953.

Pauly-Wissowa-Kroll. *See* Wüst.

Philippson, Paula. 'Die vorhomerische und die homerische Gestalt des Odysseus', *Museum Helveticum* IV (1949): 8–22.

Phillips, E. D. 'The comic Odysseus', *Greece and Rome* n.s. VI (1959): 58–67.

Prevelakis, Pandelis. *Nikos Kazantzakis and his Odyssey,* translated by P. Sherrard, New York 1962.

Radermacher, L. 'Die Enzählungen der Odyssee', *Sitzungsberichte d. Kaiserl. Akad. in Wien, Phil-hist. Kl.* CLXXVII (1916): 3–59.

Rahner, H. *Greek myths and Christian mystery,* translated by B. Battershaw, London 1963.

Reinhardt, K. 'Die Abenteuer der Odyssee', *Tradition und Geist* (Gottingen 1960): 47 ff.

Roehrich, L. 'Die mittelalterlichen Redaktionen des Polyphem-Märchens und ihr Verhaltnis zur ausserhomrischen Tradition', *Fabula* V (1962): 48–71.

Roscher, W. H. *See* Schmidt.

Rossi, M. M. 'Dante's conception of Ulysses', *Italica* XXX (1953): 193–202.

Schmidt, J. 'Ulixes posthomericus', *Berliner Studien* II (1885): 403–90; 'De Ulixe in fabulis satyricis persona', *Commentationes Ribbeckianae* (Leipzig 1888): 99–114; 'Ulixes comicus', *Jahrbücher für class. Phil.,* Suppl. Vol. (1888): 361 ff.

Schmidt, J. 'Odysseus in der bildenden Kunst', in W. H. Roscher, *Ausführliches Lexikon der griechischen und römischen Mythologie* III (Leipzig 1902): 602–81.

Schreyer, E. *Das Fortleben homerischer Gestalten in Goethes Dichtung,* Gütersloh 1893.

Scott, J. A. 'Inferno XXVI: Dante's Ulysses', *Lettere Italiane* XXIII (1971): 145–86.

Séchan, L. Article on *Ulysses* in Daremberg-Saglio, *Dictionnaire des Antiquités Grecques et Romaines* (Paris 1912): 574–83.

Sheppard, J. T. 'Great-hearted Odysseus', *JHS* LXVI (1936): 36–47.

Stanford, W. B. *The Ulysses theme,* 2nd ed., rev., Oxford 1968; 'On the *Odysseus automolos* of Epicharmus', *CP* XLV (1950): 167–9; 'Studies in the characterization of Ulysses III: the lies of Odysseus', *Hermathena* LXXV (1950): 35–48; 'The mysticism that pleased him', *Envoy* V (1951): 62–9; 'The Homeric etymology of the name Odysseus', *CP* XLVII (1952): 209–13; 'Dante's conception of Ulysses', *Cambridge Journal* VI (1953): 239–47; 'Ulyssean qualities in Joyce's Leopold Bloom', *Comparative Literature* V (1953): 125–36; 'The ending of the *Odyssey*', *Hermathena* C (1965): 5–20; 'A new name for Ulysses' daughter?', *CR* XXIII, No. 2 (Dec. 1973): 126.

Stephens, W. C. 'Two Stoic heroes: Hercules and Ulysses', *Ovidiana,* edited by Herescu (Paris 1958): 273–82.

Svoronos, J. N. 'Ulysse chez les Arcadiens et la Télégonie d'Eugammon', *Gazette Archéologique* XIII (1888): 257–85.

Thomson, J. A. K. *Studies in the Odyssey,* Oxford 1911.

Tolstoi, J. 'Einige Märchenparallelen zur Heimkehr des Odysseus', *Philologus* LXXXIX (1933): 261–74.

Trahman, C. R. 'Odysseus' lies', *Phoenix* VI (1952): 31–43.

Trencsenyi-Waldapfel, I. 'Le symbole d'Ulysse chez Cicéron et chez Joachim du Bellay', *Actes du Congrès Budé* (Paris 1958): 376–7.

Ungnad, A. 'Gilgamesh Epos und Odyssee', *Kulturfragen* IV–V, Breslau 1923.

Vikentiev, V. 'Le retour d'Ulysse du point de vue égyptologique et folklorique', *Bullétin de l'Institut d'Egypte* XXIX (1946–7): 183–241.

Waern, I. 'Odysseus bei Sophokles', *Eranos* LX (1962): 1–7.

Wilamowitz-Moellendorff, U. von. *Die Heimkehr des Odysseus,* Berlin 1927; *Homerische Untersuchungen,* Berlin 1884.

Wilhelm, J. 'Odysseus in Fénelon's "Aventures de Télémaque"', *Zeitschrift für Französische Sprache und Literatur* LXVI (1956): 231–40.

Wüst, E. Article on *Odysseus* in Pauly-Wissowa-Kroll, *Real-Encyclopädie der classischen Altertumswissenschaft* XXXIII (Stuttgart 1937): 1905–96.

Wyspiański, Stanisław. *The Return of Odysseus,* translated with an introduction by H. Clarke, Indiana 1966.

Ziegler, K. 'Odysseus, Utuse, Utis', *Gymnasium* LXIX (1962): 396–8.

Ziolkowski, T. 'The Odysseus theme in recent German fiction', *Comparative Literature* XIV (1962): 225–41.

ART AND ARCHAEOLOGY

Allan, J. 'A Tabula Iliaca from Gandhara', *JHS* LXVI (1946): 21–3.

Amelung, W. *Die Skulpturen des Vaticanischen Museums,* Berlin 1908.

Baumeister, A. *Denkmaler des klassischen Altertums,* Munich 1889.

Beazley, J. D. *Attic black-figure vase-painters,* 2nd ed., Oxford 1956; *Attic red-figure vase-painters,* 2nd ed., Oxford 1963; *Etruscan vase-painting,* Oxford 1947; *Paralipomena. Additions to Attic black-figure vase-painters and to Attic red-figure vase-painters,* Oxford 1971.

Beyen, H. G. *Die Pompejanische Wandekoration,* The Hague 1960.

Bianchi-Bandinelli, R. *Hellenistic-Byzantine miniatures of the Iliad,* Olten 1955.

Blanckenhagen, P. H. von. 'The Odyssey frieze', *Mitt. des Deutschen Archaeol. Inst. (Röm. Abt.)* LXX (1963): 100–46.

Bland, D. *A history of book illustration,* 2nd ed., London 1969.

Boardman, J. *Archaic Greek gems,* London 1968; *Greek gems and finger rings,* London 1970; *Island gems* London 1963.

Bolte, J. 'De monumentis ad Odysseam pertinentibus', Dissertation, Berlin 1882.

Bordenache, G. 'La grotta di Tiberio a Sperlonga', *Studii Clasice* XIV (1972): 223–30.

Brandt, E., *et al. Antike Gemmen in deutschen Sammlungen,* 4 vols, Munich 1968–72.

Brommer, J. 'Odysseus als Bettler', *Archaeologischer Anzeiger* LXXX (1965): 115–19; *Vasenlisten zur griechischen Heldensage,* Marburg 1960.

Bruns, G. *Das Kabirenheiligtum bei Theben,* Berlin 1940.

Buchthal, H. *Historia Troiana. Studies in the history of medieval secular illustration,* London 1970.

Bulas, K. *Les illustrations antiques de l'Iliade,* Lwow 1929; 'New illustrations to the Iliad', *AJA* LIV (1950): 112–18.

Bush, J. E. 'Homer's *Odyssey* and numismatics', *Turtle* VI (1967): 197–9.

Chase, G. H., and Vermeule, C. *The classical collection of the Museum of Fine Arts of Boston,* 2nd ed., Boston 1963.

Comstock, M., Graves, A., Vermeule, E., and Vermeule, C. *The Trojan War in Greek art,* Boston n.d.

Courcelle, P. 'Quelques symboles funéraires du néo-platonisme latin', *Revue des Études Anciennes* XLVI (1944): 65–93.

Cumont, F. 'Une mosaic de Cherchel, figurant Ulysse et les Sirènes', *Comptes Rendus, Académie des Inscriptions et Belles Lettres* (Paris 1941): 103–9.

Dawson, C. 'Romano-Campanian mythological landscape painting', *Yale Classical Studies* IX (1944).

Detienne, E. 'Ulysse sur le stuc central de la Basilique de la Porta Maggiore', *Latomus* XVII (1958): 270–86.

Dimier, L. *French painting in the sixteenth century,* London 1904; *Le Primatice,* Paris 1928.

Eichler, F. *Die Reliefs des Heroons von Gjölbaschi-Trysa,* Vienna 1956.

Enciclopedia dell'Arte. Rome 1958 (under *Omeriche Illustrazioni,* and under *Ulisse*).

Forti, L. 'Una mnesterophonia canosina', *Atti e Memorie della Società Magna Grecia* VIII (1967): 99–112.

Friis-Johansen, K. *The Iliad in early Greek Art,* Copenhagen 1967.

Furtwängler, A. *Die antiken Gemmen,* Leipzig 1900.

Gallina, A. *Le pitture con paesaggi dell' Odissea dall'Esquilino,* Rome 1961.

Gillen, O. *Iconographische Studien zum Hortus Deliciarum der Herrad von Landsberg,* Berlin 1931.

Greifenhafen, A. 'Zwei Kopgefässe. Odysseus und Achilleus', *Gymnasium* LXXIV (1967): 532–4.

Hampe, R., and Simon, E. *Griechischen Sagen in der frühen Etruskischen Kunst,* Mainz 1964.

Harrison, J. *Myths of the Odyssey in art and literature*, London 1882.

Hauser, A. *Mannerism*, 2 vols., London 1965.

Hinks, R. P. *Catalogue of the Greek, Etruscan and Roman paintings in the British Museum*, London 1933.

Inghirami, F. *Galleria Omerica*, 3 vols., Friesole 1831–6.

Jacobsthal, P. *Die melischen Reliefs*, Berlin 1931.

Jacopi, G. *L'antro di Tiberio a Sperlonga*, Rome 1963.

Jongkees, J. H., and Verdenius, W. J. *Platenatlas bij Homerus*, Haarlem 1955.

Kekule von Stradonitz, H. F. R. *Die antiken Terracotten*, Stuttgart 1880–1911.

Lavagne, Henri. 'Le nymphée du Polyphème de la *Domus Aurea*', *Mélanges d'archéologie et d'histoire* LXXXII (1970): 673–721.

Levey, M. 'Tiepolo's treatment of classical story at Villa Valmarana', *Journ. Warburg and Courtauld Inst.* XX (1957): 298–317.

Levi, D. *Antioch mosaic pavements*, 2 vols., Princeton 1947.

Müller, F. *Die antiken Odyssee-Illustrationen*, etc. Berlin 1913.

Nogara, B. *Le nozze aldobrandine. I paesaggi con scene dell'Odissea*, Milan 1907.

'Notor'. *L'Iliade illustrée*, Paris 1956; *L'Odysseé illustrée*, Paris 1951.

Oswald, F. *Index of figure types on terra sigillata*, Liverpool 1936–7.

Picard, C. 'La grande peinture de l'hypogée funéraire dit du Viale Manzoni à Rome, et les tentations d'Ulysse', *Comptes rendus, Académie des Inscriptions et Belles-lettres* (Paris 1945): 26–51.

Poulsen, V. 'Odysseus in Boston', *Acta Archaeologica* XXV (1954): 301–4.

Renard, M. 'Ulysse et Polyphème. A propos d'une mosaïque de Piazza Armerina', *Hommages à Leon Hermann* (Brussels 1960): 655–68.

Richter, G. M. A. *Engraved gems of the Greeks, Etruscans and Romans*, 2 vols., London 1968, 1971; *Handbook of Greek Art*,' 6th ed., London 1969; *The Metropolitan Museum of Art: a handbook of the Greek collection*, Cambridge, Mass. 1953.

Rizzo, G. E. *La pittura ellenistico-romana*, Milan 1929.

Robert, C. *Homerische Becher*, Berlin 1890.

Sadurska, A. *Les tables iliaques*, Warsaw 1964.

Säflund, Gösta. *The Polyphemus and Scylla groups at Sperlonga*, Stockholm 1972.

Saxl, F. 'Classical mythology in medieval art', *Metropolitan Museum Studies* IV 2, 1933.

Saxl, F., and Meier, H. *Verzeichnis astrologischer und mythologischer illustrierter Handschriften des lateinisches Mittelalters* I–III, Heidelberg 1915, 1927, London 1953.

Schefold, K. *Myth and legend in early Greek art*, London 1966; *Die Wände Pompeijis*, Berlin 1957.

Scherer, M. R. *The legends of Troy*, London and New York 1963.

Schlie, F. *Die Darstellungen des troischen Sagenkreises auf etruskischen Aschenkisten*, Stuttgart 1868.

Schmidt, J. 'Odysseus in der bildenen Kunst', in Roscher, W. H., *Ausführliches Lexikon der griechischen und römischen Mythologie* III (Leipzig 1902): 602–81.

Schubring, P. *Cassoni, Truhen und Truhenbilder der italienischen Frührenaissance*, 2nd ed., Leipzig 1923.

Sparkes, B. A. 'The Trojan Horse in classical art', *Greece and Rome* n.s. XVIII (1971): 54–70.

Thomson, W. G. *A history of tapestry*, rev. ed., London 1930.

Touchefeu-Meynier, O. *Thèmes Odysséens dans l'art antique*, Paris 1968.

Trendall, A. D. *The red-figured vases of Lucania, Campania and Sicily*, 2 vols, Oxford 1969; *Phlyax vases*, 2nd ed., London 1967.

Weege, F. *Etruskische Malerei*, Halle 1921.

Weitzmann, K. *Illustrations in roll and codex*, Princeton 1970; 'A Tabula Odysseaca', *AJA* XLV (1941): 166–81.

Wiencke, M. I. 'An epic theme in Greek art', *AJA* LVIII (1954): 285 ff.

Wilpert, J. *I Sarcofagi cristiani antichi*, 5 vols., Rome 1929–36.

Zancani Montuoro, P. 'Odisseo a Caridde', *La Parola del passato* XV (1959): 221–9.

Zancani Montuoro, P., and Bianco, Z. *Heraion alla Foce del Sele,* 4 vols., Rome 1951–4.

Zazoff, P. *Etruskische Skarabäen,* Mainz 1968.

Zori, N. 'The house of Kyrios Leontis at Beth Shean', *Israel Exploration Journal* XVI (1966): 123–34.

Chapters 3–6

Allen, T. W. *The Homeric Catalogue of Ships,* Oxford 1921.

Benton, S. 'Antiquities from Thiaki', *BSA* XXIX (1927–28): 113–16; 'The Ionian Islands', *BSA* XXXII (1931–32): 213–46.

Bérard, J. *La Colonisation Grecque de l'Italie Méridionale et de la Sicilie dans l'Antiquité,* 2nd ed., Paris 1957.

Bérard, V. *Les Navigations d'Ulysse,* 4 vols., Paris 1927–9; *Les Phéniciens et l'Odyssée,* 2nd ed., Paris 1927.

Blegen, C. W., and Rawson, M. *The Palace of Nestor at Pylos in Western Messenia,* Princeton 1966–.

Blegen, C. W., *et al. Troy,* 4 vols., Princeton 1950–58.

Boardman, J. *The Greeks Overseas,* Harmondsworth 1964.

Bradford, E. *Ulysses Found,* London 1963.

Brea, L. Bernabò. *Sicily before the Greeks,* London 1957.

Brewster, F. 'Ithaca: A study of the Homeric Evidence', *HSCP* XXXI (1920): 125–66; 'Ithaca, Dulichium, Samê, and wooded Zakynthus', *HSCP* XXXVI (1925): 43–90.

British Excavations in Ithaca: Reports in *BSA* XXXIII (1933); XXXV (1934–5); XXXIX 1938–9; XL (1939–40); XLIII (1948); XLIV (1949); XLVIII (1953); L (1955).

Bunbury, E. H. *A History of Ancient Geography,* London 1879.

Chadwick, J. *The Decipherment of Linear B,* Cambridge 1958.

Coldstream, J. N. *Greek Geometric Pottery,* London 1968.

Desborough, V. R. d'A. *The Last Mycenaeans and their Successors,* Oxford 1964.

Dörpfeld, W. *Alt-Ithaka,* 2 vols., Munich 1927.

Dunbabin, T. J. *The Western Greeks,* Oxford 1948.

Edwards, I. E. S., *et al. Cambridge Ancient History,* Vol. 2, 3rd ed., rev., Cambridge 1971–.

Gell, Sir William. *The Geography and Antiquities of Ithaca,* London 1807.

Graham, A. J. 'The Date of the Greek Penetration of the Black Sea', *BICS* V (1958): 25–42.

Gray, D. 'Houses in the Odyssey', *CQ* V (1955): 1–12.

Hammond, N. G. L. *Epirus,* Oxford 1967; 'Tumulus-burial in Albania, the Grave Circle of Mycenae, and the Indo-Europeans', *BSA* LXII (1967): 77–105.

Hesiod, *Theogony,* edited by M. L. West, Oxford 1966.

Hood, M. F. S. *The Home of the Heroes,* London 1967.

Hope Simpson, R., and Lazenby, J. F. *The Catalogue of the Ships in Homer's Iliad,* Oxford 1970.

Hope Simpson, R., and Waterhouse, H. 'Prehistoric Laconia, Parts I and II', *BSA* LV (1960): 67–107; and LVI (1961): 114–75.

Huxley, G. L. *Achaeans and Hittites,* Oxford 1960; 'Odysseus and the Thesprotian Oracle of the Dead', *La Parola del Passato* XIII (1958): 245–48.

Johnson, F. P. 'Chthamalē Ithakē', *AJP* I (1929): 221–38.

Kirk, G. S. *The Songs of Homer,* Cambridge 1962.

Leake, W. M. *Travels in Northern Greece,* Vol. III, London 1835.

Luce, J. V. *The End of Atlantis,* London 1969.

McDonald, W. A. 'Overland Communications in Greece during LH III, with special reference to the south-west Peloponnese', *Mycenaean Studies* (edited by E. L. Bennett Jr.), Madison 1964.

McDonald, W. A., and Hope Simpson, R. 'Prehistoric Habitation in Southwestern Peloponnese', *AJA* LXV (1961); 'Further Exploration in Southwestern Peloponnese: 1962–1963'; *AJA* LXVIII (1964): 229–45.

Minns, E. H. *Scythians and Greeks*, Cambridge 1913.

Mylonas, G. E. *Mycenae and the Mycenaean Age*, Princeton 1966.

Nilsson, M. P. *Homer and Mycenae*, London 1933.

Ormerod, H. A. *Piracy in the Ancient World*, Liverpool 1924.

Page, D. L. *History and the Homeric Iliad*, Berkeley 1959.

Partsch, J. *Kephallenia und Ithaka*, Gotha 1890.

Phillips, E. D. 'Ulysses in Italy', *JHS* LXXIII (1953): 53–67.

Philippson, A. *Die Griechischen Landschaften* (edited by Kirsten), Frankfurt am Main 1950–59.

Pocock, L. G. *Odyssean Essays*, Oxford 1965.

Rennell of Rodd, Lord. 'The Ithaca of Odysseus', *BSA* XXXIII (1933): 1–22.

Schliemann, H. *Mycenae,* New York 1880; *Tiryns,* New York 1885.

Shewan, A. 'Beati Possidentes Ithakistae', *CP* XII (1917): 132–42; *Homeric Essays,* Oxford 1935.

Strabo. *Geography,* Bk. 1: 2; Bk. 10: 2, 8–20 (Vols. 1 and 5 in the Loeb edition by H. L. Jones, London 1928).

Stubbings, F. 'The Principal Homeric Sites: Ithaca', *A Companion to Homer,* edited by A. J. B. Wace and F. Stubbings (London 1962): 398–421.

Taylour, Lord William. *Mycenaean Pottery in Italy and Adjacent Areas,* Cambridge 1958; *The Mycenaeans,* London 1964.

Thomas, C. G. 'A Mycenaean Hegemony? A Reconsideration', *JHS* XC (1970): 184–92.

Thomson, J. O. *History of Ancient Geography,* Cambridge 1948.

Trump, D. *Central and Southern Italy before Rome,* London 1966.

Ventris, M., and Chadwick, J. *Documents in Mycenaean Greek,* Cambridge 1956.

Vermeule, E. *Greece in the Bronze Age,* Chicago 1964.

Vollgraff, W. 'Fouilles d'Ithaque', *BCH* XXIX (1905): 145–68.

Wace, A. J. B. 'Houses and Palaces', *A Companion to Homer,* edited by A. J. B. Wace and F. Stubbings (London 1962): 489–97; *Mycenae,* Princeton 1949.

Wade-Gery, H. T. 'The Dorian Invasion: What happened at Pylos', *AJA* LII (1948): 115–18.

List of Illustrations

The authors and publishers are grateful to the many official bodies, institutions and individuals mentioned below for their assistance in supplying illustrative material.

243

27 Ulysses, guided by Hermes, meets Elpenor in the underworld, from an Attic red-figure pelike by the 'Lykaon painter', c. 450-40 BC. Photo: by courtesy of the Museum of Fine Arts, Boston. William Amory Gardner Fund. 34.79.

28 Ulysses and the Sirens, drawing from a Corinthian aryballos, c. 570 BC. Photo: by courtesy of the Museum of Fine Arts, Boston. H. L. Pierce Fund. 01.8100.

29 Ulysses' ship sailing past the Sirens. Campanian terracotta relief (much restored and painted over), 1st century AD. Photo: by courtesy of the Service de Documentation Photographique de la Réunion des Musées Nationaux, Paris.

30 Decorative relief on a Roman bronze cup from Boscoreale, near Pompeii, 1st century AD, showing Skylla and a ship. Photo: by courtesy of the Trustees of the British Museum.

31 Ulysses and Calypso, on a terracotta from Tanagra. Photo: Giraudon.

32 Ulysses, Athena, Nausikaä and her maidens, from an Attic red-figure amphora, c. 450-40 BC. Museum für Antike Kleinkunst, Munich. Photo: Phaidon Archives.

33 Attic red-figure stamnos, c. 475 BC, from Vulci, showing Ulysses and the Sirens. Photo: by courtesy of the Trustees of the British Museum.

34 Pellegrino Tibaldi: *Cattle of the Sun*. Fresco in the Università di Bologna. Photo: Scala.

35 Penelope mourning. Terracotta relief, Roman period. Photo: by courtesy of the Trustees of the British Museum.

36 Ulysses recognized by his dog, Argos. Roman sarcophagus relief, 2nd century AD. Museum of San Martino, Naples. Photo: Phaidon Archives.

37 Ulysses recognized by Eurykleia. Campanian terracotta relief, probably from Tusculum, 1st century AD. Museo delle Terme, Rome. Photo: by courtesy of the Deutsches Archäologisches Institut, Rome.

38 Ulysses and Penelope. Terracotta relief from Melos, 460-50 BC. Musée du Louvre, Paris. Photo: Maurice Chuzeville.

39, 40 Ulysses slays the Suitors, from an Attic red-figure skyphos by the 'Penelope painter', c. 435 BC. Photos: by courtesy of the Staatliche Museen, Berlin.

41 Ulysses slays the Suitors, from a relief on the west wall of the Heroon of Gjölbaschi-Trysa, Lycia, early 4th century BC. Photo: by courtesy of the Kunsthistorisches Museum, Vienna.

42 Sons and grandsons of Ulysses according to the post-Homeric tradition.

43 The Wooden Horse, from the neck of a relief pithos found in Mykonos, c. 675 BC. Archaeological Museum, Mykonos. Photo: Phaidon Archives.

44 The blinding of Polyphemos, from a Proto-Attic amphora found at Eleusis, c. 675-50 BC. Photo: Phaidon Archives.

45 The François vase, made by Ergotimos and painted by Kleitias, c. 570 BC. Museo Archeologico, Florence. Photo: Alinari.

46 Ulysses riding a turtle, from a black-figure skyphos from Palermo, 6th century BC. Photo: Phaidon Archives.

47 Rock-crystal bowl in the form of a duck, from Grave Circle B at Mycenae, 1550-1500 BC. National Archaeological Museum, Athens. Photo: Phaidon Archives.

48 Chronological table of the Late Bronze Age and Early Iron Age. Drawn by G. March.

49 Detail of a gold cup from Vapheio, c. 1500-1450 BC. National Archaeological Museum, Athens. Photo: Alison Frantz.

50 Gold death mask from Grave Circle A, Mycenae, c. 1550 BC. National Archaeological Museum, Athens. Photo: Alison Frantz.

51 Map of the Mycenaean world in the Late Bronze Age. Drawn by G. March.

52 The Lion Gate, Mycenae. Photo: Peter Clayton.

53 Grave Circle A, Mycenae. Photo: J. Powell.

54 Aerial view of the citadel, Mycenae. Photo: Royal Hellenic Air Force.

55 Chariot scene, from a grave-marker from Mycenae, 16th century BC. Photo: by courtesy of the Deutsches Archäologisches Institut, Athens.

56 The entrance to the Treasury of Atreus, Mycenae, c. 1250 BC. Photo: Peter Clayton.

57 Genealogical tables of the principal Achaean families.

58 Amethyst portrait gem, from Grave Circle B, Mycenae. National Archaeological Museum, Athens. Photo: T.A.P. Service, Athens.

59 The Hill of Hissarlik. Photo: J. V. Luce.

60 Section of the circuit wall of Troy VI. Photo: J. V. Luce.

61 Bronze arrowhead from Troy VIIA. From Carl W. Blegen *et al.*, *Troy*, Vol. IV, Part 2, Fig. 219. Published for the University of Cincinnati by Princeton University Press, 1958. Reprinted by permission of the Princeton University Press and the University of Cincinnati.

62 A room of a house at Troy VIIA. Photo: J. V. Luce.

63 Plastic vase from Ialysos, Rhodes, 12th century BC. Archaeological Museum, Rhodes. Photo: T.A.P. Service, Athens.

64 View of Ithaca from Mt. Aetos. Photo: J. V. Luce.

65 Drawing of a ship, from a stirrup jar from Skyros, 12th century BC. After Hansen.

66 Drawing of a ship, from the outer walls of the Mortuary Temple of Ramesses III at Medinet Habu. From Landström, *Ships of the Pharaohs* published by George Allen & Unwin Ltd. in 1970.

67 Portion of the circuit wall on the west of the citadel of Tiryns. Photo: Alison Frantz.

68 Map of Ithaca. Drawn by G. March.

69 The northern promontory of Ithaca. Photo: J. V. Luce.

70 A cist grave cut into the rock in the Late Bronze Age, near Pilikata, Ithaca. Photo: J. V. Luce.

71 View of 'Rocky Ithaca', south of Marathia. Photo: J. V. Luce.

113 The embassy to Achilles, from an Attic pelike, *c.* 500 BC. Villa Giulia, Rome. Photo: Deutsches Archäologisches Institut, Rome.

114 The embassy to Achilles, from the inside of an Attic cup by Douris. Photo: by courtesy of the Trustees of the British Museum.

115 The capture of Dolon, from an Attic oinochoë, 5th century BC. Photo: by courtesy of the Ashmolean Museum, Oxford.

116 Ulysses and Circe, from an oinochoë, *c.* 460 BC. Musée du Louvre, Paris. Photo: Giraudon.

117 Ulysses, directed by Athena, advances to seek food and clothing from Nausikaä, from the cover of an Attic red-figure pyxis by Aison, late 5th century BC. Photo: by courtesy of the Museum of Fine Arts, Boston. H. L. Pierce Fund. 04.18.

118, 119. Two sides of an Attic red-figure skyphos by the 'Penelope painter', from Chiusi, *c.* 440 BC, showing Penelope and Telemachos, and the washing of Ulysses' feet. Museo Nazionale, Chiusi. Photos: Mansell Collection and Phaidon Archives.

120 Ulysses on a raft of amphorae, from a black-figure Boeotian skyphos, *c.* 400 BC. Photo: by courtesy of the Ashmolean Museum, Oxford.

121 Ulysses and Circe, from a black-figure Boeotian skyphos, *c.* 400 BC. British Museum, London. Photo: Phaidon Archives.

122 Burlesque on the theft of the Palladium, from a red-figure Apulian oinochoë, 4th century BC. Photo: by courtesy of the Trustees of the British Museum.

123 The return of Ulysses. Greek terracotta relief from Melos, *c.* 460 BC. Photo: by courtesy of the Metropolitan Museum of Art, Fletcher Fund, 1930.

124 Eurykleia washing the feet of Ulysses in the presence of Penelope and Telemachos. Greek terracotta relief from Melos, 5th century BC. Photo: by courtesy of the Metropolitan Museum of Art, Fletcher Fund, 1925.

125 Clay impression of a metal belt-buckle, showing Ulysses mourning, 5th century BC. Photo: by courtesy of the American School of Classical Studies at Athens.

126 Bronze cheek-piece of a helmet from Megara, 4th century BC, showing Ulysses mourning. Staatliche Museen, Berlin. Photo: Phaidon Archives.

127 Roman statuette of Ulysses holding up a wine-bowl. Vatican, Rome. Photo: Phaidon Archives.

128 Ulysses creeping. Marble statue from Rome, *c.* AD 50. Photo: by courtesy of the Isabella Stewart Gardner Museum, Boston.

129 A gem, now lost, showing Ulysses on a turtle. Drawn by J. Wickman.

130 Gold ring, with engraved design on oval bezel, 4th century BC, showing Ulysses and his dog, Argos. Photo: by courtesy of the Soprintendenza alle Antichità della Puglia, Taranto.

131 Cover of an Etruscan mirror-case from Cervetri, showing the meeting of Ulysses and Penelope. Photo: by courtesy of the Trustees of the British Museum.

132 Coin of C. Mamilius Limetanus, 82–79 BC, showing Ulysses and his dog, Argos. Photo: American Numismatic Society.

133 Ulysses as a charioteer. Small bronze plate from the foot of an Etruscan cist from Chiusi, 6th century BC. Photo: by courtesy of the Bibliothèque Nationale, Paris.

134 Ulysses threatening Circe. Etruscan sarcophagus relief from Torre San Severo, *c.* 300 BC. Museo dell'Opera del Duomo, Orvieto. Photo: Alinari.

135 The Suitors banquet. Etruscan alabaster funeral urn, from Volterra. Photo: by courtesy of the Museo Etrusco Guarnacci, Volterra.

136 Ulysses and the Sirens. Etruscan burial urn, from Volterra. Museo Etrusco Guarnacci, Volterra. Photo: Alinari.

137 Ulysses blinding Polyphemos. Etruscan mural-painting from the 'Tomb of the Underworld' at Tarquinia, 3rd century BC. From R. Engelmann, *Bilder-Atlas zum Homer*, 1889.

138 A Roman lamp from Pozzuoli showing Ulysses and Circe. Photo: by courtesy of the Trustees of the British Museum.

139 The Wooden Horse brought into Troy. Roman wall-painting from Pompeii, 1st century AD. Museo Nazionale, Naples. Photo: Phaidon Archives.

140 Ulysses and his Companions attacked by the Laistrygonians. Graeco-Roman wall-painting from the Esquiline Villa in Rome, 1st century BC. Photo: Scala.

141 The Laistrygonians destroy the ships of Ulysses' Companions. Graeco-Roman wall-painting from the Esquiline Villa in Rome, 1st century BC. Photo: Scala.

142 Ulysses in Hades. Graeco-Roman wall-painting from the Esquiline Villa in Rome, 1st century BC. Photo: Scala.

143 Mosaic of Ulysses and the Sirens, from the House of Dionysos at Dougga, Tunisia, 3rd century AD. Photo: by courtesy of the Direction des Musées Nationaux, Le Bardo.

144 *Ulysses and Penelope.* Roman wall-painting from Pompeii, 1st century AD. Photo: Phaidon Archives.

145 Silver cup from Hoby, Roman copy of a 5th century BC work, showing Ulysses addressing Philoctetes on Lemnos. National Museum, Copenhagen. Photo: Phaidon Archives.

146 Ulysses and Circe, from a Roman relief acquired by the Marquis Rondanini in 1757 (now lost). From R. Engelmann, *Bilder-Atlas zum Homer*, 1889.

147 The Stroganoff bowl: silver dish, 6th century AD, showing the Judgement of Arms. Photo: by courtesy of the State Hermitage Museum, Leningrad.

148 Ulysses and Diomedes demand the return of Helen. Franco-Flemish tapestry from Tournai, 1472–4. Photo: by courtesy of the Burrell Collection, Glasgow Art Gallery and Museum.

149 Ulysses and the Sirens. Christian sarcophagus, 4th century AD. Photo: by courtesy of the Deutsches Archäologisches Institut, Rome.

150 Ulysses and the Sirens. From Herrade de Landsberg, *Hortus Deliciarum*. Recueil ... par Joseph Walter, ...—Strasbourg, Paris, F.X, Le Roux, 1952, Pl. XXXIX. Photo: by courtesy of the Bibliothèque Nationale et Universitaire, Strasbourg.

151, 152 Illustrations from the Rylands English manuscript of John Lydgate's *Siege of Troy*, 1420, folios 155v, 168r. Photos: by courtesy of the John Rylands University Library of Manchester.

153, 154 Illustrations by Jean Mielot in a later manuscript of Christine de Pisan's *Letter of Othea to Hector*, 1461. Copyright Bibliothèque royale Albert 1er, Brussels B.R. Ms. 9392, folios 99v, 22v. Photos: by courtesy of the Bibliothèque royale Albert 1er, Brussels.

155, 156 A pair of Franco-Flemish wool tapestries, 1480–3, depicting Ulysses and Penelope separately. Photos: by courtesy of the Museum of Fine Arts, Boston. Maria Antoinette Evans Fund. 26.53 and 26.54.

157 The Trojan Horse disgorges its burden. Illustration from a late 15th century manuscript of Raoul Lefèvre's *Recueil*. Bibliothèque Nationale, Paris. Ms. fr. 22552, folio 277v. Photo: Félicien Faillet.

158 Dosso Dossi: *Circe and her lovers in a landscape*, detail. Samuel H. Kress Collection. Photo: by courtesy of the National Gallery of Art, Washington, D.C.

159 Majolica plate illustrating Ulysses and Ajax, probably from the Duchy of Urbino, late 16th century. Photo: reproduced by permission of the Trustees of the Wallace Collection.

160 Ulysses and Circe. Illustration from a printing of a play entitled *Ulisse et Circé* by 'Monsieur L.A.D.S.M.', published in *Le Théâtre Italien de Gherardi*, 5th edn., Vol. III, Amsterdam 1721. Photo: M. O'Regan.

161 Francesco Primaticcio: *Penelope and Ulysses embrace*. Drawing for the Ulysses series at Fontainebleau, now destroyed, mid-16th century. Photo: by courtesy of the Nationalmuseum, Stockholm.

162 Francesco Primaticcio: *Ulysses and Penelope*, c. 1563. The Toledo Museum of Art, Toledo, Ohio. Gift of Edward Drummond Libbey. Photo: by courtesy of the Toledo Museum of Art.

163, 164 Annibale Carracci: *Ulysses and Circe* and *Ulysses and the Sirens*. Lunettes in the Camerino Farnese, Rome. Photos: Alinari.

165 Giulio Romano: *The Trojan Horse*. Fresco in the Ducal Palace, Mantua. Photo: Alinari.

166 Pellegrino Tibaldi: *The Blinding of Polyphemos*. Fresco in the Università di Bologna. Photo: Alinari.

167 Pellegrino Tibaldi: *Ulysses and the sea-nymph Leukothea*. Fresco in the Università di Bologna. Photo: Scala.

168 Pintoricchio: *Telemachos and Penelope*, c. 1509. National Gallery, London. Photo: Phaidon Archives.

169 Rubens: *Ulysses and Nausikaä* (figures by Rubens, landscape by Lukas van Uden). Palazzo Pitti, Florence. Photo: by courtesy of the Soprintendenza alle Gallerie Gabinetto Fotografico, Florence.

170 Pieter Lastman: *Ulysses and Nausikaä*, 1609. Photo: by courtesy of the Herzog Anton Ulrich-Museum, Braunschweig.

171 Nicolas Poussin: *Achilles on Skyros*, c. 1656. The Virginia Museum of Fine Arts, Richmond. Arthur and Margaret Glasgow Fund, 1957. Photo: Phaidon Archives.

172 Tiepolo: *The building of the Trojan Horse*, c. 1760. Photo: by courtesy of the Wadsworth Atheneum, Hartford, Connecticut. The Ella Gallup Sumner and Mary Catlin Sumner Collection.

173 Turner: *Ulysses deriding Polyphemos*, 1829, detail. National Gallery, London. Photo: Phaidon Archives.

174 Claude Lorrain: *Ulysses returns Chryseïs to her father*. Musée du Louvre, Paris. Photo: Scala.

175 Bouchardon: *Ulysses conjures up the ghost of Teiresias*. Photo: by courtesy of the Bibliothèque Nationale, Paris.

176 Henry Fuseli: *Ulysses slaying the Suitors*. Pen and watercolour drawing, 1802. Kunsthaus, Zürich. Photo: Phaidon Archives.

177 Henry Fuseli: *Ulysses escaping from the cave of Polyphemos*, 1802. Private Collection, Zurich. Photo: Phaidon Archives.

178 Ingres: *Ambassadors of Agamemnon at the tent of Achilles*, 1801. École Nationale des Beaux-Arts, Paris. Photo: Phaidon Archives.

179 Edward Burne-Jones: *The wine of Circe*, 1863–9. Collection of the Marquis of Normanby. Photo: Phaidon Archives.

180 William Etty: *Ulysses and the Sirens*, 1836–7. Photo: by courtesy of the City of Manchester Art Galleries.

181 Ulysses and Athena. Scene from Monteverdi's opera, *Il ritorno d'Ulisse in patria*, realized and conducted by Raymond Leppard, produced by Peter Hall and designed by John Bury at the Glyndebourne Festival in 1972 and 1973. Photo: Guy Gravett, by courtesy of the Glyndebourne Festival Opera.

182 Honoré Daumier: *Penelope's Nights*. Lithograph, from the series *Histoire Ancienne*, in *Charivari*, 24 April 1842. Photo: Phaidon Archives.

183 Honoré Daumier: *Ulysses and Penelope*. Lithograph, from the series *Histoire Ancienne*, in *Charivari*, 26 June 1842. Photo: Phaidon Archives.

184 Henry Moore: Illustration to Edward Sackville-West, *The Rescue*. Photo: A. C. Cooper.

185 Picasso: *Ulysses and the Sirens*. By courtesy of the Musée Picasso, Antibes. Photo: Lelaurain.

186 Salvador Dali: *Return of Ulysses*, 1936. Ink transfer, pen and ink, $9\frac{3}{8} \times 15\frac{5}{8}$ in. Private Collection. Photo: by courtesy of the Museum of Modern Art, New York.

187 Bryson Burroughs: *Calypso's Island*, 1928. Collection of Mrs Bryson Burroughs, Baltimore. Photo: Phaidon Archives.

188 Marc Chagall: *Ulysses and the Sirens and the death of Ulysses*, 1968. Right-hand side of the mosaic in the Faculté de Droit et des Sciences Economiques de Nice. Photo: Copyright J. R. Simkin, Antibes, France.

189 André Bauchant: *Ulysses and Circe*, 1942. Right-hand side. Photo: Copyright Luc Joubert.

190, 191 Henri Matisse: *The Cyclops*, and *Nausikaä*. Two etchings from James Joyce's *Ulysses*, from a series made by Henri Matisse for The Limited Editions Club. Reproduced by arrangement with the Cardavon Press, Inc., Avon, Connecticut. Copyright 1935, © 1963.

192–194 Drawings by Ghika in Nikos Kazantzakis, *The Odyssey: A modern sequel*, translated by Kimon Friar, published by Martin Secker & Warburg Ltd., London, and Simon & Schuster Inc., New York. Copyright © 1958 by Simon & Schuster.

Index